The L.A. Theatre Works Audio Docudrama Series

The L.A. Theatre Works Audio Docudrama Series

PIVOTAL MOMENTS IN AMERICAN HISTORY

The Great Tennessee Monkey Trial
The Real Dr. Strangelove
RFK: The Journey to Justice
The Chicago Conspiracy Trial
Top Secret: The Battle for the Pentagon Papers

methuen | drama
LONDON • NEW YORK • OXFORD • NEW DELHI • SYDNEY

METHUEN DRAMA
Bloomsbury Publishing Plc
50 Bedford Square, London, WC1B 3DP, UK
1385 Broadway, New York, NY 10018, USA

BLOOMSBURY, METHUEN DRAMA and the Methuen Drama logo are trademarks of
Bloomsbury Publishing Plc

First published in Great Britain 2020

Introduction copyright © L.A. Theatre Works, 2020
Top Secret: The Battle for the Pentagon Papers copyright © Geoffrey Cowan and Leroy Aarons, 2020
The Great Tennessee Monkey Trial copyright © Peter Goodchild, 2020
The Real Dr. Strangelove copyright © Peter Goodchild, 2020
RFK: The Journey to Justice copyright © Murray Horwitz and Jonathan Estrin, 2020
The Chicago Conspiracy Trial copyright © Peter Goodchild, 2020

L.A. Theatre Works have asserted their right under the Copyright, Designs and Patents Act, 1988, to be identified as editor of this work.

Cover design: Ben Anslow

All rights reserved. No part of this publication may be reproduced or transmitted in any form or by any means, electronic or mechanical, including photocopying, recording, or any information storage or retrieval system, without prior permission in writing from the publishers.

Bloomsbury Publishing Plc does not have any control over, or responsibility for, any third-party websites referred to or in this book. All internet addresses given in this book were correct at the time of going to press. The author and publisher regret any inconvenience caused if addresses have changed or sites have ceased to exist, but can accept no responsibility for any such changes.

No rights in incidental music or songs contained in the work are hereby granted and performance rights for any performance/presentation whatsoever must be obtained from the respective copyright owners.

All rights whatsoever in these plays are strictly reserved and application for performance etc. should be made before rehearsals by professionals and by amateurs to the following agents: for *Top Secret: The Battle for the Pentagon Papers* by Geoffrey Cowan and Leroy Aarons to L.A. Theatre Works, audiosales@latw.org, for *The Great Tennessee Monkey Trial*, *The Real Dr. Strangelove*, and *The Chicago Conspiracy* by Peter Goodchild to The Marton Agency Inc, info@martonagency.com, for *RFK: The Journey to Justice* by Murray Horwitz and Jonathan Estrin to The Barbara Hogenson Agency, Inc, Bhogenson@aol.com

No performance may be given unless a licence has been obtained.

A catalogue record for this book is available from the British Library.

A catalog record for this book is available from the Library of Congress.

ISBN: HB: 978-1-3501-3578-9
PB: 978-1-3501-3579-6
ePDF: 978-1-3501-3580-2
eBook: 978-1-3501-3581-9

Typeset by RefineCatch Limited, Bungay, Suffolk

To find out more about our authors and books visit www.bloomsbury.com
and sign up for our newsletters.

Contents

Introduction   *Michael Hackett*   vii

The Great Tennessee Monkey Trial   Peter Goodchild   1
The Real Dr. Strangelove   Peter Goodchild   55
RFK: The Journey to Justice   Murray Horwitz and Jonathan Estrin   109
The Chicago Conspiracy Trial   Peter Goodchild   181
Top Secret: The Battle for the Pentagon Papers
Geoffrey Cowan and Leroy Aarons   247

Introduction

The five plays of this anthology—*The Great Tennessee Monkey Trial, The Real Dr. Strangelove, RFK: The Journey to Justice, The Chicago Conspiracy Trial,* and *Top Secret: The Battle for the Pentagon Papers*—focus on extraordinary crisis points in the history of the United States. At a time when many of our basic liberties as citizens are being questioned, it is deeply compelling to hear these voices and to witness their engagement with the world in situations not so dissimilar from our own. Our present political debates—concerning science and religion, nuclear proliferation, racial injustice, political protest, First Amendment rights—find their antecedents in the issues represented in these plays.

Although the anthology will be especially appealing to readers of American history, it also will excite the general public. These docudramas, based on primary sources and historical research, provide a vivid context and imaginative entryway into some of the most important events of the twentieth century in the United States. Key sections of *The Great Tennessee Monkey Trial*, for example, are taken directly from the trial transcripts—the famous orations of William Jennings Bryan and Clarence Darrow are included as are speeches made by Robert Kennedy and Martin Luther King in *RFK: The Journey to Justice*. Those readers drawn to the post-war periods of World War I, World War II, the Korean, and the Vietnam Wars, will find the plays particularly interesting as the anthology concentrates specifically on the core years of the "American Century" from the 1920s through the 1970s.

These plays are also about the power of words and about those who use words, both printed and spoken, for their seeming alchemical power to persuade and to transform the hearts and minds of the listeners. The anthology is a compendium of American language as it evolves through the twentieth century—language as speech, rhetoric, diatribe, propaganda, legal argument, debate. Can there be anything more disparate than the clash of words between Judge Julius Hoffman and the Chicago Seven? Yet they are united in their essential understanding of the power of language.

L.A. Theatre Works believes in the efficacy of words as theater, as political action, as agents of social change. Since 1985, the company has recorded over five hundred plays, both classic and contemporary. These productions are broadcast nationally on eighty radio stations and internationally in China and Germany. They are also streamed and podcast worldwide. Some of the plays in this anthology have toured the country presented as "live-in-performance" radio dramas in two hundred separate civic and performing arts venues and universities. The effect can be riveting as the audience is drawn into the "argument" of our ongoing national dialogue

And this has been as true in Beijing as it has been in New York, when L.A. Theatre Works made its first international tour of China in 2011 with the play *Top Secret: Battle for the Pentagon Papers*. In the middle of the performance, the audience broke into cheers when the character of Ben Bradlee announced that the *Washington Post* would publish the Pentagon documents.

These plays have the capacity to provoke, challenge, and activate the historical and political imagination—it is exciting to have them in one volume and to know that the ideas they contain will be read, analyzed, debated, and performed.

Michael Hackett
Professor of Theater
UCLA School of Theater, Film and Television
May 27, 2019

Setting

Dayton, Tennessee, the Rhea County Courthouse

Time

July 7–21, 1925

About the Play

L.A. Theatre Works' production of *The Great Tennessee Monkey Trial*, written by Peter Goodchild, is based entirely on original transcripts of the famous 1925 Tennessee v. John Scopes "Monkey Trial," which challenged the newly passed Tennessee legislature's Butler Act banning the teaching of evolution in the state's public schools. Recreated by a renowned cast of actors, the play transports audiences back to Dayton, Tennessee's sweltering, tension-filled courtroom during the summer of 1925 where they will experience first-hand the dramatic trial as it took place.

Original Live Theatre Production

The Great Tennessee Monkey Trial by Peter Goodchild was originally commissioned and produced by L.A. Theatre Works and the BBC, in association with KCRW Santa Monica, CA. Recorded in 1994. It was directed by John Theocharis. The cast was as follows:

William Jennings Bryan	Edward Asner
Howard Morgan	Danny Cooksey
John Thomas Scopes	Jeff Corbett
Narrator	Tyne Daly
Clarence Darrow	Charles Durning
Shelton	Walt Goggins
Dudley Field Malone	Harold Gould
Arthur Garfield Hays	Gerrit Graham
Ensemble	Peter Jacobs
Ensemble	Macon McCalman
Ben McKenzie	Logan Ramsey
Judge John Raulston	John Randolph
H.L. Mencken	Joe Spano
Ensemble	Ray Stricklyn
Attorney General Tom Stewart	Harris Yulin

Additional Production

Recorded in Cambridge, Massachusetts before a live audience at the Institute of Politics at the John F. Kennedy School of Government, Harvard University in April 2007. It was directed by Brendon Fox. The cast was as follows:

William Jennings Bryan	Edward Asner
Ensemble	Bill Brochtrup
Ensemble	Kyle Colerider-Krugh
John Thomas Scopes	Matthew Patrick Davis
Clarence Darrow	John de Lancie
H.L. Mencken	James Gleason
Dudley Field Malone	Harry Groener
Judge John Raulston	Jerry Hardin
Attorney General Tom Stewart	Geoffrey Lower
Narrator	Marnie Mosiman
Arthur Garfield Hays	Kenneth Alan Williams

Characters*

Clarence Darrow
Sixty-eight-year-old Darrow was near the end of his career as the foremost trial lawyer of his time, a career in which he had defended high-profile cases involving social injustice and also famous murderers. Only the year before Dayton, he had successfully defended the self-confessed murderers Leopold and Loeb.

He delighted in challenging traditional concepts of morality and religion. He regarded Christianity as an enslaving religion. Genesis, he believed, had given man an inflated sense of self-importance. In his mind the Dayton trial was a duel with traditional religion, very different from the issues of academic freedom that concerned his colleagues from the American Civil Liberties Union (ACLU), and this was to cause friction. Two years previously he had publicly challenged Bryan to answer questions on the meaning of the Bible but Bryan had not replied.

William Jennings Bryan
In 1896, at the age of thirty-six, Bryan's oratory and enthusiasm made him the youngest Democratic presidential nominee ever. He was narrowly defeated but with popular reformist campaigns on votes for women and a minimum wage, he was twice more the Democrats' nominee—though without success.

In 1912 he had helped Woodrow Wilson to power, becoming his Secretary of State. A confirmed pacifist, he had resigned in protest when Wilson pushed to join the war in Europe. After leaving office he began his fundamentalist crusade amassing an enormous following, particularly in the Southern and Western states where he delivered up to 200 speeches a year and commanded audiences of thousands. By age sixty-five, he lived in Florida where he had become wealthy from property development.

Arthur Garfield Hays
At age forty-four, Hays was a successful corporate lawyer who turned to the ACLU out of boredom and remained one of its central figures for three decades. His belief in direct action, such as selling banned books on Boston Commons, and supporting illegal union action, had resulted in periods in jail. Some years after Dayton, Hays, a Jew, had gone to Germany to defend the radicals accused of burning the Reichstag.

Dudley Field Malone
Malone, age forty-four, was an international divorce lawyer who embraced radical causes. As a young man, he had been Bryan's Undersecretary at the State Department. Malone was the only member of the defense who was a practicing Christian.

Henry Louis Mencken
H.L. Mencken, age forty-five, of the *Baltimore Sun* was one of the most influential journalists of the time and a friend of both Darrow and Hays. His paper had helped fund Scopes' defense. His caustic and disdainful reporting of the trial brought the local police chief to fear for his safety from angry locals.

Ages given are those at the time of the trial

Tom Stewart
Stewart, age thirty-four, was Tennessee's newly appointed Attorney General who led the prosecution team. He was to surprise and frustrate the defense with his tenacity and grasp of the law. He himself was not a fundamentalist but resented interference in state affairs by outsiders. Later he became a member of the Senate.

Judge John Raulston
Raulston was a local judge and lay preacher, more used to trying bootleggers and petty thieves. At the time of the trial he was coming up for re-election to his post. After the trial he was to declare himself against evolution.

John Thomas Scopes
Scopes, age twenty-four, was a general science teacher and part-time football coach at Rhea County High School in Dayton. He played little part in the proceedings, other than to resist those in the ACLU who wanted to replace Darrow as his counsel. During the trial, he received numerous lucrative offers from newspapers and of film work in Hollywood, all of which he turned down.

Producing Director Notes

Susan Loewenberg

In 2005 we were approached to do a national tour—to share a behind-the-scenes look at how we created our weekly radio show *The Play's the Thing*. We had no idea how it would—to borrow a word from Mr. Darwin—evolve.

We chose Peter Goodchild's *The Great Tennessee Monkey Trial* after we discovered that out of all the recordings we had given to public school teachers across the country this was the most utilized play. The play was so well received that we toured it again in 2007–2008 and in 2009. The issues that fuel the drama of Goodchild's work were headlines of every newspaper and debated on television and radio talk shows with as much controversy as the original trial in 1925. Politicians, from the President to the Speaker of the House, stated their opinion. School boards in Kansas and other states voted on whether or not evolution can be taught as science. The terms have changed—what was once a battle between science and faith had now become reframed as a debate between evolution and intelligent design, an approach to life's beginning put forth by the Seattle-based Discovery Institute—but the passion on both sides remained as divisive as ever.

The Great Tennessee Monkey Trial resonates today for many reasons. It is a fascinating piece of real drama set in 1925 when America was changing. A world war had ended, social traditions were under strain, jazz played in the background, and a great wave of revivalism swept the country. Dayton, Tennessee was a sleepy town looking for a way to put itself on the map and in the Butler Act a few of its citizens found a way, with the help of the ACLU, to stage what would turn out to be the trial of its time.

John Thomas Scopes, a young science teacher and part-time football coach, was persuaded to volunteer to challenge the state's law forbidding the teaching of evolution in the classroom. The trial attracted a most unlikely set of lawyers and observers—from the three-time Presidential candidate and former Secretary of State turned religious speaker William Jennings Bryan, on the prosecution side, to Clarence Darrow, a famed criminal attorney for the defense. Arthur Garfield Hays, a prominent free speech advocate, joined Darrow, as did international divorce lawyer Dudley Field Malone, who was to make one of the most powerful speeches during the trial.

A circus atmosphere pervaded the town—from the 1,000 people who swarmed the courtroom the first day, to the side-show chimpanzees said to have been brought in by the prosecution, the evangelists preaching to crowds of the faithful, and the Anti-Evolution League members selling copies of T.T. Martin's book *Hell and the High School*. Eventually the trial would be moved outside to the lawn, where several thousand more came to listen. Journalists, including H.L. Mencken, came from around the country, and the trial would become the first court case ever to be broadcast on national radio. The whole country was listening and avidly following the case's arguments and testimonies. On trial were both Darwin's theories as well as the Bible's claims and the debate between the two sides was often acrimonious and fiery.

Fast-forward to today and the same questions are before us. What is it that makes this particular branch of science so controversial? Why are we, over ninety years after that famous trial, still echoing the arguments of its great orators, Clarence Darrow and William Jennings Bryan?

We have found, we hope, a different way to approach these difficult and complex questions. By going backward and taking another look at what actually happened in that hot and dusty courtroom, perhaps we can go forward in our thinking with new ways to approach this highly charged debate. From a backstage look at how a radio drama is created, we found ourselves creating something else, something that perhaps only theater can do in its alchemical mix of intimacy and community. We found ourselves staging a national conversation—one that began with the docudrama by Peter Goodchild and will go on to include those in our towns and cities who are a part of this drama today. Scientists, theologians, politicians, historians, legal scholars, and more joined the actors in this great road show and we ask you, our reader, to do so as well.

Author's Notes

Peter Goodchild

The trial is perhaps best known from the play *Inherit the Wind*, later made into a film starring Spencer Tracy and Fredric March. For all their dramatic power, both the play and the film significantly distort events and simplify the issues surrounding the legendary confrontation between Clarence Darrow and William Jennings Bryan in Dayton, Tennessee eighty years ago. The trial in "Inherit the Wind" is seen as a clash between open-mindedness and dogmatism, but both Darwinism and the original Scopes trial raise more complex issues.

When first published in 1859, the impact of Darwin's *Origin of the Species* was truly profound. According to Darwin, species arose by the "natural selection of numerous, slight, favorable variations" and these variations, over time, proved beneficial in the battle for "survival of the fittest." Not only did this theory challenge the authority of the Bible and its account of creation but it also raised questions about the relationship of man to his universe. His position as the crowning creation of a universe created by a loving God was no longer secure. Instead he could be seen as just the latest arrival in an impersonal universe, which operated by the random rules of natural selection and was tainted by the cruelty of survival of the fittest.

Darwin himself had been deeply disturbed by his own findings. However, after the furor at the time of publication, a majority of scientists came to accept the fact of evolution—albeit without understanding the mechanism—and many faithful came to accept it as the means by which a still benevolent God worked his will.

The First World War changed that. Its brutality and the apparent breakdown of traditional values that followed generated widespread concern, and among conservative Christians Darwinism was seen to have much to answer for. Not only had it weakened the moral authority of the Bible, but it was argued that, through the writings of Friedrich Nietzsche, Darwinism had provided the Germans with the justification for a violent and competitive struggle "for the good of the world." Furthermore a 1916 study of religious belief among college students and professors showed that, while 15 percent of freshmen were "unbelievers," the number had grown to nearly 40 percent by the time they graduated. Furthermore the greatest number, over 80 percent, was found amongst biologists.

These criticisms of the social impact of Darwinism were embraced by the one-time reformist politician William Jennings Bryan. He declared that "to destroy the faith of Christians and lay the foundations for the bloodiest war in history would seem enough to condemn Darwinism."

In Bryan, the Baptists, Methodists, and Pentecostalists who, in 1919, had collaborated to create the World Christian Fundamentals Association, found a leader powerful enough to turn their campaign into political action. In 1921, Bryan joined the Baptists in Kentucky calling for a state law against teaching evolution in public schools. The resolution just failed, but over the next four years the anti-evolution crusade attempted restrictive legislation in seven states, and succeeded in four of them. The last had been the Butler Act, passed by the Tennessee legislature in early 1925. It stated:

> That it shall be unlawful for any teacher in the public schools of the state to teach any theory that denies the story of the Divine Creation of man taught in the Bible, and to teach instead that man has descended from a lower order of animals.

With these attacks on religious freedom, its involvement in issues ranging from prohibition to abortion and its links in some areas to the violent Ku Klux Klan, fundamentalism was being seen as a threat to civil liberties. So concerned was the newly formed American Civil Liberties Union (ACLU) that they decided to mount a test case. They advertised throughout Tennessee for a teacher of evolution who would challenge the new law, and their call was answered by a group of businessmen in the once prosperous mining town of Dayton. They hoped that such an event in Dayton would restore its fortunes and they approached a general science teacher at the local high school, John Scopes. Scopes proved a willing collaborator and went off to have himself arrested.

The businessmen of Dayton may have relished the trial but the state legislature knew the strength of liberal opinion nationwide against the law, and feared both ridicule and accusations of bigotry. They were determined to avoid any debate of the broad issues of academic and religious freedom, which the ACLU wished to publicize through the trial. Instead they intended to limit the case to the simple question of John Scopes' guilt under the Act. The prosecution was led by the able 34-year-old state Attorney General, Tom Stewart. Bryan himself was invited to join the team but had not tried a case in thirty years. However, he was expected to make both an opening and closing speech.

Arthur Garfield Hays led the ACLU's legal team defending Scopes and he had welcomed an offer from the leading trial lawyer of the day, Clarence Darrow, to join the defense. Darrow, in turn, brought with him Dudley Malone, a wealthy Irish Catholic divorce lawyer, and along with them came one of the best-known journalists of the time, H.L. Mencken of the *Baltimore Sun*.

By the time the trial opened in sweltering heat on Friday, July 10, 1925 there were estimated to be some 200 journalists covering the case, and telegraph operators wired stories to Europe and Australia. It was also going to be the first American trial to be broadcast nationally by radio. Outside the court, evangelists shared the streets of Dayton with monkeys and chimpanzees dressed in suits and ties, and stalls selling "Monkey Fizz" soda, celebrating man's alleged common ancestry with the apes. On his arrival, Bryan had set the tone by declaring that, "If evolution wins, Christianity goes." Everyone was hoping for a momentous event, a battle royal between science and faith.

Act One

The opening (fade up gospel music: "We Will Understand It Better By and By"):

Narrator   It was the trial of the century—two of the most famous men in America locked in ideological combat. For the press it was the headline story of the decade, and it marked the first time the new medium of radio was used to broadcast a trial to listeners all across the nation. The issues were as controversial then as they are today. It was an event that came to be known as . . . THE GREAT TENNESSEE MONKEY TRIAL.

Sound of crowd in an expectant state. Train whistle is heard. Crowd cheers approaching train.

Narrator   Tuesday, July 7, 1925, the Royal Palm Limited train from Florida was making a special stop at the tiny train station in Dayton, Tennessee.

A crowd numbering several hundred was there to greet one of the most celebrated men to ever visit this backwater town; one-time Secretary of State and three-time Democratic Presidential candidate—William Jennings Bryan. He had come to join the prosecution in the case of John Thomas Scopes versus the state of Tennessee

Bryan   Well, I'm here.

Crowd cheers.

Long have I looked forward to getting to Dayton and I'm ready for anything that is to be done. John Scopes has been indicted for the teaching of evolution in our public schools, which is against the law in this state.

Make no mistake, my dear friends, the contest between evolution and Christianity is a duel to the death; a battle between the unbelievers that attempt to speak through so-called "science," and the defenders of the Christian faith speaking through the legislature of Tennessee.

Cheers.

If the Butler Act is upheld and evolution is banned from our schools—and the morals of our children protected—there will be millions of Christians everywhere who—with hearts full of gratitude—will call you, the people of Dayton, blessed.

Cheers, the band begins to play and fades out.

Narrator   It was in the aftermath of the First World War that religious fundamentalism was re-ignited in America and brought men like William Jennings Bryan to its ranks.

The shock of a brutal conflict, and the perceived breakdown of traditional values, created a search for causes; for reasons; and among conservative Christians one of the main targets was Darwin's theory of evolution.

By 1925, Bryan was heading a formidable movement, using state legislation to prevent the teaching of evolution across the nation. Tennessee was the first to pass such an act, introduced by farmer-senator John Butler.

Butler   It shall be unlawful for any teacher in any of the Universities, Normals and all other public schools in the state of Tennessee to teach any theory that denies the story of the Divine Creation of man as taught in the Bible, and to teach instead that man has descended from a lower order of animals.

Narrator   Known as the Butler Act, it was passed by the Tennessee legislature on March 21, 1925. The fundamentalists cheered.

The American Civil Liberties Union, however, saw it as a threat to the constitution and decided to mount a test case.

They advertised throughout Tennessee for a teacher who would challenge the new law, and this was where the little town of Dayton got involved.

An attractive and once prosperous iron and coal-mining town, with eleven churches serving only 1800 inhabitants, Dayton had fallen on hard times and was desperately looking to better itself. So they turned to a popular science teacher by the name of John Thomas Scopes.

Scopes   On May 5, a group of local businessmen asked to meet with me in Frank Robinson's Drug Store and Soda Fountain.

To them.

Morning, Mr. Robinson.

Robinson   John.

Scopes   Mr. White

White   John.

Scopes (*to audience*)   Frank Robinson handed me the *Chattanooga News* where the American Civil Liberties Union was offering to pay the expenses of anyone willing to test the constitutionality of the Butler Act.

Robinson   It's an opportunity to put this little town back on the map.

White   John, we need a volunteer.

Scopes (*to audience*)   I knew that, sooner or later, someone would have to take a stand against the stifling of freedom the Butler Act represented.

(*To* **Robinson**.) Sure, I'll volunteer, provided you can prove I've taught evolution.

Robinson   Well, you filled in as a biology teacher when the principal was sick, didn't you?

White   Didn't you cover evolution?

Act One   11

Scopes (*to audience*)   To tell the truth, I wasn't sure I had, but Robinson and the others weren't concerned about this technicality. I had expressed a willingness to stand trial and that was enough. Frank walked over to the phone and called the *Chattanooga News*.

Robinson   This is F.E. Robinson in Dayton; I'm chairman of the school board here. We've just arrested a man for teaching evolution. What'd ya think about that?!

Narrator   In fact, John Scopes had to find the sheriff to get *himself* arrested; after that Scopes returned to playing tennis.

Robinson then sent a cable to the American Civil Liberties Union and there was a prompt reply . . .

Sound of telegraph.

Hays   "We will cooperate Scopes case with financial aid, legal advice, and publicity."

White   Frank, we're in business!

Narrator   As intended, the trial became national news almost immediately and the giants of both the liberal and fundamentalist causes came and answered the call to battle.

The first to step up to the plate was William Jennings Bryan. He had been Woodrow Wilson's Secretary of State during the First World War, but now, with his political career in decline, he attached himself to a variety of causes. By 1925 he had found fame as a leader of the fundamentalists.

Renowned as a preacher and great orator there were many who were put off by his messianic approach. Back in Nebraska, his home state, he was described as:

Nebraskan   "Like the River Platte—a mile wide at the mouth, but only six inches deep."

Narrator   Bryan's involvement in the trial galvanized another great American into joining the fray. The country's most famous criminal lawyer and one of its most public agnostics: Mr. Clarence Darrow.

Darrow   I was in New York when I saw that Mr. Bryan had volunteered to assist in the prosecution. At once I volunteered to assist in the defense—free of charge.

My only object was to focus attention on the evil at hand—the program of Mr. Bryan and the other fundamentalists in America.

With me came my friends, Arthur Garfield Hays, attorney for the American Civil Liberties Union; and Dudley Field Malone, international divorce lawyer.

Narrator   And so they assembled from far 'n' wide in Dayton, Tennessee; two titans of the American scene preparing for battle or, as Bryan liked to say, "a duel to the death."

John Scopes may have been on trial for a misdemeanor carrying a likely penalty of only $100, but there were some 200 journalists in town, and not just from the U.S. Of A., but from all over the world.

H.L. Mencken, the renowned journalist with the acid tongue, set the scene best:

Mencken   Thursday, July 9, 1925: The town I confess, greatly surprised me. I expected to find a squalid Southern village, with darkies snoozing on the horse blocks, pigs rooting under the houses and the inhabitants full of hookworm and malaria.

What I found instead was a country town of charm and even beauty. The town boomers have banqueted Darrow as well as Bryan, but there is no mistaking which of the two has the crowd. What Bryan says doesn't seem to these congenial Baptists and Methodists to be argument; it seems to be a mere graceful statement of the obvious.

Narrator   The trial began on Friday, the 10th of July, in the surprisingly large and elegant courthouse at the centre of Dayton.

The crowd murmurs.

Darrow   At the top of the grand staircase, we entered the largest courtroom I have ever seen; able to accommodate a thousand of its townspeople.

Above the judge's seat, and in other places around the courtroom, were monster signs saying, "Read Your Bible Daily"—it looked as though there was a discount sale somewhere.

Bailiff   All rise.

Narrator   The court was presided over by John Raulston, a local judge and lay preacher, more used to trying bootleggers and petty thieves than issues of national importance. Tennessee's ambitious Attorney General, Tom Stewart, led the prosecution.

Bailiff   All be seated.

Raulston   Gentlemen, I desire to show you that we are glad to have you here—the foreign lawyers for both the state and the defense. I shall accord you the same privileges accorded to local counsel and I assure you again that we are delighted to have you with us. Mr. Attorney General Stewart, are you ready to proceed with the selection of the jury?

Stewart   Yes, Your Honor.

Raulston   Are you ready, Colonel Darrow?

Darrow   Yes, sir.

Narrator   By local custom attorneys on both sides were graced with the title "Colonel."

Raulston   Good. I would like to invite Rev. Cartwright to open the court with a prayer.

Cartwight Oh, God, our divine Father, we recognize Thee as the Supreme Ruler of the universe. We are incapable alone of thinking pure thoughts or performing righteous deeds. Hear our prayers and grant that the President of the United States down to the most insignificant officer of this court seek thy Wisdom and Honor and Glorify thy name . . .

Narrator The entire prayer ran over five minutes.

Raulston Thank you, Reverend Cartwright.

Gentlemen, shall we have the names drawn?

Narrator And so it was on the "First Day" the jury was examined. A four-year-old boy, perched on the corner of Judge Raulston's desk, drew the names of possible jurors from a large wooden box.

Stewart Mr. Riley, are you related by blood or marriage to John T. Scopes?

Riley No, sir.

Stewart Have you formed an opinion about him?

Riley No opinion, just what I've heard.

Stewart Just rumor talk?

Riley Yes sir.

Stewart Pass him on to you, Colonel.

Darrow Mr. Riley, you a farmer?

Riley Yes. And I was a coal miner too . . . for awhile.

Darrow I see. Member of a church?

Riley Yes, sir.

Darrow Which one?

Riley Baptist.

Darrow Do you have any feeling that evolution is a wrong teaching at this time?

Riley Well, I haven't studied very much about it.

Darrow Ever heard Mr. Bryan speak about it?

Riley No, sir.

Darrow Ever read anything he said about it?

Riley No, sir. I can't read.

Darrow Well, you're fortunate. With those glasses do you have a problem with your eyes?

Riley No, sir. I am uneducated, just uneducated.

Narrator Few of the prospective jurors knew what "evolution" was, but some who did had a very particular view.

Darrow You say you are a pastor, Mr. Massingill?

Massingill (*proudly*) Yes, I am pastoring four churches at this time.

Darrow Ever preach on evolution?

Massingill I'm strictly for the Bible.

Darrow I'm talking about evolution, I'm not talking about the Bible! Did you preach for or against evolution?

Massingill I preached against it, of course!

Darrow I challenge for cause. Your Honor.

Raulston Well, I want every juror to start with an open mind. I will have to excuse you, Reverend Massingill.

Mencken Friday, July 10: The selection of a jury went on all afternoon in the atmosphere of a blast furnace. It was obvious after a few rounds that the jury would be unanimously hot for Genesis.

The most that Mr. Darrow could hope for was to sneak in a few men bold enough to declare publicly that they would have to hear the evidence against Scopes *before* condemning him.

This is a strictly Christian community. For them, to be accused of heresy by their peers is like being accused of boiling their grandmother to make soap in Maryland.

Narrator By the end of the day the choices had been made—ten farmers, a teacher and a former U.S. Marshall.

Sound of crowd exiting the courtroom.

It was now the weekend and the crowds dispersed. Dayton, for the first time in its life, experienced a traffic jam as the visitors headed for the cool of the mountains. But when Darrow went out for an evening stroll, he found Dayton far from deserted.

Darrow Like mushrooms on every corner: "Hot Dog" booths, fruit peddlers, ice cream vendors had sprung into existence. Evangelists' tents were propped up everywhere. It sounded like hordes of howling dervishes were holding forth crying out against the wickedness of Darwin.

Sound of dance-hall music.

Scopes On Saturday night an old girlfriend asked me to walk her back from the dance pavilion. As we walked, suddenly, and to my great surprise, she enveloped me in a passionate embrace.

Kiss.

Simultaneously the path was flooded with light and a horde of photographers snapped away. After that, I was not so keen to accept even the most harmless invitation.

Sound of court spectators.

Narrator The court reconvened on Monday, July 13—the "Second Day."

Raulston Rev. Moffett would you please lead us in prayer.

Moffett Oh God, our Father. Thou who art the creator of the heavens and the earth and the sea and all that is in them; bless this court this morning. Guide our presiding judge, bless the jury, each member of it, that they shall be able to make a decision *according to the law* . . .

Narrator . . . When the prayer was finished Stewart read the indictment.

Stewart The grand jurors for the state of Tennessee present that John Thomas Scopes did willfully teach in the public schools certain theories that deny the story of the divine creation of man as taught in the Bible and did teach instead that man has descended from a lower order of animals.

Raulston So what is your plea, gentlemen? Colonel Hays.

Hays Your Honor, we the Defense make a motion to quash the indictment, and we would like simply to present our thirteen reasons for that motion.

Narrator In this attempt to quash the indictment at the lower court, the defense was challenging the constitutionality of the new law.

If they failed, they hoped to appeal the case to the federal court. This higher court would be bound to consider the constitutionality of the Butler Act.

The prosecution, on the other hand, was determined to stick to a narrow interpretation; simply establishing that Scopes was guilty of his teaching offence as indicted.

Stewart Your Honor, it has occurred to me that the jury should leave the courtroom.

Hays I object.

Stewart It doesn't make any difference whether you do or not, Colonel Hays. I addressed the Court.

Hays Your Honor, the jury has got to be the judge of the law.

Stewart There is no issue before the jury. Let the jury leave the room.

Hays Your Honor . . . we would like to present "experts" . . .

Stewart You don't need experts to explain a statute that explains itself. Mr. Scopes taught evolution. He was a school teacher in a school funded by the state of Tennessee. The questions have all been settled in Tennessee. If these gentlemen have any laws in the great metropolitan city of New York or in the *great white cities* of the . . .

Malone I would like to say here that I do not consider further allusion to geographical parts of the country as particularly necessary . . .

Raulston Please, please! Do not take offense! I want you gentlemen from New York or any other foreign state, to always remember that you are our guests and . . .

Stewart   It was not my intention, Your Honor, to insult or hurt the feelings of either one of these various gentleman, but . . .

Narrator   And so it went the whole morning as both sides jockeyed for position and for what was or was not to be "admitted." The jury was eventually dismissed.

That afternoon Stewart and Darrow clashed over the preferential treatment the Butler Act gave to the Bible.

Darrow   Your Honor.

Stewart (*in mid-argument*)   The Butler Act does not even approach interference with religious worship.

Darrow   It gives preference to the Bible.

Stewart   To the Bible?

Darrow   Yes, why not the Koran?

Stewart   It does not mention the Koran?

Darrow   Then doesn't it prefer the Bible to the Koran?

Stewart   We are not living in a heathen country so how could it prefer the Bible to the Koran?

Derisive laughter at the defense table.

Stewart   Are you saying teaching the Bible in the public schools is a religious matter?

Malone (*jumping in*)   It is an invasion of the right of the citizen . . .

Stewart   Because it imposes an opinion?

Malone   Because it imposes a *religious* opinion!

Darrow (*picking up*)   What we mean is this: to impose on a *science course* a particular view of creation from the Bible is, in our view, *interfering* with the civil rights . . .

Stewart (*jumps in*)   The Butler Act is not an invasion of a man's religious rights! He can go to church on Sunday or any other day, and there worship according to the dictates of his conscience. Mr. Scopes, the defendant, can do this. So this is not an invasion of religious liberty.

The legislature has simply directed through the Butler Act that public money shall not be spent in the teaching of theories that conflict or contravene the story of creation—*as stated in the Bible*—which the legislature have a right to do . . .

Darrow   Can I proceed, Your Honor?

Raulston   I will hear you, Colonel Darrow.

Stewart   Your Honor?! . . .

Raulston Sit down, General Stewart. It's Colonel Darrow's turn.

Darrow Thank you, and I shall always remember that this court, Your Honor, is the first one that ever gave me the great title of "Colonel" and I hope it will stick to me when I get back North—(*Dig to* **Stewart**.) to those *great white cities*!

Raulston I want you to take it back to your home, Colonel.

Darrow I shall try do that, Your Honor. Now the case we have to argue is a case at law; and hard as it is for me to bring my mind to conceive it—almost impossible as it is to put my mind back into the sixteenth century—I am going to argue this law as if it were serious and as if it were a death struggle between two civilizations.

What we find here today is as brazen and bold an attempt to destroy learning as was ever made in the Middle Ages. The only difference is we have not provided that Mr. Scopes shall be burned at the stake. But there is time for that, Your Honor. We have to approach these things gradually.

Now we have been informed that the legislature has the right to prescribe study in the public schools. Within reason, they no doubt have.

But the people of Tennessee adopted a piece of legislation that says you shan't teach any theory on the origin of man, *except* the divine account contained in the Bible.

No legislature is strong enough to pick any book as being divine. The state of Tennessee has no more right to teach the Bible as the Divine Book than that the Koran is the one, or the Book of Mormon, or the books of Confucius or the Buddha, or the essays of Emerson, or any one of a thousand books to which human souls have gone for consolation.

Now I ask you; what *is* the Bible? The Bible is made up of sixty-six books written over a period of about 1,000 years, some of them very early and some of them comparatively late.

It is a book primarily of religion and morals. It is not a book of science—never was and never was meant to be. There is nothing prescribed that would tell you how to build a railroad, or a steamboat, or how to make anything that would advance civilization.

It is not a book on biology—they knew nothing about it. They thought the earth was created 4,004 years before the Christian era. We know better. I doubt if there is a person in Tennessee who does not know better.

And there are in America at least 500 different sects or churches, all of which quarrel with each other on the importance or non-importance of certain things or the construction of certain passages. So, who is the chief mogul who is going to tell us what the Bible means?

No criminal statute can rest that way. There is not a chance for it. And the Butler Act is a criminal statute, and every criminal statute must be plain and simple. My friend the Attorney General says John Scopes knows what he is here for. Yes, I know what he is here for. He is here because the fundamentalists are against anyone who thinks.

Voice   Heathen!

The crowd reacts loudly.

Darrow   I know John Scopes is here because ignorance and bigotry are rampant. That is a pretty strong combination, Your Honor, and it makes him fearful. But the indictment the state uses to bring him here must be clear, it must be plain and simple.

I am a pseudo-scientist, and I believe in evolution; a pseudo-scientist so named by somebody from Florida. Mr. Bryan neither knows nor cares what science is, except to grab it by the throat and throttle it to death.

Now as a pseudo-scientist, can a legislative body say to someone like me, "You cannot read a book or take a lesson, or make a talk on science until you first find out whether you are saying anything against Genesis?"

It could, if it were not for the work of Thomas Jefferson, which is woven into every state constitution including this one and which says that no preference shall be given to any religion by law.

Yet here we have the state of Tennessee teaching evolution for years, and then along comes somebody who says we have to believe it as *they* believe it. And they publish a law—the Butler Act—inhibiting learning.

It makes the Bible the yardstick to measure every man's intellect; to measure every man's intelligence; and to measure every man's learning.

Is your mathematics good? Turn to Elijah. Is your astronomy good? See Genesis chapter two, verse seven. Is your chemistry good? See Deuteronomy three, six, or anything that tells about brimstone.

Every bit of knowledge that the mind has must be submitted to a religious test, and that is a travesty of justice and of the constitution. Show me that barber's case will you, Mr. Hays?

Now, Your Honor, I have got a case here—a Tennessee case where somebody had passed a law which said it was a misdemeanor for any barber to shave, shampoo, cut hair, or keep the bathrooms open on Sunday.

Laughter in the court.

Well, of course, I suppose it would be wicked to take a bath on Sunday—I don't know.

More laughter.

But that was not the trouble with the statute. The trouble was a barber could not give a bath on Sunday: but anybody else could.

Now I do not question the right of the legislature to fix the courses of study in a school.

What the state of Tennessee cannot do is make it a criminal act for this teacher to teach evolution and then permit books on evolution to be sold in every store and to permit newspapers from foreign countries to bring into your peaceful community the horrible utterances of evolution.

Oh no, nothing like that. Your Honor knows the fires that have been lighted in America to kindle religious bigotry and hate. If today . . .

Raulston   Sorry to interrupt your argument, Colonel, but it is adjourning time.

Darrow   If I may, I can close in five minutes. I shall . . .

Raulston   Proceed tomorrow.

Darrow   I shall not talk long, Your Honor. I will tell you this.

If today you can take a thing like evolution and make it a crime to teach it in the public school, tomorrow you can make it a crime to teach it in the private schools and then at the hustings or in church.

At the next session you may ban books and the newspapers. If you can do one you can do the other and, after a while, Your Honor, it is the setting of man against man, and creed against creed, until with flying banners and beating drums we are marching backwards to the sixteenth century when bigots burned the men who dared to bring any intelligence and enlightenment and culture to the human mind. Tomorrow I will say a few more words.

The crowd reacts with hissing.

Raulston   Court is adjourned to 9 o'clock tomorrow morning.

Mencken   Darrow's speech was not designed for reading but for hearing. It rose like a wind and ended like a flourish of bugles. The very judge on the bench, towards the end of it, began to look uneasy. But the morons in the audience, when it was over, simply hissed it.

During the whole delivery, the old mountebank, Bryan, sat tight-lipped and unmoved. He has these Hillbillies locked up and he knows it. His nonsense is their idea of sense.

Narrator   The third day of the trial was as hot as ever—97 degrees. It was Raulston's intention to adjourn the court while he completed his opinion.

The judge raps for order. The crowd does not respond immediately.

Raulston   Reverend Stribling, you may open with prayer . . .

Stribling   Our Father, help us to be loyal . . .

Darrow   Your Honor, I want to make an objection before the jury comes in.

Raulston   What is it, Colonel Darrow?

Darrow I object to prayer and I object to the jury being present when the court rules on the objection.

Stewart (*having not heard*) What is it?

Raulston Colonel Darrow objects to the court being opened with prayer, especially in the presence of the jury.

Stewart The jury is not here.

Raulston No? Well, I do not want to be unreasonable about anything but it has been my custom since I have been a judge to have prayers in the courtroom when it was convenient. I believe in prayer. I constantly invoke divine guidance myself when I'm on the bench. Reverend.

Motions to continue the prayer.

Stribling Our Father, help us to be . . .

Darrow Just a minute.

Raulston Yes.

Darrow I understand that His Honor has sometimes opened a court with prayer and sometimes not, and we took no exception on the first day or the second; but seeing that this has persisted and that this case is one where it is claimed by the state that there is a conflict between science and religion, then above all other cases there should be no attempt by means of prayer to influence the jury.

Stewart The state makes no contention that this is a conflict between science and religion. It is a case as to whether or not a schoolteacher has taught a doctrine prohibited by statute—that is all! The ideas extended by the agnostic counsel for the defense are foreign to the thoughts and ideas of the people of this state.

Hays I take exception to the statement "agnostic counsel for the defense."

Malone (*joining in*) Your Honor, those prayers we have already heard have been duly argumentative in that they help to increase a atmosphere of hostility to our point of view.

Stewart I would advise, Mr. Malone, that this is a God-fearing country.

Malone And it is no more God-fearing than that from which I come and in which I live!

Raulston Gentlemen, gentlemen, do not turn this into an argument.

Beat.

I've instructed the ministers leading the prayers to make no reference to the issues involved in this case. Therefore I am pledged to overrule the objection of counsel and invite Dr. Stribling to open the court with prayer.

Darrow I note an exception, Your Honor.

Raulston Dr. Stribling, please, please . . .

Stribling Our Father, to Thee we give all praise for every good thing in life and we invoke thy blessings upon us this morning—

Narrator When the prayer ended and Raulston adjourned the court he continued working on his opinion as to whether the case should proceed or be dismissed. However, when the court reconvened later in the afternoon, the defense raised the issue of prayers yet again.

Raulston (*banging gavel*) The court will come to order. I have—

Hays You Honor, may I present a petition to the court from religious representatives here in Dayton? "We, the following petition Your Honor that, if you continue opening the court of Rhea County with prayer . . ."

Stewart Your Honor, just a minute. I submit that Colonel Hays is absolutely out of order . . .

Hays Your Honor . . .

Stewart . . . Your Honor has passed upon the motion of prayer!

Hays I insist upon making this motion.

Stewart (*shouting*) I am making my exception to the court, would you please keep your mouth shut!

Hays Will Your Honor hear my motion?

Stewart I am making an exception . . .!

Raulston I will hear it, Colonel Hays.

Stewart This is entirely out of order, and I except to it with all the vehemence of my nature.

Hays ". . . It is requested that you select officiating clergymen from among *other* than fundamentalist churches." The signatories are eminent men, Your Honor: A Rabbi, two Unitarians and a Congregationalist.

Raulston I shall ask the Pastors' Association from now on to name the man who is to conduct prayer.

Laughter and loud applause.

Hays Your Honor knows that the men of the Pastors' association are not among the class of men that signed this petition.

Raulston Some are perhaps fundamentalists—I don't know.

Another round of applause.

Narrator Days of baking heat, along with delays in the judge's decision, were fueling an already hostile situation.

That evening the defense lawyers took some time to relax. As a publicity stunt, they enjoyed dinner with a "distant relative"—the immaculately dressed chimpanzee—Big Joe Mendi—who ate ketchup—daintily—with a spoon.

Sound of monkey slurping.

When the court opened on Wednesday—the fourth day—Judge Raulston, at last, presented his ruling.

Raulston   The courts are not concerned in questions of public policy and the motive or wisdom of a statute is the responsibility of the legislature, not of these courts.

Further, public schools are not maintained as places of worship; the relationship between the teacher and his employer are purely contractual, and if his conscience constrains him to teach evolution then he can find opportunities elsewhere. The court having passed on each ground is now pleased to overrule the whole motion and require the defendant to plead further.

Narrator   And there it was! After three and a half days of legal haggling, Raulston had set the exact limits on the case that the prosecution wanted. But the defense was determined to keep the broader issues in play. Stewart estimated that his whole case would take only an hour; while the defense believed their case would take weeks. Scopes pleaded . . .

Scopes   Not guilty.

Stewart   Yesterday afternoon, near the hour of adjournment, I said a thing which upon reflection I feel sorry for. As soon as I said it I knew I had said the wrong thing and I want to say to Mr. Hays that there was nothing back of what I said at all, except a temporarily ruffed temper. I am sorry for it and I apologize.

Hays (*taking no prisoners*)   I am happy to accept the apology of the Attorney General on condition that there be no further reference or allusions that are disrespectful to the state from which counsel for the defense come; and no reference or allusions to the economic, political, social, or religious views of the counsel for the defense; and further I wish to warn counsel for the prosecution that if statements of that sort are made in the presence of the jury we will regard them as prejudical.

Narrator   After that little dust-up, Dudley Malone, the New York Irish Catholic divorce lawyer, began preparing the ground for the defense's case.

Raulston (*interrupts*)   Before you get started, Colonel . . . I want to thank the little girl or whoever it may be that is so mindful to the court as to send up this beautiful bouquet of flowers.

Great applause all around.

Raulston (*continues*)   Now, Col. Malone, I don't want any argumentative statement made in front of the jury. I just want a brief statement of your theory.

Malone   I understand, Your Honor. The defense believes that "God is a spirit and they that worship Him must worship Him in spirit and in truth." That said, we the defense will show that there are millions of people who believe in evolution as well as in the creation stories set forth in the Bible and who find no conflict between the two.

And that we, the defense, maintain that such opinions are a matter of faith and interpretation, which each individual must determine for himself.

The defense also thinks that there is no conflict between evolution and Christianity. There may be between evolution and peculiar ideas of Christianity, which are held by Mr. Bryan, but we deny that the evangelical leader of the prosecution is an authorized spokesman for the Christians of the United States.

Now I wish to read from a commentary in praise of Jefferson's Statute of Religious Freedom. It reads, quote, "to attempt to compel people to accept a religious doctrine by act of law is to make not Christians but hypocrites." End quote

And what could be more true than this statement? And who wrote these words—William Jennings Bryan.

Stewart   Your Honor, I except to that part of the statement that was brought in Mr. Bryan's name and . . .

Malone   My relations with Mr. Bryan have been such for so many years, he would be the last one to think anything I have to say would have my personality in it. I do not think, Your Honor, that Mr. Bryan is the least sensitive about it.

Bryan   Not a bit. I ask no protection from the court. When the proper time comes I shall be able to show the gentleman that I stand today just where I did.

Great applause. Repeated banging of the gavel.

Mencken (*over the gavel*)   It was the first time Bryan spoke and it is clear that he is no longer thought of as a politician and job seeker in these godly regions, but has become half man and half archangel—in brief, a sort of fundamentalist pope.

Malone   Can I continue?

Raulston   Proceed, yes, Colonel Malone.

Malone   We shall prove that Christianity is bound up with no scientific theory, and that it has survived 2,000 years in the face of all the discoveries of science.

And for the purpose of illustration, we hope to show you from embryology the development of a child from a single cell to its birth.

Stewart   But we do not want him to read that part about the embryo . . .

Raulston   Carry on, Mr. Malone, please.

Malone   We shall show how, during its development in the womb, the embryo actually recapitulates the stages of evolution. And we also expect to show you how vital the theory of evolution is to geology.

And finally, the defense denies that it is part of any movement or conspiracy on the part of scientists to destroy the authority of Christianity or the Bible. The defense maintains that Genesis is in part a hymn, in part an allegory, written by men who thought the earth was flat and whose authority simply cannot be accepted to control the teachings of science in our schools.

Raulston   Have you finished, Colonel Malone? Any further statement from the state's side?

Stewart   None whatever.

Narrator   After Malone's opening statement the jury was sworn in and the first witness was called: Walter White, Superintendent of the Rhea County schools.

Stewart   Your Honor, I may use a few leading questions to get the evidence out.

Darrow *consents.*

Stewart   Mr. White, you were one of those present at the meeting in Robinson's Drug Store which began this case?

White   Yes, sir.

Stewart   Do you know what book Mr. Scopes used?

White (*strays a little*)   Mr. Scopes was the science teacher. He taught chemistry, biology, and other science courses . . .

Stewart   Did he teach from Hunter's biology book . . .

White   Yes sir.

Stewart   That is all.

Darrow *takes over.*

Darrow   What was the conversation between you and Mr. Scopes as to the teaching of Hunter's biology?

White   He said that he had reviewed the book, as was customary for a teacher to do, and that he couldn't teach the book without teaching evolution, and he could not teach evolution without violating the statute.

Darrow   Did the defendant say it was unconstitutional?

White   Yes. He defended his action by saying that the statute was unconstitutional.

Darrow   "Hunter's biology" was the official book adopted by the Tennessee Textbook Commission, was it not?

White   Yes. The official book.

Darrow   Now, do you know how long this book has been used?

White   It has been used since 1909. That's be sixteen years.

Darrow   That is all.

Raulston   Step down.

New witness for the prosecution.

Stewart   Your name is Howard Morgan?

Morgan   Yes, sir.

Stewart   And how old are you?

Morgan Fourteen years old, sir.

Stewart You're Luke Morgan's son. Your father works in the bank?

Morgan Yes, sir.

Stewart Now just state in your own words, Howard, what Professor Scopes taught you and when that was.

Morgan Yes, sir. It was along about April 2nd and he said the earth was once a hot molten mass too hot for plant or animal life to exist upon it. He said that in the sea, after the Earth cooled off, there was a little germ of a one-cell organism formed and it kept on evolving, and from this was man.

Stewart Good. Now, Howard, how did he classify man with reference to other animals? What did he say about them?

Morgan Well, the book and Mr. Scopes both classified man along with cats and dogs, cows, horses, monkeys, lions, and all that.

Stewart What did he say they were?

Morgan Mammals.

Stewart And classified them along with cats and dogs, horses, monkeys, and cows?

Morgan Yes, sir.

Stewart Cross-examine, Colonel Darrow.

Darrow *stands.*

Darrow Now, Howard, what do you mean by classify?

Morgan Well, it means classifying these animals we mentioned, that men were just the same as them. In other words—

Darrow He didn't say a cat was the same as a man, did he?

Morgan No, sir, he said man had a reasoning power that these animals did not.

Darrow There's some doubt about that, but that is what he said . . .

Laughter.

Stewart With some men.

Darrow A great many. Now, Howard, he said they were all mammals didn't he?

Morgan Yes, sir.

Darrow But did he tell you what distinguished mammals from other animals?

Morgan I don't remember.

Darrow But he said dogs, and horses, monkeys, cows, man, whales, they were all mammals?

Morgan Yes, sir, but I don't know about the whales.

Laughter.

Raulston   Order.

Darrow   And you didn't know that the definition of a mammal was a species that suckled its young, did you?

Morgan   No, sir.

Darrow   Well, did he tell you anything else that was wicked?

Morgan   No, sir.

Darrow   And it has not hurt you any, has it?

Morgan   No, sir.

Darrow   That's all.

Narrator   The last witness to appear for the prosecution was F.E. Robinson, in whose drug store the famous meeting took place.

Darrow   General Stewart showed you the book *Civic Biology,* which I hold in my hand. You were selling them? Were you not?

Robinson   Yes, sir.

Darrow   And you were also a member of the school board?

Robinson   Yes, sir.

Darrow   Would you now read pages 194 and 195, "The Doctrine of Evolution."

Pages turning.

Robinson (*reads*)   "We have now learned that animal forms may be arranged so as to begin with very simple one-cell forms and culminate with a group which contains man himself."

Darrow   And this part on page 195 on "Man's Relationship with the Monkeys."

Stewart   Oh yes, please, just go right on.

Darrow   I will. Continue, Mr. Robinson.

Robinson   "In their method of learning, although monkeys do not reach the human stage of ideas, yet in the number of things he learns, the complex habits he can form, the monkey justifies his inclusion with man."

Darrow   That is what was read in class?

Robinson   Yes, sir.

Darrow   How do you get these books, Mr. Robinson?

Robinson   From the state depository at Chattanooga.

Darrow   You got them from the state authorities . . .?

Robinson   By the State Board of Education? Yes, sir.

Darrow   Thank you . . .

Stewart   Perhaps as Mr. Darrow has seen fit to read from that part of the biology, Your Honor, I want at this point to read the first two chapters of Genesis.

Fades away.

"In the beginning God created the heaven and the earth. And the earth was without form and void . . ."

Mencken   There is, in fact, considerable heat in the trial. The high point was reached with the appearance of Dr. Metcalf, the eminent zoologist, of the Johns Hopkins. The instant the doctor was asked a question Bryan came out from behind the table and planted himself not ten feet away.

Bryan *is standing across from* **Darrow**.

Darrow   Give us your name.

Metcalf   Maynard M. Metcalf.

Darrow   Dr. Metcalf, are you an evolutionist?

Metcalf   Surely, under certain circumstances that question would be an insult, but under these circumstances I do not regard it as such.

Darrow   Do you know any scientific man in the world that is not an evolutionist?

Stewart   We except to that, of course. Though if you want them all to take a vote . . . ?

Hays   Our whole case depends upon proving that evolution is a reasonable scientific theory.

Raulston   I do not know how you can prove it reasonable by proving what some other person believes. That would be hearsay testimony.

Hays   But we expect to prove what all science says.

Raulston   Then bring them here and offer them. I will hear you. Exception sustained.

Darrow   Professor Metcalf, what would you say, that practically all scientists . . .

Stewart   Your Honor, as we do not yet know if Dr. Metcalf's evidence will be admissible, I suggest the court reporter and the council go close to the witness so that they can hear but the jury cannot.

Raulston   As you say, Colonel Stewart.

Darrow (*quietly*)   So what would you say, that practically all scientific men were or were not evolutionists?

Metcalf   Evolution and the theory of evolution are fundamentally different things. The "fact" of evolution is perfectly clear but I doubt any two scientists would agree on the exact method by which evolution has been brought about.

Darrow Will you state what evolution is then with regard to the origin of man?

Stewart We except to that.

Darrow How is that?

Stewart We are excepting, Your Honor, to everything that mentions evolution . . .

Darrow How is the jury, only one of whom ever read about evolution, expected to pass on this question without being told what it is?

Stewart Your Honor, we want the jury excluded now. We do not want them to hear any more questions along this line.

Hays If Your Honor please, I am learning every day more about the procedures in the state of Tennessee. First, our opponents object to the jury hearing the law; now, they are objecting to the jury hearing the facts!

Raulston Objection sustained.

Slight confusion.

That is I agree with *you*, General Stewart. The jury is to vacate.

Narrator And so the jury, much to their annoyance, *again* left the courtroom. Darrow continued to question Metcalf for possible use in a later appeal.

Darrow Dr. Metcalf, when did the earliest organism appear?

Metcalf It is awfully hard to answer in years—geologists talk in ages, not years—but . . .

Darrow More than 6,000 years?

Metcalf Well, I would say 600 million years is a modest guess. And during that time this whole great fundamental evolutionary series, seen throughout the whole realm of organic life, has continued; making it extremely probable that man evolved in the same fashion.

Mencken Wednesday, July 15, 1925: The doctor was never at a loss for a second, yet there was no cocksuredness in him. What he got over was a superb counter-blast to the fundamentalist bunkum. The jury, at least in theory, heard nothing of it, but it went whooping into the radio and it went banging into the face of Bryan.

It is a tragedy, indeed, to begin life as a hero and to end it as a buffoon. But let no one, laughing at him, underestimate the magic that lies in his black, malignant eye, his frayed but still eloquent voice. He can shake and inflame these poor ignoramuses as no other man can.

Narrator The next morning, Thursday, July 16—the "fifth day," the legal wrangle began on whether to admit the expert evidence. Joker and raconteur Ben McKenzie, the former Attorney General, made the prosecution's case.

McKenzie May it please Your Honor, since the beginning of this lawsuit, and upon meeting these distinguished gentlemen, I have begun to love them—every one. I love the great men!

Now on to the question in controversy: the defense, Your Honor, with the evidence of their scientists are trying to put words into God's mouth. So when He said, "And God created man in his own image out of the dust of the ground," they would have us say instead that He issued some sort of protoplasm, or soft dishrag, and put it in the ocean and said, "Old boy, if you wait around about 6,000 years, I will make something out of you."

Laughter.

The divine story is a much more reasonable story to me than that.

Raulston   General, let me ask you a question. Is it your position that the story of the divine creation is so clearly set forth in the Bible that no reasonable minds could differ?

McKenzie   Yes.

Raulston   That God created Adam *first* as a complete man.

McKenzie   That is right.

Raulston   And that the cell of life did not develop in time.

McKenzie   That is right. Man did not descend from a lower order of animals and then changed from one animal to another and finally a man's head shot up. I don't know where your witnesses have got their evidence but they are putting it up against the Word of God . . .

Hays   May I interrupt . . .

McKenzie   Do you believe the story of divine creation, Mr. Hays?

Hays   Well . . . that's none of your business.

McKenzie   Then don't interrupt me with impertinent questions . . .

Applause from the courtroom.

Raulston   Before we get started with the afternoon session I'd like to announce that the floor on which we are now assembled is burdened with a great weight. I do not know how well it is supported but sometimes buildings and floors give way; so I suggest you be as quiet as you can. Now, I believe, Mr. Bryan, you are going to speak for the state.

Mencken   Word that the great Bryan was to speak made the court house a magnet. Outside under the cool of the cotton wood trees, even greater crowds gathered to hear the story from the brazen mouths of the loudspeakers. The whole town was one great sounding board of oratory.

Bryan   A few remarks, Your Honor, before I get started: I've been tempted to speak before this but I've been able to withstand the temptation; even though I've been drawn into the case by the lawyers for the other side.

The principal attorney has often suggested that I am the arch conspirator responsible for the ignorance and bigotry he believes inspires this law. So you will understand why I'm overjoyed that Mr. Malone has seen fit to honor me by quoting my opinion on religious liberty. It tickles me no end.

As to the "so-called" experts . . . this is not the place to prove that the law ought never to have been passed. The place to prove that was in the legislature.

If the people of Tennessee were to go into a state like New York and try to convince those good people that a law they had just passed ought not to be enforced don't you think it would be resented as an impertinence?

New York just passed a law repealing prohibition—maybe we should send some Tennessee lawyers up there and set you folks straight.

Laughter.

And lastly, that little Howard Morgan; that boy is going to make a great lawyer some day.

Mr. Darrow thought that little boy was talking about evolution coming up from one cell. That's not evolution, that's growth! I'm not surprised the gentlemen of the defense are confused. Let me see if I can set them straight.

We have this book, Mr. Hunter's *Civic Biology*, the book Mr. Scopes was teaching. Has the court seen this diagram?

Raulston No, sir, I have not.

Bryan Well, sir, you must see it. On page 194 it purports to give someone's family tree. Man, I think. Not only his ancestors but his collateral relatives as well—518,900 of them branching off in increasingly developed groups. There are 8,000 protozoans, 35 hundred sponges! I am satisfied from some people I have seen, there must be 35 *thousand* sponges.

And then the insects: 360,000 of them, and in the hot weather we feel we've become intimately acquainted with every one.

And now we're getting up near our kinsfolk: 13,000 birds, 3,500 reptiles, 13,000 fishes—same number as birds, well, well—and then the mammals: 3,500 of them all in a little circle and man is in that same circle. Find him; find man. This book teaches your children that man is a mammal, and so undistinguishable that they leave him there with 3,499 other mammals. Including elephants!

Talk about putting Daniel in the Lion's Den!

How dare those scientists put man in a little circle like that, with lions and tigers and everything bad? Shutting man up with all these animals that have an odor that extends way beyond the circumference of the circle.

Mr. Scopes tells the children to copy this diagram, which effectively detaches them from the throne of God, and links their ancestors with the jungle. I quote page 195 . . . "from the old world monkeys, at a remote period, came man; the wonder and glory of the universe." Not even from American monkeys but from "old world monkeys" mind you! It's a great game to be put into the public schools, to find men among animals.

And then, my friend, if these children believe it, they go back home to scoff at the religion of their parents! But these parents have a right to say that no teacher paid by their money shall rob their children of faith in God and send them back to their houses skeptical infidels, or agnostics, or atheists!

They call us ignoramuses and bigots because we don't throw away our Bible, and yet they demand that we allow them to teach this stuff to our children!

They think life is a mystery that nobody can explain. Not one word about God at the back of it. They want to come in with their little padded up evolution that commences with nothing and goes nowhere.

They do not explain the great riddle of the universe; they do not deal with the problems of life; they do not teach the great science of how to live. There is no place for miracles in this train of evolution. They eliminate everything supernatural from the Old Testament and the New. They eliminate the Virgin Birth, the resurrection of the body and with it the doctrine of atonement.

They don't tell us in this long period of time between the cell and man, where man became endowed with the hope of immortality. They believe that man has been rising all the time; that he never fell from Grace and that when the Savior came, there was no reason for his coming, and that he was born of Joseph or some other corespondent, and that he lives in his grave.

Evolution is a doctrine that not only destroys their belief in God but takes from them every moral standard that the Bible gives us. It is the doctrine that gives us Nietzsche; the survival of the fittest; and the philosophy of the Superman—that supreme being who is unaffected by suffering, who has no pity for or tolerance of the weak.

We have the testimony of Mr. Darrow, my distinguished friend from Chicago, in the Leopold and Loeb murder case that, because Leopold read Nietzsche, the boy was not responsible for his premeditated murder of a weaker fellow student . . .

Darrow There is not a word of truth in this, Your Honor. Nietzsche never taught that.

Bryan I will read you what you said . . .

Darrow If you will read it all.

Bryan I will read that part I want; you can read the rest. "Is there any blame attached because somebody took Nietzsche's philosophy seriously and fashioned his life on it? The university would be more to blame than he is."

And now my friends, you have heard Mr. Darrow ask Howard Morgan; "Did it hurt you? Did it do you any harm?" Why did he not ask the boy's mother?

Darrow She did not testify, Your Honor.

Bryan Your Honor; here we have our greatest criminal lawyer stating that it is the universities, the teachers who are poisoning the minds of our children . . .

Darrow I object to the Leopold and Loeb case being brought into this one.

Bryan The Bible is the word of God: the Bible is the only expression of man's hope of salvation. The Bible is not going to be driven out of this court by "experts" who have come hundreds of miles to testify that they can reconcile evolution with a man made by God in His image and put here for purposes as part of the divine plan.

Applause.

Darrow Your Honor, what I went on to say was "you cannot destroy thought because some brain may be deranged by a thought. Every new religious doctrine has created its victims, there is no great idea but does both good *and* harm and we cannot stop because it may do harm."

Bryan (*a little out of control*) Nietzshe praised Darwin. He put him as one of the three great men of his century . . .

Darrow (*takes the bait*) Darwin didn't make half as many . . .

Bryan And Nietzsche himself became an atheist and tried to kill his father, his mother and his uncle . . . !

Darrow (*takes the bait*) Darwin didn't make half as many people insane as Jonathan Edwards, your great theologian!

Raulston All right, Colonels, that will be all. Mr. Malone, you speak last for the defense.

Narrator In the stifling heat, Malone had been the only one to remain fully clothed. But now as he rose to answer Bryan, he carefully took off his jacket, folded it neatly and laid it carefully on the counsel's table. Every eye was on him before he said a single word.

Malone If the court please, it does seem to me that we have gone far afield in this discussion.

What does this law, this Butler Act, do? We have been told it is not about a religious question. I defy anybody, after Mr. Bryan's speech, to believe that this is not a religious question.

Moreover the burden is on the prosecution to prove its case. And we maintain that even if everything the state has said in its testimony be true, and we admit that it is true. Then the defendant, Scopes, has still not violated this statute. To explain, let us for a moment take this law which says, quote; "It shall be unlawful to teach anything that denies the story of divine creation of man as taught in the Bible, and to teach that man is descended from a lower order of animals." End quote. It doesn't say "or" it says "and." So the prosecution has to prove not only that Scopes taught evolutionary theory, but that he also taught the theory that denies the theory of divine creation in the Bible.

So we believe we have the right to introduce evidence from witnesses to show that the defendant's evolutionary theory is not in conflict with the theory of creation in the Bible.

But these gentlemen say, "The Bible contains the truth and if the world of science produces any truth or facts not in the Bible as we understand it, then destroy science and keep our Bible."

But we say, "Keep your Bible." Keep it as your consolation, keep it as your guide but keep it where it belongs, in the world of your conscience, and in the world of theology and do not try to tell an intelligent world that these books—written by men who knew none of the accepted fundamental facts of science—can be put into a course of science, because what's it doing there?

Raulston Mr. Malone, is it your opinion that the theory of evolution is reconcilable with the story of the divine creation.

Malone Yes, sir.

Raulston And that out of that one single-life cell God created man by a process of development? Is that your theory?

Malone Yes, sir. But that's just one way, Your Honor. It could happen in many ways. But what we ask for is the right to bring to the court the evidence of scientists, God-fearing men who believe in the Bible but who support our view—that the Bible is not to be taken literally as an authority on science.

Raulston That is what I was trying to get—that you believe you have the right to introduce proof to show what the true interpretation of the Bible is . . .

Malone Yes, because what is the issue here that has gained the attention of people around the world? The mere technical question as to whether John Scopes taught a couple of paragraphs from that book? Oh no. The issue is as broad as Mr. Bryan has published it. And that is what we want to scrutinize with our experts.

And yet why the fear? Who has been excluding the jury for fear they might learn something? Have we? Why the fear of meeting issues? I don't understand it.

Is it as the prosecution would have us believe that the teachers and scientists of this country really are in combination to destroy the morals of the children to whom they have dedicated their lives?

Are preachers the only ones who care about our youth? Is the church the only source of morality? We should have no fears about the young people of America. They are a pretty smart generation. We have just had a war with 20 million dead. Civilization need not be so proud of what the grown-ups have done.

For God's sake, let the children have their minds kept open, close no doors to their knowledge. Let them have both theology *and* science. Let them both be taught.

We want everything we have to say on science and religion told, and we are ready to submit our theories to the direct and cross-examination of the prosecution. We have come here ready for a battle, for a duel.

Is our only weapon—the witnesses who shall testify to the accuracy of our theory—to be taken from us? That is not my idea of a duel, but there isn't going to be a duel. There is never a duel with the truth. The truth always wins and we are not afraid of it. The truth is no coward, the truth does not need the law—or Mr. Bryan. The truth is imperishable, eternal, and immortal, and needs no human agency to support it.

We are ready to tell the truth as we understand it. We feel we stand with progress, with intelligence, with science. Where is the fear? We defy it. We ask Your Honor to admit the evidence as a matter of correct law, as a matter of sound procedure, and as a matter of justice to the defense in this case.

Prolonged applause.

Scopes The courtroom went wild when Mr. Malone finished. The Chattanooga policeman applauded too, pounding the table with his night-stick—actually splitting the table top. The judge couldn't control it; but I was concentrating on watching Bryan and I realized that Malone had penetrated his flinty armor. There was only dejection on his face; the victory that had been his only minutes before was suddenly and disastrously dissipated. The people wanted to hear it all!

Several minutes later, the courtroom was cleared and only three persons remained, Bryan, Malone and myself. Bryan was sitting alone and as he tried to cool himself, he slowly would let the palm leaf drop and then he would stare at a spot in front of him. Then, without turning he said,

Bryan Dudley, that was the greatest speech I ever heard.

Malone Thank you, Mr. Bryan. I'm sorry it was I who had to make it.

Scopes (*beat*) I shall never forget that moment.

End of Act One.

Act Two

Spectators chatter as they enter the courtroom.

Narrator Friday, July 17th, the sixth day, was short but eventful. It began with Judge Raulston's ruling on the subject of "expert testimony."

Brings court to order.

Raulston In Tennessee, an act should be construed to carry out the purpose for which it is intended. In this case the legislature clarified their intention for the act as a whole when they stated that it was unlawful to teach that man descended from a lower order of animals. The ordinary non-expert mind can comprehend this simple language "descended from a lower order of animals." It is not ambiguous or complex, though I personally would suggest the substitution of the word "ascend" for the word "descend."

If the court is correct in this, then there is no justification for calling expert witnesses.

Therefore, the court is content to sustain the notices of the Attorney General to exclude expert testimony.

Hays Your Honor will permit me to take an exception? We say it is a denial of justice not to permit the defense to make its case on its own theory. It assumes the court has full knowledge on a subject which has been under study for generations.

Raulston Let the exception be entered on record.

Stewart I desire to except to the exceptions of the court's ruling. I think it is a reflection on the court.

Hays May I respectfully move that the court hear evidence in order to inform itself, in the presence of the court only, and in the absence of the jury?

Stewart Your Honor, they have no right to conduct a long, drawn-out examination and make a farce of Your Honor's opinion.

Bryan May I ask? If these witnesses are allowed to testify as experts for the information of the judge, I presume they will be subject to cross-examination.

Raulston They will if they go on the stand.

Darrow The prosecution has no right whatever to cross-examine any witness, when we are offering simply to show what we expect to prove.

Raulston I will say this: if they put the witness on the stand and the state decides to cross-examine them, I shall allow them to do so.

Darrow We except to it and take an exception.

Raulston Yes, sir: always expect this court to rule correctly.

Darrow No, sir, we do not.

Oohs and laughter.

Raulston I suppose you anticipated it?

Darrow Yes, otherwise we should not be taking our exceptions here, Your Honor. We expect to protect our rights in some other court. Now can we have the rest of the day to . . .

Raulston The rest of the day . . .?!

Darrow If Your Honor takes half a day to write an opinion surely we can have . . .

Raulston I have not taken . . .

Darrow We want to make a statement here of what we expect to prove. I do not understand why every request of the prosecution should meet with an endless waste of time, while the barest suggestion of anything that is perfectly competent on our part should be immediately overruled.

Raulston I hope you do not mean to reflect upon the court?

Darrow Well, Your Honor has the right to hope.

Crowd murmurs.

Raulston I have the right to do something else, perhaps.

Darrow All right, all right.

Raulston Mr. Darrow is certainly laboring under a mistake when he says this court has taken a day to prepare an opinion. It was perhaps five hours . . .

Stewart Your Honor needed that time.

Darrow I ask, is it unreasonable for me to ask for the rest of the day to prepare the statements? They will be read tomorrow.

Stewart They wouldn't be read: just filed. And they can be filed anytime after the lawsuit is done.

Malone We have these witnesses here who cannot stay; these men have been brought here at great expense; we want to make use of them while they are here.

Stewart What would be the purpose? For the enlightenment of the crowd perhaps?

Hays Will Your Honor hear the question about statements Monday morning?

Raulston I will hear it Monday morning.

Malone Eight o'clock, Monday morning.

Raulston Nine o'clock.

Stewart I object!

Raulston That is all.

Gavel.

Narrator And so ended Friday, the sixth day. It seemed to observers like H.L. Mencken that the case was over, effectively over.

Act Two 37

Mencken July 17, 1925: All that remains of the great cause of the state of Tennessee against the infidel Scopes is the formal business of bumping off the defendant. There may be some legal jousting or some gaudy oratory, but the main battle is over, with Genesis completely triumphant.

But let no one mistake this trial for comedy, farcical though it may be in all its details. Let this trial serve notice that Neanderthal man is organizing in these forlorn backwaters of the land, led by a fanatic devoid of conscience.

There are other states that had better look to their arsenals before the Hun is at their gate.

Narrator This was Mencken's final report from Dayton before he left. And not a moment too soon in the view of the local police chief who had to rescue him from locals angered by his acid comments.

Sound of band.

Over the weekend, however, Darrow was planning his comeback. And so, Monday, July 20th—the seventh day (not a day of rest!) promised excitement none of the departing journalists had expected.

Raulston Last Friday, contempt and insult were expressed in this court by Mr. Clarence Darrow, and therefore I order that a citation for contempt be served upon the said Clarence Darrow requiring him to appear here on Tuesday, July 21st to make answer. He will be required to execute a bond for $5,000 and not depart the court without leave.

Darrow What is the bond, Your Honor?

Raulston $5,000.

Darrow I have to put up this money?

Raulston When the papers are served.

Darrow I do not know whether I could get anybody, Your Honor . . .

There is a growing noise in the court.

Fighting to be heard.

Spurlock If Mr. Darrow is willing, I can provide the bond—Frank Spurlock, Your Honor.

Darrow Thank you, Mr. Spurlock.

Raulston Come forward would you, Mr. Spurlock, and then let the day's proceedings commence.

Narrator Eminent scientists from the universities of Chicago, Harvard, Missouri, Johns Hopkins, and others provided written statements and Arthur Hays, after much wrangling, was allowed to read from some of them.

Hays If the Hebrew Bible were properly translated and understood, one would not find any conflict with the theory of evolution. In the translation of the Hebrew Bible, from which the King James Protestant version is derived, there are many errors. The word "create" purports to be a translation of "bara." This word "bara" is used to represent the whole cosmic scheme and the correct translation is "to set in motion." From that incorrect translation great confusion has resulted.

Then, in the first chapter of Genesis, the word "Adam" is used. The word "Adam," or Adam does not mean a man but actually a living organism containing blood. If that is a lower order of animal, then Genesis itself teaches that man is descended from a lower order of animals.

Narrator   And so the accumulation of evidence continued in readiness, everyone thought, for the appeal to the federal court. But just after lunch, Darrow asked to speak.

Darrow   Your Honor, I have been practicing law for forty-seven years and never have I been criticized for anything I have done in court. I do think, however, Your Honor, that I went further than I should have done. I overstepped the mark and Your Honor could not help taking notice of it.

Personally, I don't think it constitutes contempt, but I am quite certain that the remark should not have been made, and I am sorry that I made it and I want to apologize to the court.

Raulston   Anyone anything else to say? Then, my friends, and Colonel Darrow, the man that I believe came into the world to save man from sin taught that it was godly to forgive. I believe in that Christ. I believe in these principles and I accept Colonel Darrow's apology.

Applause.

Bailiff approaches the judge and whispers.

Raulston   It's been brought to my attention that the there are now cracks in the ceiling below. It a glorious day outside and I believe that the wider audience outside would welcome hearing the closing speeches. I hereby move the proceedings to the courthouse lawn.

Sound of crowd moving outdoors.

Narrator   It was a striking scene. Under the cottonwood trees, Judge Raulston sat at a little wooden table in the centre of a raised speaker's platform, with the state's attorneys at his right and the defense at his left. In front was a sea of upturned faces.

Hays   The defense desires to call Mr. Bryan as a witness, and to place him on the stand now.

Crowd reacts.

Stewart *leaps to his feet—huffing and puffing—only to sit down a few moments later.*

Raulston   Do you think you have a right to Mr. Bryan's testimony or evidence like you did the others? If you ask him about any confidential matter, I will protect him, of course.

Darrow   I do not intend to do that. On the scientific matters, Colonel Bryan can speak for himself.

Bryan   If Your Honor please, I insist that Mr. Darrow can be put on the stand, and Mr. Malone, and Mr. Hays.

Raulston   Call anybody you desire. Ask them any questions you wish.

Bryan   Then we will call all three of them.

Darrow   Not at once?

Raulston   Mr. Bryan, you are not objecting to going on the stand?

Bryan   Not at all. Where do you want me to sit?

Raulston   These are extraordinary circumstances. Do you want Mr. Bryan sworn?

Bryan   I can say, "So help me God, I'll tell the truth."

Darrow   No, I take it you will tell truth, Mr. Bryan.

Narrator   The news that Darrow was to question Bryan traveled like wildfire and soon more than 3,000 spectators spread out across the lawn.

It was a shrewd move on Darrow's part. Two years earlier, Darrow had challenged Bryan in the press with a series of questions on the literal truth of the Bible. Sensing a trap, Bryan had refused to respond. But here, in front of the world's press, a man of Bryan's vanity could not refuse.

Darrow   You have given considerable study to the Bible, haven't you, Mr. Bryan?

Bryan   Yes, sir, I have tried to.

Darrow   Well, we all know you have—we are not going to dispute that at all.

Bryan   Good.

Darrow   Also you have written and published articles almost weekly, and sometimes have made interpretations of various things?

Bryan   I would not say interpretations, Mr. Darrow, but comments on the lesson.

Darrow   But you have made a general study of it?

Bryan   Yes, I have. I have studied the Bible for about fifty years. I have studied it more as I have become older than when I was but a boy.

Darrow   Do you claim that everything in the Bible should be literally interpreted?

Bryan   I believe everything in the Bible should be accepted as it is given. Some of the Bible is given illustratively. For instance: "ye are the salt of the earth." I would not insist that man is actually salt, or that he had flesh of salt, but it is used in the sense of salt as saving God's people.

Darrow   But when you read that Jonah swallowed the whale—or that the whale swallowed Jonah, excuse me, please—how do you literally interpret that?

Bryan When I read that a big fish swallowed Jonah—it does not say whale.

Darrow Doesn't it? Are you sure?

Bryan That is my recollection of it, a big fish: and I believe it. And I believe in a God who can make a whale and can make a man, and make both do what he pleases.

Darrow Now, you say, the big fish swallowed Jonah and he remained—how long—three days and then he spewed him up on the land? You believe that the big fish was made to swallow Jonah?

Bryan I am not prepared to say that. The Bible merely says it was done.

Darrow You don't know whether it was in the ordinary run of fish or made for that purpose?

Bryan You may guess: you evolutionists tend to guess.

Darrow But when we do "guess," we have the sense to guess right.

Bryan But you do not do it often. Let me add: one miracle is just as easy to believe as another.

Darrow It is for me.

Bryan It is for me.

Darrow Just as hard?

Bryan It is hard to believe for you but easy for me. A miracle is a thing performed beyond what man can perform. When you get beyond what man can do, you get within the realm of miracles. And it is just as easy to believe the miracle of Jonah as any other miracle in the Bible.

Darrow Perfectly easy to believe that Jonah swallowed the whale?

Bryan If the Bible said so. But the Bible doesn't make as extreme statements as evolutionists do. You use a definition of fact that includes imagination.

Darrow And you have a definition of fact which is nothing but imagination.

Stewart I object to that as argumentative.

Darrow So, you consider the story of Jonah and the whale a miracle?

Bryan I think it is.

Darrow Do you believe Joshua made the sun to stand still for the purpose of lengthening the day?

Bryan I accept the Bible absolutely.

Darrow Do you believe that the men who wrote it thought that the day could be lengthened, or that the sun could be stopped?

Bryan I don't know what they thought. I think they wrote the fact without expressing their own thoughts.

Act Two   41

Stewart   I want to object, Your Honor. This line of questioning has gone beyond the pale of any issue that could possibly be relevant into this lawsuit.

Raulston   I will hear Mr. Bryan.

Bryan   It seems to me it would be too exacting to confine the defense to the facts. If they're not allowed to get away from the facts, what have they to deal with?

Raulston   Mr. Bryan is willing to be examined. Go ahead.

Darrow   Have you an opinion as to whether—whoever wrote the book, I believe it was Joshua, the Book of Joshua—thought the sun went around the earth or not?

Bryan   I believe he was inspired.

Darrow   Can you answer my question?

Bryan   When you let me finish the statement.

Darrow   It is a simple question, but finish it.

Bryan   You cannot measure the length of my answers by the length of your question.

There is laughter around the court.

Darrow   No, except that the answer will be longer.

More laughter.

Bryan   I believe the author of the Bible was inspired by The Almighty; and that he may have been directed to use language that could be understood at that time, instead of using language that could not be understood till Darrow was born.

More laughter.

Darrow   So do you believe that, in order to explain the lengthening of the day, it would have to be construed that the earth stood still and not the other way around?

Bryan   I would not attempt to say that would have been necessary; but if my puny hand can hold up a glass of water and overcome the all powerful law of gravitation, I would not set limit to the power of the hand of the Almighty God that made the universe.

Darrow   I read that years ago. Now can you answer my question directly? If the day was lengthened by stopping either the earth or the sun, it must have been the earth?

Bryan   Well I would say so, yes. But saying it was the sun that stood still, that was the understanding at the time. In saying the sun stopped moving, the Lord was using language at that time that the people understood.

Darrow   Now, Mr. Bryan, have you ever pondered what would have naturally happened to the earth if it had stood still?

Bryan   No.

Darrow You have not?

Bryan No. The God I believe in could have taken care of that, Darrow.

Darrow Don't you know that it would have been converted into a molten mass of matter?

Bryan You testify to that when you get on the stand. I will give you a chance.

Darrow Don't you believe it?

Bryan I would want to hear expert testimony on that.

Darrow Or ever thought of it?

Bryan I have been too busy on things that I thought were of more importance than that.

Darrow Mr. Bryan, you believe the story of the flood to be a literal interpretation?

Bryan Yes.

Darrow When was that flood?

Bryan I wouldn't attempt to fix the date.

Darrow About 4004 BC? That estimate is printed in the Bible.

Bryan That was the estimate given. I would not say it is accurate.

Darrow Don't you know how it is arrived at?

Bryan I never made a calculation.

Darrow A calculation from what?

Bryan I could not say.

Darrow From the generations of man described in the Bible?

Bryan I would not want to say that.

Darrow What do you think?

Bryan I do not think about things I don't think about.

Darrow Do you think about things you do think about?

Bryan Well, sometimes . . .

Laughter.

Darrow You want to say now you have no idea how the dates for this flood were computed?

Bryan No, I don't say that. I say I don't know how accurate it was.

Stewart Your Honor, I am objecting to his cross-examining his own witness.

Darrow He is a hostile witness.

Act Two 43

Raulston   I am going to let Mr. Bryan control.

Bryan   I want him to have all the latitude he wants. For I'm going to have some latitude when he gets through.

Darrow   You can have latitude and longitude.

Laughter.

Stewart   Your Honor, this is not competent evidence.

Bryan   These gentlemen have not had much chance. They did not come here to try the case in hand. They came here to try revealed religion. I am here to defend it and they can ask me any questions they please.

There is applause.

Darrow   Great applause from the bleachers!

Bryan   From those you call "yokels."

Darrow   I never called them yokels.

Bryan   That is, the ignorance of Tennessee, the bigots you talk about.

Darrow   You mean who are applauding you?

Bryan   Those are the people you insult.

Darrow   You insult every man of science and learning in the world, because he does not believe in your fool religion.

Raulston   I will not stand for that.

Darrow   For what he is doing?

Raulston   I am talking to both of you.

Stewart   This has gone beyond the pale of a lawsuit, Your Honor. I have a public duty to perform, under my oath, and I ask the court to stop it. Mr. Darrow is making an effort to insult the gentleman on the witness stand and I ask this to be stopped.

Raulston   To stop it now would not be just to Mr. Bryan. He wants to ask the other gentleman questions along the same line.

Stewart   This is all incompetent.

Darrow   How long ago was the flood, Mr. Bryan?

Bryan   Let me see Archbishop Usher's calculation about it. They are the dates in the margin.

Darrow   Surely.

Foley sound of pages turning.

Bryan   Ah, yes here it is. It is given here as 2348 years BC.

Darrow And you believe that all living things that were not contained in the Ark were destroyed?

Bryan I think the fish may have lived.

Darrow The fish. Outside of the fish?

Bryan I cannot say.

Darrow You cannot say?

Bryan No. I accept that just as it is. I have no proof to the contrary.

Darrow I am asking you whether you believe.

Bryan I do.

Darrow That all living things outside the fish were destroyed.

Bryan What I say about the fish is merely a matter of humor.

Darrow I understand. And you believe every nation, every organization of men, every animal in the world—outside of the fish—were wiped out by the flood?

Bryan At that time but I want you to understand that the fish is merely a matter of humor!

Darrow At that time. And then, whatever human beings, including all the tribes that inhabited the world, and who run their pedigree straight back, and all the animals, have come on the earth since the flood?

Bryan Yes.

Darrow Within 4,000 years? Do you know any scientific man on earth that believes any such thing?

Bryan I cannot say, but I know some scientific men who dispute entirely the antiquity of man as testified to by other scientific men.

Darrow Oh, that does not answer the question. Let me ask it again.

Beat.

Bryan I don't think I have even asked a scientific man that direct question.

Darrow Quite important, isn't it?

Bryan Well, I don't know as it is.

Darrow You've never had any interest in the age of the various races and people and civilizations and animals that exist upon the earth today, is that right?

Bryan I have never felt a great deal of interest in the effort that has been made to dispute the Bible.

Darrow Do you know that there are thousands of Christians who believe the earth and the human race is much more ancient?

Act Two 45

Bryan   There may be.

Darrow   . . . but you've never investigated.

Bryan   I never found it necessary.

Darrow   Don't you know that the ancient civilizations of China are six or seven thousand years old, at the very least?

Bryan   No, but they would not run back beyond the creation, according to the Bible—6,000 years.

Darrow   You don't know how old they are, is that right?

Bryan   I don't know how old they are, but possibly you do.

Laughter around the court.

I think you would give preference to anybody who opposed the Bible.

Darrow   Do you have any idea how old the Egyptian civilization is?

Bryan   No.

Darrow   Do you know of any record in the world, outside the story of the Bible, which conforms to any statement that it is 4,300 years ago, or thereabouts, that all life was wiped off the face of the earth—except for the fish?

Bryan   I think they have found records.

Darrow   Do you know of any?

Bryan   Outside the Bible?

Darrow   Yes.

Bryan   Records reciting the flood exist in other religions, but the Christian religion has satisfied me and I have never felt it necessary to look up some competing religion.

Darrow   Like the religions of Confucius and Buddha?

Bryan   I can tell you something about that, if you want to know.

Darrow   Did you ever investigate them?

Bryan   Somewhat.

Darrow   Do you regard them as competitive?

Bryan   No. I think they are very inferior. There are those, Mr. Darrow, who say that Jesus brought nothing into the world and talk about Confucius' Golden Rule. But Confucius said, "Do not do unto others what you would not have done to you." That is purely negative while Jesus taught, "Do unto others what you would have done to you." There is all the difference between negative harmlessness and positive Christian helpfulness.

Darrow   Mr. Bryan, but do you know how old the Confucian religion is?

Bryan   No, sir.

Darrow   Do you know anything about how many people there were in Egypt 3,500 years ago, or how many people in China 5,000 years ago?

Bryan   No.

Darrow   Have you ever tried to find out?

Bryan   No, sir, you are the first man I ever heard of who was interested in it.

Laughter around the court.

Darrow   Mr. Bryan, am I really the first person you ever heard of who has been interested in the age of human societies and primitive man?

Bryan   You are the first man I ever heard speak of the numbers of people at these different periods.

Darrow   Where have you lived all your life?

Bryan   Not near you.

More laughter and applause.

Darrow   Nor anybody of learning?

Bryan   Oh, don't assume you know it all.

Darrow   Do you know there are thousands of books in the libraries on all these subjects, but you don't care how old the earth is, how old man is, and how long the animals have been here, do you?

Bryan   No, sir. I have been so well satisfied with the Christian religion that I have spent no time trying to find arguments against it. I have all the information I want to live by and to die by.

Darrow   All right. Can you tell me how old the earth is?

Bryan   No, I have never made a study of it. Although I could probably come as near as the scientists . . .

Darrow   Mr. Bryan, you don't think much of scientists, do you?

Bryan   Yes, I do, sir.

Darrow   Can you name one whose opinion you value on this subject?

Bryan   I can think of George Price; he was at a notable college near Lincoln, Nebraska, and he is a professor of geology at Lodi in California now.

Darrow   That is a small college.

Bryan   You judge a man by the size of his college but I would rather find what he believed.

Darrow   Whether his belief corresponds with your views and your prejudices?

Bryan I am no more prejudiced for the Bible than you are against it.

Darrow You mention Price, because he is the only human being in the world, so far as you know, that signs himself as a geologist and who believes like you do?

Bryan No, there is a man named Wright who . . .

Darrow We will get to Mr. Wright in a moment. Who publishes Price's book?

Bryan I can't tell you. I can get you the book.

Darrow Don't you know it is Revell and Co., Chicago?

Bryan I couldn't say.

Darrow They publish yours, don't they?

Bryan Yes, sir.

Stewart Will you let me make an exception? The man's publisher is not pertinent.

Darrow He has quoted a man that every scientist in this country knows is a mountebank and a pretender, and not a geologist at all.

Raulston You can ask him about the man but don't ask him about who publishes his book.

Darrow As you wish. So to return, have you any idea how old the earth is?

Bryan No.

Darrow The Bible you have introduced in evidence tells you, doesn't it?

Bryan I don't think it does, Mr. Darrow.

Darrow Let's see whether it does.

Foley sound of turning pages.

It says 4004 BC. Right here!

Bryan That is Bishop Usher's calculation.

Darrow Would you say that the earth was only 4,004 years old?

Bryan Oh, no. I think it is much older than that.

Darrow Really?! How much?

Bryan I couldn't say.

Stewart Your Honor, what is the purpose of this examination?

Bryan The purpose is to cast ridicule on everybody who believes in the Bible; and I am perfectly willing that the world shall know that these gentlemen have no other purpose than ridiculing every person who believes in the Bible.

Darrow We have the purpose of preventing bigots and ignoramuses from controlling the education of the United States and you know it, and that is all.

Bryan So now we have it, Mr. Darrow's purpose from his own mouth. And I am trying simply to protect the Word of God against him, the greatest atheist and agnostic in the United States.

There is prolonged applause.

Darrow I wish I could get a picture of these clackers.

Stewart Your Honor, I respectfully ask in the name of all that is legal to stop this examination and stop it now.

Hays I rather sympathize with the General, but Mr. Bryan is produced as a witness because he is one of the foremost students of the Bible in the United States. Mr. Bryan has already stated that the world is older than 6,000 years, and that is very helpful to us. And where is your evidence coming from? Your Bible—which states 4004 BC.

Bryan You think the Bible says that?

Hays The one you have taken in evidence says that.

Bryan I don't concede that.

Stewart It's absolutely worthless, Your Honor, even for the record in the Supreme Court.

Hays Not worth anything when Mr. Bryan, as Bible student, states you cannot take the Bible as literally true?

Stewart The Bible speaks for itself.

Hays You mean to say, General Stewart, that the Bible itself says whether these are parables? Does it?

Stewart Your Honor, this is just a harangue between Colonel Darrow and his witness.

Bryan Your Honor, the reason I am answering is to keep these gentlemen from saying I was afraid to meet them and let them question me.

Raulston Are we about through, Colonel Darrow?

Darrow I want to ask a few more questions about the creation.

Raulston We are going to adjourn for the day when Mr. Bryan comes off the stand, so be very brief, Mr. Darrow.

Darrow Mr. Bryan, do you believe that the first woman was Eve?

Bryan Yes.

Darrow Do you believe she was literally made out of Adam's rib?

Bryan I do.

Darrow Did you ever discover where Cain, Adam and Eve's son, got his wife?

Act Two   49

Bryan   No, sir, I leave the agnostics to hunt for her.

Darrow   All right. Does the statement "The morning and the evening were the first day" and "The morning and the evening were the second day" mean anything to you?

Bryan   I do not think it necessarily means a twenty-four-hour day.

Darrow   You do not?

Bryan   No.

Darrow   What do you consider it to be?

Bryan   Let me have the Bible. I have never attempted to explain it. The word "day" here is used to describe a whole period of creation. Therefore I do not see any necessity for construing the words "evening and the morning" as meaning necessarily a twenty-four-hour day.

Darrow   Does it or doesn't it?

Bryan   A great many people think so.

Darrow   But what do you think?

Bryan   I do not think it does.

Darrow   You think those were not literal days.

Bryan   I do not think they were twenty-four-hour days.

Darrow   I see.

Bryan   But I think it would be just as easy for the kind of God we believe in to make the earth in six days or in six years, or in six million years or in 600 million years. I do not think it important whether we believe one or the other.

Darrow   Have you any idea of the length of the periods?

Bryan   No, I don't.

Darrow   Do you think the sun was made on the fourth day?

Bryan   Yes.

Darrow   And they had evening and morning without the sun?

Bryan   I am simply saying it is a period.

Darrow   They had evening and morning for three periods without the sun, d'you think?

Bryan   I believe in creation, as told, and if I am not able to explain it, I will accept it.

Darrow   Can you not answer the question?

Bryan   I have answered it! I believe that it was made on the fourth day.

Darrow And they had the evening and the morning before that time for three days? Without the sun?

Bryan They might.

Darrow All right, that settles it. Now, if you call those "periods," they may have been a very long time?

Bryan They might have been.

Darrow The creation might have been going on for a very long time?

Bryan It might have continued for millions of years.

Darrow Yes. All right. But let me ask you now, you believe in the temptation of Eve by the serpent.

Bryan I do.

Darrow And the reason women have childbirth pains is because Eve tempted Adam in the Garden of Eden, just as it says?

And that, and I'll quote, "The Lord God said unto the serpent because thou has done this . . . upon thy belly thou shalt go and dust shalt thou eat all the days of thy life."

Bryan I believe that.

Darrow Any idea how the snake went around before that time.

Bryan Your Honor, I think I can shorten this testimony. The only purpose Mr. Darrow has is to slur at the Bible. I want the world to know that this man who does not believe in a God, is trying to use a court in Tennessee . . .

Darrow I object to that . . .

Bryan —to slur at it, and while it will require time, I am willing to take it.

Darrow I object to your statement. I am examining you on your fool ideas that no intelligent Christian on earth believes.

Sound of an excited audience and attorneys shouting—banging of gavel.

Raulston Order. Order. Can we have order? The court is adjourned.

Narrator As the crowd dispersed, scores of people clamored around Darrow, while Bryan, "the great commoner," sat exhausted, virtually alone with his thoughts.

Before the court opened the next day, a secret meeting took place between Raulston and a number of local politicians and police. In essence they warned the judge that things had developed to such a fever pitch that they could not be responsible for what might happen if the cross-examination continued.

At the same time Bryan had been told by Stewart that he would dismiss the case if there was any attempt to continue the duel with Darrow.

Raulston I fear I may have committed error yesterday in my over-zeal to ascertain any new insights; but now I feel that the testimony of Mr. Bryan can shed no light upon any issues pending before the higher courts. The lawsuit now is whether or not Mr. Scopes taught that man descended from a lower order of animals—and is not one of these broader issues. And so, I am pleased to expunge this testimony, given by Mr. Bryan yesterday, from the records of this court and it will not be considered further.

Darrow   If Your Honor please, we have no further witnesses, no proof to offer on the issues the court has just laid down; so we will thus ask the court to instruct the jury to find the defendant guilty. It will save a lot of time and I think it should be done.

Stewart   For the prosecution, we are pleased to accept Mr. Darrow's suggestion.

Bryan   May it please the court . . .

Raulston   I will hear you, Mr. Bryan.

Bryan   I fully agree that the testimony taken yesterday was not legitimate or proper. But now that the testimony is ended, I assume that you will expunge yesterday's questions as well as the answers.

Raulston   I have expunged the whole proceedings.

Bryan   What is more I have not had a chance to answer the charges the defense has made to my ignorance and bigotry.

Darrow   I object, Your Honor. What is all this about?

Bryan   Let me finish. Now that there is a plea of guilty, I realize I cannot make any closing statement; and so I am not asking to make a statement here.

Raulston   But I will hear what you have to say, Mr. Bryan.

Bryan   Your Honor, I shall have to trust to the justice of the press, to report what I will say to them later when I give them the questions I would have asked the defense had I been able to call them.

Darrow   Why don't you take us out with the press and ask us the questions and then they will have both the questions and the answers.

Bryan   The gentleman who represents the defense not only differs so much from me but also in the manner of the court. I think it hardly fair for them to have brought into the limelight my views on religion, and then to stand behind the dark lantern, which throws light on others but conceals themselves. The country should know the religious attitudes of these people who come down here to deprive the people of Tennessee of the right to run their schools.

Darrow   I object to that.

Raulston   I overrule the objection.

Bryan   That is all.

Narrator   After that, the case moved swiftly to its inevitable conclusion. The jury did not even bother to retire but stood huddled in one of the corridors before returning nine minutes later.

Raulston Mr. Foreman, will you tell us whether you have agreed on a verdict.

Foreman Yes, sir.

Raulston What do you find?

Foreman We have found for the state; we find the defendant guilty.

Raulston Did you fix the fine?

Foreman No, sir.

Raulston You leave it to the court?

Foreman Leave it to the court.

Raulston Mr. Scopes, will you come forward, please, sir? Mr. Scopes, the jury has found you guilty under the law. Have you anything to say as to why the court should not impose punishment upon you?

Scopes Your Honor, I feel I have been convicted of violating an unjust statute. I will continue in the future, as I have in the past, to oppose this law in any way I can. Any other action would be in violation of my ideal of academic freedom—that is, to teach the truth as guaranteed in our Constitution, of personal and religious freedom. I think the fine is unjust.

Raulston The court now imposes on you a fine of $100 and costs, which you will arrange with the clerk.

Narrator After a series of effusive final speeches, the trial of John Thomas Scopes ended and the court was adjourned just after midday on July 21, 1925. The defense now expected the case to go to the Tennessee Supreme Court.

However, with the case causing the politicians of Tennessee increasing embarrassment, playing as it did to its "hayseed" image, the state Supreme Court used a legal nicety to relieve the embarrassment.

There was a requirement that fines greater than $50 had to be set by the jury, but Judge Raulston, in his rush, had set the fine himself.

On the basis of that procedural slip-up, Scopes' conviction was overturned, leaving Darrow with no conviction to appeal.

This was a serious blow, but the defense's cause had already been overshadowed by an event that took place just a few days after the trial ended.

Bryan had been deeply wounded by the trial, but he was a fighter. By the week's end he was hard at work publishing a rebuttal to Darrow's charges.

On Sunday, July 26th, Bryan spent the morning discussing plans to take a party of 500 to the Holy Land. He lunched well that day—he had a reputation as a trencherman—and then retired to bed for a nap. He died in his sleep. Great throngs of people visited the little house in Dayton to take a last look at their hero.

Then he lay in state in the nation's capital. Thousands filed past his coffin while across the land flags flew at half-mast.

In the immediate aftermath, such an upwelling of popular feeling overwhelmed any critical response to the trial, and Bryan's cause bloomed. Anti-evolution bills were passed in Arkansas and Mississippi, while in Texas and elsewhere across the country, school textbooks were actually re-written.

There it remained until the 1950s when Sputnik and the importance of science in the national defense awakened concern.

Across the country, legislation like Tennessee's Butler Act was declared unconstitutional and repealed.

Lately, however, the politicizing of religious faith has given a platform to more sophisticated concepts.

One of them—"intelligent design"—tries to use scientific method to find evidence of a "grand designer" shaping the universe.

However, in a case in 2005, in Dover, Pennsylvania, the judge saw it differently.

Raulston (*new judge*) I find that "intelligent design" to be a religious view, a mere relabelling of creationism, and not a scientific theory.

Narrator So do we still live in the shadow of Dayton? Many share Bryan's deep-seated fears.

Bryan They think life is a mystery that nobody can explain. That it commences with nothing and goes nowhere.

They do not explain the great riddle of the universe; do not teach the great science of how to live. There is no place for miracles.

Voiceover of **Darrow** *speech—altered to sound old, with pops, scratches, etc.*

Light fade on stage during speech.

Darrow (*V.O.*) If today, you can take a thing like evolution and make it a crime to teach it in public school, tomorrow you can make it a crime to teach it in the private schools, and or in church. It is the setting of man against man, creed against creed, until with flying banners and beating drums, we are marching backwards, to the sixteenth century, when bigots burned the men who dared to bring any intelligence and enlightenment and culture to the human mind.

End.

Setting

1952–54, various locations in Cold War America and South Sea Islands.

About the Play

The birth of Armageddon. The first hydrogen bomb detonates and the proud father is Edward Teller. But he's on a collision course with Robert Oppenheimer, the inventor of the bomb that obliterated Hiroshima. Now Oppenheimer has turned pacifist and the government will stop at nothing to "neutralize" him. And Teller is their star witness!

Original Live Theatre Production

The Real Dr. Strangelove by Peter Goodchild was originally commissioned and produced by L.A. Theatre Works, with lead funding from the Alfred P. Sloan Foundation, bridging science and the arts in the modern world. It premiered and was recorded before a live audience at the Skirball Cultural Center, Los Angeles in June 2006. It was directed by Matt August. The cast was as follows:

Rose/Newsreader #3/PA Announcement	Jordan Baker
Borden/Colgate/Pilot	Corey Brill
Lewis Strauss	John de Lancie
Robb/Christy/Newsreader #3	Reed Diamond
Luis Alvarez	J. Michael Flynn
Lawrence/Bethe	Raphael Sbarge
Enrico Fermi	Joe Spano
Blair/Court Official/Photographer/Narrator	Matt St. James
Edward Teller	Simon Templeman
J. Robert Oppenheimer/Newsreader #1	Granville Van Dusen
Bradbury/Garrison	Geoffrey Wade
Mici/Nurse/Secretary/Receptionist	Margaret Welsh

Touring Production

The Real Dr. Strangelove by Peter Goodchild was originally commissioned and produced by L.A. Theatre Works, with lead funding from the Alfred P. Sloan Foundation, bridging science and the arts in the modern world. It toured nationally to ten American cities before live audiences during the 2010–11 season, and was directed by Shannon Cochran. The touring cast was as follows:

Mici/Rose/Newsreader 1/Receptionist/Secretary/Ann/Nurse	Diane Adair
Strauss/FBI Agent/Bethe/Fermi/Crouch	Michael Canavan
Robb/Pilot/Officer 2/Reston/Borden	Kyle Colerider-Krugh
J. Robert Oppenheimer/Christy	John Getz
Marks/Bradbury/Newsreader 2/Rabi/Photographer	Peter McDonald
Edward Teller	John Vickery
Alvarez/Justice Dept. Lawyer/Newsreader 3/Gray/Officer 1/Colgate	Geoffrey Wade

Characters

Edward Teller
Hungarian-born American nuclear physicist, known colloquially as "the father of the hydrogen bomb." Of Jewish descent, Teller immigrated to the United States in the 1930s, and was an early member of the Manhattan Project charged with developing the first atomic bombs. He was involved in a ten-year struggle to develop the H-bomb in which he saw Oppenheimer as one of his main obstacles.

Enrico Fermi
Italian theoretical physicist and Nobel Laureate who emigrated to the U.S. in 1935. Fermi won the 1938 Nobel Prize in Physics for his work on induced radioactivity.

Mici Teller
Teller's childhood sweetheart. A mathematician and an independent spirit.

William Borden
A Yale law graduate, and bomber pilot with the 8th USAF in World War II. Influential executive director of the Joint Committee on Atomic Energy until sacked in 1953. He was suspicious that there was a second spy at Los Alamos during World War II which led him to investigate Oppenheimer.

Lewis Strauss
Began life as a shoe salesman who by his early twenties was assistant to Herbert Hoover, organizing post-war food relief. Became a wealthy banker who rose to the rank of Rear Admiral during World War II. Eisenhower's unlikely appointee to run nuclear affairs, he resisted disarmament and was prominent in efforts to displace Oppenheimer.

Ernest Lawrence
Inventor of the cyclotron, Nobel Laureate, and first U.S. entrepreneur of "big" science. Provided crucial backing to the U.S. A-bomb program, as well as the H-bomb and Teller's second laboratory at Livermore. Originally a friend of Oppenheimer, he eventually came to distrust him.

Luis Alvarez
Worked under Lawrence at the Berkeley Radiation Laboratory for twenty years. Nobel Laureate in 1968. One of the few senior scientists to give evidence against Oppenheimer at the latter's security hearing.

J. Robert Oppenheimer
Scientific director of Los Alamos during World War II. Post-war became director of the Institute of Advanced Studies at Princeton and influential member/chairman of countless government defense committees. He was believed by Teller to have deliberately obstructed the H-bomb's development.

Clay Blair
Time journalist. Co-authored *The Hydrogen Bomb: The Men, the Menace, the Mechanism* with James Shepley in 1954.

Lloyd Garrison
Lawyer, partner in a distinguished New York practice, and a man whose hobbies included bird watching, philosophy, and Greek literature.

Roger Robb
Well-established trial lawyer who prepared the government case for the hearing.

Norris Bradbury
Physicist who succeeded Oppenheimer as director of Los Alamos in 1945, a job he held for twenty-five years. He was increasingly at odds with Teller over his lack of support for the H-bomb.

Stirling Colgate
Physicist and protégé of Teller's.

Hans Bethe
German who immigrated to the U.S. in 1935. Head of the Theoretical Division at Los Alamos during World War II and a government adviser for five decades thereafter. Nobel Laureate in 1967. A close early friend of Teller's, their friendship was put to the test as their views on the nuclear program diverged.

Rose Bethe
Bethe's wife.

Rosie Colgate
Colgate's wife.

Bob Christy
A physicist who had known Teller at Los Alamos. Their families had shared a house in Chicago directly after the war.

Producing Director Notes

Susan Loewenberg

Almost seventy years have passed since the United States was gripped by the threat of nuclear holocaust. The Cold War—rooted in a fear of Communism's spread—was permeated by the threat that the Soviet Union's nuclear power posed to the American way of life. Along with the era's dominant images of President Eisenhower, Senator McCarthy's relentless hearings to pursue government subversives, and happy families playing games in basement bomb shelters, there loomed the omnipresent image of ever more powerful mushroom clouds.

A central question faced by Teller and Oppenheimer (and one that Peter Goodchild explores in his play) regards the use of power: if and when to use it, and for what purpose. That question persists today, and dogs the American government in a way quite different from what Eisenhower and his administration encountered. In the 1950s, the U.S. faced one main enemy: Communism. And as contemplated by the average citizen, the Communist threat emanated from the Soviet Union. This bi-polar world lasted until the collapse of the Soviet Union in 1991. Today we live in a very different world and the nature of the threat has changed. Instead of facing a single enemy, the American government faces rogue and failed states and individual terrorists; instead of just the Soviet Union, we have to keep an eye on Iran, al-Qaeda, ISIS, Pakistan, Somalia, and North Korea among others.

How we as Americans perceive the threats to our security and way of life are very different, too. The days of trusting in elected officials are long gone, replaced by suspicion and disgruntlement. As access to information and the ability to both dispense and receive it has grown exponentially because of technology, so has the threat to our security morphed from a single known entity to a much more complex, moving target. Perhaps history has shown that Teller was right—that deterrence was an effective means of containment because it was in the hands of two superpowers with everything to lose. Today, however, that thinking may pose an even greater danger to humanity. Nuclear proliferation is a major item on our government's agenda. And while the threat of nuclear proliferation is far more ominous, in reality, than it was seventy years ago, domestically the cultural and political focus on that threat has been replaced by the day-to-day struggles Americans are experiencing. In the prosperous 1950s, the government could afford to focus on the Cold War. The present administration, on the other hand, faces an ever growing plethora of domestic and international challenges. Nor, it could be argued, does the United States have the same ability to wield influence on the rest of the world.

Today, the responses to contemporary dangers must be both strategic and tactical—how to counter nimble enemies that don't recognize armies in uniform, that can move about like ordinary citizens, and can transport weapons of mass destruction in their pockets.

Author Notes

Peter Goodchild

Edward Teller died in 2003, aged ninety-five. He already had a distinguished career as a scientist when, in 1940, he became involved with Einstein in warning Roosevelt on the dangers of a German atomic bomb. He was deeply involved in nuclear strategy throughout the next sixty years. How to find a focus to do dramatic justice to such a man? That was the problem I faced when starting to write this play.

I first met Edward Teller in September 1978 at one of his sponsor's homes just off Rodeo Drive. I was researching a drama series on Robert Oppenheimer for the BBC in which Teller was to be a character. I had a fragmented view of him as a prima donna at wartime Los Alamos, who obsessively "fathered" the H-bomb and then became Oppenheimer's nemesis when the wartime director of Los Alamos stood in the way of his plans. That knowledge saved me from the demonic view of him so current at the time as a real life "Strangelove," though when I met him he certainly played up to that image. The series writer and I sat in a room lined with original Modiglianis while he delivered an hour-long impassioned attack on Oppenheimer without allowing us to take a single note. I was fascinated by his passion, the monomania which still obsessed someone of the highest intellect twenty-five years after he and Oppenheimer had clashed at the security hearing at the center of this play, and a decade after Oppenheimer's death. He was one of the most remarkable people I had ever met.

Nearly thirty years had passed since that initial brush with him but when, after years as an executive in BBC television, I had the opportunity to write a biography, I unhesitatingly picked him. When Susan Loewenberg suggested I write a play about him, I jumped at the chance. But how to find the dramatic focus I needed? After numbers of false starts, I picked one main incident.

Back in 1954, Teller was almost alone among scientists to give evidence at Oppenheimer's security hearing which ostensibly questioned his security clearance. This, in effect, was a trial for treason. The hearing had been a centerpiece in our BBC drama series, but I had learnt new things about Teller's involvement. The night before he was due to testify, Teller had arrived in Washington to find himself staying in the hotel which was hosting the annual meeting of the American Physical Society. The whole of the U.S. physics fraternity were there and were up in arms, having just heard that the Oppenheimer "secret" hearing was taking place in the city. What is more, Teller was thought to be preparing an incriminating testimony.

During my research for my book, numbers of those present in the hotel that night told me of their desperate effort to persuade Teller not to testify. One of them, the Nobel Laureate Hans Bethe (an old friend of Teller's), described the meeting he and his wife had with Teller that evening as one of the worst of his life. So much was at stake surrounding Teller's testimony. He could well support the view that Oppenheimer was a security risk. If he did, then Oppenheimer could lose his clearance, and would no longer act as a moderating influence on a nuclear arms race, which would affect everyone's lives for decades to come. What's more, only nine months after the Rosenbergs had been executed for spying, Oppenheimer could well find himself fighting off charges of espionage and treason. I had the focus for my play.

Interview Excerpt

Susan Loewenberg Joining me now is Richard Rhodes, America's preeminent historian of the nuclear age. He is the author of the Pulitzer Prize-winning book *The Making of the Atomic Bomb* and its companion book, *Dark Sun: The Making of the Hydrogen Bomb*. In addition to editing or authoring more than twenty other books, Rhodes has been a visiting scholar at Harvard and MIT, and has testified before the U.S. Senate on nuclear energy. Richard Rhodes, welcome to L.A. Theatre Works and thanks for being with us.

How did the development of the bomb and the subsequent nuclear arms race change the American public's perception of nuclear physicists?

Richard Rhodes Yes that's very interesting. I got to know some of the men who worked on the first bombs in the Manhattan Project during the Second World War. One of them, Louis Alvarez, Nobel Laureate physicist from Berkeley, told me that in the 1930s when he got his Ph.D. in physics, physics was such an unknown field of science that when he was at a cocktail party and people asked him what his field was, he would say he was a chemist because he didn't want to go through all the trouble of explaining what a physicist did.

That of course all changed. so that by 1945, the English physicist and novelist C.P. Snow could write an essay about all of this, and that by 1945 physicists had become the most valuable asset that a nation state had.

Susan Loewenberg But did people blame the physicists for this harsh new Cold War reality, or did they champion them as patriots or heroes?

Richard Rhodes I think it's pretty consistent across and from nation to nation as these countries developed nuclear weapons that they cheered their physicists. I'm thinking even as late as the development of the Pakistani bomb, when Pakistan erupted in national celebration for A.Q. Khan, the man who led the enrichment of uranium program that enabled them to develop their bombs. If you look back in 1945, at the close of the Second World War, there's almost no protest in the public literature with the single exception of the National Council of Churches, which objected to the use of weapons of mass destruction. I think people forget when they think about the bombings of Hiroshima and Nagasaki that the real decision about mass killing with weapons of mass destruction had been made in 1943 with the decision by the United States and Great Britain to begin the mass bombing of cities. The only thing that changed with the development of those first small low-yield nuclear devices that were used in Japan was that only one plane was needed to carry them. But the yield of the first bombs, 15 kilotons and 22 kilotons for Hiroshima and Nagasaki—that is the equivalent of 15,000 tons of TNT and 22,000 tons—was not different in scale from the fire bombings that had been going on in Japan since the previous April. We completely burned out Tokyo—18 square miles of downtown Tokyo—in the first major firebombing with a thousand B-29s carrying each 20,000 lbs of fire bombs and high explosives. We completely burned out downtown Tokyo, killed 140,000 people in one night by starting a fire storm that destroyed the city.

When people like the physicist Philip Morrison went to Hiroshima and Nagasaki after the war to inspect the damage of those atomic bombings, his first observation was that it didn't look any different from what he had already just seen in Tokyo.

Susan Loewenberg   Except the effect, the radiation damage to people . . .

Richard Rhodes   You know, because the bombs were deliberately exploded about 18 hundred yards above the ground, the only radiation that hit the people below was the prompt radiation from the fireball itself. Most of the people who were seriously irradiated were also killed either by the blast from the bomb, or by the ensuing firestorm that burned out the city. There were relatively few people who experienced severe radiation injuries in the aftermath of either one of those bombings. We've seen it, images of their injuries. Their injuries are primarily injuries from fire, or from the direct light. the very intense light of the fireball. So it's true of course there was radiation injury as well as the firebombing. My point simply is that the scale of destruction really was not different from what had preceded it. And I think that's one of the reasons why people in the immediate aftermath of the war didn't really perceive atomic bombs as being something Armageddon-like.

Susan Loewenberg   What were the nuclear scientists saying, and what do they say today, regarding their responsibility for a profoundly changed way of life?

Richard Rhodes   You know there was a range of responses; some people were really profoundly horrified. The Hungarian physicist Leo Szilard was one of those who really had pushed the idea of developing the bomb in the first place. Because he understood that Germany was probably working on a bomb and the idea of the Third Reich under Adolf Hitler with nuclear weapons was far more horrifying than one could even think today. People like Szilard were so disturbed by our deliberate use of these weapons to bomb cities, that he actually left physics and moved over to biology, but continued to promote the notion that we had to find a solution to this new weapon. He was one of the founders of some of the peace movements that followed from the post-war. And in fact he had interesting negotiations with Nikita Khrushchev about standing down and stepping back.

Act One

Scene One

Teller's *office* (*July 1952*).

Teller *is being interviewed by the FBI. The agent is setting up a small recorder.*

FBI Agent (*speaking into mike*)   For the record; Agents Kaufmann and Reinhardt interviewing Dr. Edward Teller, July 21, 1952.

Teller   Can I be absolutely certain, gentlemen, that this meeting is strictly confidential? And your director knows it?

FBI Agent   We have been told to give you that assurance, Dr. Teller.

Teller   You want to know, do I think Robert Oppenheimer is a danger to the security of this country?

FBI Agent   Correct, sir.

Teller   You ask me, maybe, if he's even a traitor.

FBI Agent   We would welcome your views.

Teller   Well, I will answer you this way. Any spy would be proud to have done what he has done to hinder our nuclear weapons program, delaying our hydrogen bomb programme by seven years during these crazy times with the Russians. Any agent would have been proud to have done that.

The best I can say about him is that he is like a general who doesn't want to fight, who has qualms, moral qualms which, with the Russians as our foes, is sheer madness. The worst I can say is the worst thing you can imagine. The father of the atomic bomb, the most powerful scientist in the country, who knows every detail of our nuclear program, is a sleeper, a sleeper who for two decades has been receiving orders directly from Moscow and passing all our secrets back to them. That's what I am talking about. That's why I am so angry, so frustrated that no one feels they can touch him.

FBI Agent   And when did you begin doubting his integrity?

Teller   It was at the time of the Eniwetok test in 1951.

Fade up music, cross-fade to:

Scene Two

Beach, Eniwetok Atoll (*Spring 1951*).

Cross-fade music into sounds of waves gently lapping on a shingle beach. Low voices can be heard, the odd laugh, as a group of scientists move across the beach. The occasional ship's foghorn can be heard.

Teller We were up early that May morning, the morning of the first ever thermonuclear test. We walked through the tropical heat to the beach by the Pacific atoll's placid lagoon. There we looked out to sea where the lights of the naval support vessels shone through the dawn mist and reflected on the water. We put on dark glasses, just as we had done at the first Trinity test in 1945.

Countdown over a tannoy begins.

Once again we listened to the countdown, and awaited the stunning brilliance of another nuclear explosion.

The countdown ends. Gasps of surprise from the scientists.

Teller Then the blast wave.

An enormous rumbling explosion drowns out the scientists' reactions and applause.

At fifteen times bigger than the Hiroshima bomb, this was the largest explosion ever at the time. At its heart a vial containing less than an ounce of heavy hydrogen had been ignited—the nuclear fusion fire of the sun had been recreated here on earth for the first time. My six-year struggle, working alone at Los Alamos laboratory against powerful resistance from the laboratory's founder, Robert Oppenheimer, had borne fruit. The U.S. would be first with the hydrogen bomb. Now, surely, there would be a rapid push from an experimental to a usable bomb, and I went to meet Oppenheimer.

Scene Three

Los Alamos, **Oppenheimer***'s office* (*Spring 1951*).

Oppenheimer *and* **Teller** *are together.*

Oppenheimer It's a wonderful result, Edward. It's hard to believe that only a month ago many of us believed fusion was an impossibility. Not you of course. But this realization that the heat alone from the initiating explosion is not enough—

Teller —that you need to separate the fusion fuel from the explosion just long enough—

Oppenheimer Yes, long enough to allow the radiation to compress the fuel first—once you see it, it's so simple, so elegant, so sweet.

Teller I'm glad you think that.

Oppenheimer Oh, I do, quite seriously, so the question is what to do now?

Teller There can be no question—we have to move straight to a deliverable weapon and that is why I asked to see you, to talk about who should be on the development team.

Oppenheimer You'd think that a Presidential Order for a crash program would make recruiting easier, wouldn't you, but it doesn't. Because it's like we're casting a Broadway show here.

Teller Well, then, let us talk about individuals. Who do you think can be available?

Oppenheimer The theoretical side of things is well covered by your little group. The problem is on the engineering and project direction side.

Teller As long as there is someone like Jacob Weschler on engineering I think quite junior people on project direction will suffice. I've been talking around and there are two guys working—

Oppenheimer Edward, are we on the same wavelength? If I'm getting your drift, you're seeing yourself as director of the next phase. Am I right?

Teller I have been working on this project for seven years, and against all the odds, I have made it happen. All I am asking is that I mastermind things just as you did at the first Trinity test.

Oppenheimer Of course, but being realistic, this is a massive logistical operation. There were 10,000 Army and Navy personnel on that last test.

Teller I expect to delegate, of course I do. But I need to be absolutely certain about the science, that we don't lose momentum again.

Oppenheimer Then believe me, as head of theory you would stand the best chance of doing that.

Teller The theory is done, and you were much more than that on Trinity.

Oppenheimer Please, Edward. You are pushing me to say things that are best left unsaid. I am so hoping things will be better between us now.

Teller (*flares*) I have had enough of knock backs, enough of excuses, enough delays, and enough bitchiness. From now on it has to be different.

Oppenheimer Then I will speak straight. You have a brilliant mind, but you are indecisive, unreliable, fly off the handle when you need to be calm, and the result is you are mistrusted and almost no one wants to work with you. There, I've said it. I would be irresponsible if I allowed you to take on such a task.

Pause.

Teller Well. Then who will you put in charge?

Oppenheimer Marshall Holloway. I'm putting Marshall in charge.

Teller You say I'm disliked. What about him?

Oppenheimer Nobody disputes his competence.

Teller I knew something like this would happen. You knew I could never work with him, and yet you take the project I have nurtured all these years, construct an impossible mismatch with him, and thus spirit it away from me. You have stolen my baby.

Oppenheimer   I am not stealing anything. You can't really be so blind to your own virtues and vices to think you could really do that job. I really want you as part of this project, it will be the poorer without you, but we have to be realistic.

Teller   You said our discovery was so sweet, so simple. So simple, in fact, that the Russians could have it and be ahead of us already. Yet you still create this disastrous mismatch. You know, I find something very deliberate, very calculating, about what you are doing.

Oppenheimer   What are you saying?

Teller   Suffice it to say it is a good thing we have the new lab at Livermore starting up.

Oppenheimer   Funded by the Air Force, and we know what they are looking for—the biggest bang. I am surprised that first-class people like you and Ernest Lawrence are happy to service them.

Teller   At least we will listen to them, which I'm sure they will find a refreshing change.

You know, Oppie, I really do wonder why, with your conscience, you continue with the work you do. And there are lots of people who think that.

Oppenheimer   I know the rumours, Edward, and I live with them.

Teller   Well, those rumours are hardening up, Oppie, I am telling you.

Scene Four

Washington Street (*two years later, Summer 1953*).

Heavy traffic. Two FBI officers in a parked car are staking out an apartment building.

Officer 1   There's Oppenheimer—getting out of that cab.

Officer 2   I've got him. Nobody with him.

Officer 1   And look over there, that guy crossing the street.

Officer 2   Yeah. Is that Weinberg?

Officer 1   He's gone behind that truck. Here he comes. It's Weinberg—and Oppenheimer has seen him.

The sound of an automatic camera shutter.

Officer 2   They're shaking hands—and now they're heading for that bar. Is Weinberg giving him something? I can't see, damn it.

Officer 1   We got them together, that's enough.

Officer 2   Jeez, the boss of everything meeting an ex-student accused of spying. What is going on?

Scene Five

Dulles Airport, Washington (Summer 1953).

A busy airport. Tannoys announcing arriving and departing flights and passenger information.

Borden (*approaching from a distance*)   Admiral Strauss. Admiral Strauss.

Strauss   Ah, Bill. I hoped you would be able to come.

Borden   I thought I had missed you. The car is over this way. Straight to the Atomic Energy Commission offices?

Strauss   Perfect, Bill. Perfect.

Borden   A good flight?

Scene Six

Interior limousine (Summer 1953).

Borden   This is the FBI's surveillance on Oppenheimer's meeting with Weinberg last week.

Strauss   Right, and they say he handed something to Weinberg?

Borden   A few days after that meeting, an optical company in New Jersey received a job application from Weinberg and Oppenheimer was his reference. Which, given Weinberg's upcoming trial and Oppenheimer's position, is pretty extraordinary.

Strauss   So you think it's coming together?

Borden   Without a doubt. The evidence is mostly circumstantial but it's cumulative. Before the war he contributed hundreds of dollars monthly to the Communist Party. His wife, Kitty, was a communist, his mistress during the war was a communist. The ex-students like Weinberg who he recruited to Los Alamos were Communists, he was in constant contact with Communist Party agents. In sum, I have 189 points Oppenheimer should answer to, and now you have this meeting with Weinberg, a proven spy.

Strauss   But Bill, all that earlier stuff has been looked at before.

Borden   Sure, but Teller's comments on Oppenheimer's negative attitude to the H-bomb gives it a fresh relevance. It's no longer history.

Strauss   What about Ernest Lawrence? He's the only scientist they've heard of on the Hill. Will he back Teller?

Borden   No question. They're absolutely at one on the H-bomb issue

Strauss   Teller could be so useful. Are we sure he is with us—is it a certainty?

Borden It would have been once but since he's had the new Livermore lab to look after, he's gone real quiet. But I'm in Berkeley next week, I'll go see his new house and sound him out.

Scene Seven

Teller's *garden, Berkeley (Fall 1953).*

Garden sounds in the background.

Teller Bill, with this house I'm no longer a physicist, but a gardener. When we were building Livermore last year, we bought this wonderful white elephant with these big grounds—all weedy so it can't get any more, or so I thought. I was so wrong, but I shall get by.

Borden How is Livermore doing now?

Teller Very exciting—difficult—but very exciting.

Borden And is Los Alamos cooperating?

Teller Absolutely not! Bill, they are so arrogant, so poisonous—they are Oppie's boys and they won the war. We've had problems with our first tests and they have relished them. But we are out at Bikini for more tests with them again soon, and we shall show them this time. But thank goodness for good friends in Washington, like Strauss.

Borden Have you heard the latest about him?

Teller About Strauss becoming Ike's nuclear energy adviser, yes.

Borden Had you heard that he's also become Atomic Energy Commission chairman? Ike's given him both jobs.

Teller Really! That is amazing. Lewis Strauss of all people. Then it's going to be open warfare.

Borden Edward, it's already started. When Ike offered him the AEC, Strauss actually made it a condition that Oppenheimer should be gotten rid of before he accepted. And then straight away he had me going through all the files on Oppenheimer. And what I've found is devastating, just devastating.

Mici Teller *approaches carrying a jug of lemonade and glasses.*

Mici Here we are. Iced lemonade for the gardener and his guest—and cookies. You two are sounding very excited.

Teller Mici, Bill has been giving me news about Strauss, and Oppenheimer.

Mici Ah-ha. I see. Then you're going to tell him how much your family loves the Californian climate, and how much you are enjoying yourself at Livermore with your own laboratory now. No more terrible arguments and sleepless nights with that man and his stooges. And perhaps you will mention that your mother and sister are still in

Hungary, and that the Soviets interrogated them for three days when the papers mentioned your work on the H-bomb. So. Is there anything else you want?

Borden   Thank you, Mici, no. This is fine.

Mici   I'll leave you to it then. (*She moves away.*)

Teller   I don't argue with Mici, she knows exactly what she thinks, but she seems to have second guessed your intentions. Why are you here? Has Strauss sent you?

Borden   I want you to read my report on Oppenheimer. There are no less than 189 points he has to answer.

Teller   And you want my views?

Borden   Certainly, but we're hoping for more than that. We are hoping you'll become involved again.

Teller   But does Lewis Strauss know what you're doing?

Borden   Why do you ask that?

Teller   The last time you produced a document on Oppenheimer it resulted in the worst breach of security ever.

Borden   What happened was a terrible accident.

Teller   It wasn't. You deliberately sent a technical report on how Oppenheimer delayed the H-Bomb to be evaluated at Princeton. It contained a blueprint of my bomb and yet you used the regular mail, and then one of the Princeton people lost it on a train. And where did it go? Nobody knows. You engineered the loss of the H-bomb's real secrets and to God knows who.

Borden   Edward, this is totally different. Strauss has a plan and he has real power now. He hates and mistrusts Oppenheimer at least as much as the rest of us and he is determined to see him gone. He is equally determined to see you as his replacement, as the next Oppenheimer.

Teller   For a moment, Bill, I was beginning to believe you, but not that. Look, I fought Oppenheimer for seven painful years. I have my independence now and I have my family in Hungary whose safety concerns both Mici and I greatly. I have no intention of being drawn into anything until I'm clear that there is a real chance of success

Borden   Okay, Edward, but please, read the document. Because I'm certain it will show you just how much we have against him now. Then talk to Strauss, because I know he thinks as I do—that this is the best chance to unseat Oppenheimer we've ever had.

Scene Eight

Strauss's *office, AEC* (*December 3, 1953*).

Teller *is sitting waiting.* **Strauss's Secretary** *enters from the outer office.*

Secretary I'm so sorry you're having to wait so long, Dr. Teller. That was the White House on the phone to say Admiral Strauss is on his way back here now. Can I get you tea, coffee?

Teller Thank you, no.

An agitated **Strauss** *is heard arriving in the outer office.*

Secretary Oh, there he is now.

Strauss What a dreadful afternoon. Is Dr. Teller here?

Secretary Yes, he is.

Strauss Excellent. Virginia, please make sure that Dr. Teller and I are not disturbed.

Secretary Very well.

Strauss *enters the inner office.*

Strauss What a relief it is to see you, Edward. I am so sorry, I hate being late, but it's been one hell of a day. I've just come from Eisenhower. Bill Borden has really blown it this time.

Teller How do you mean?

Strauss You've seen Borden's Oppenheimer dossier?

Teller Yes, it's why I'm here.

Strauss Well, without a word to me he sent it to the FBI, to Hoover himself. And Hoover had no choice but to send it on to the White House. For them it was a complete bolt from the blue.

Teller Ike had no idea of the things it contained?

Strauss No. In one stroke the President has learned that his most senior and respected scientist is almost certainly a sleeper, and has been right from the start.

Teller What did Ike say?

Strauss A great deal! But the bottom line is he's ordered a "blank wall"—that's the expression he used—to be put between Oppenheimer and any classified material until the matter has been properly investigated.

Teller Why on earth did Borden act so suddenly?

Strauss I don't think he felt we were taking him seriously, and Ike had effectively fired him over that Princeton train fiasco. I guess Borden wanted to embarrass him—and us too.

Teller In one careless move, he's raised the stakes a hundred fold. I came here not too sure about Borden's schemes, and to find out what your plans were, but this changes everything.

Strauss   One thing he mentioned—he said you had serious worries about your family behind the Iron Curtain.

Teller   He's right. I was in the papers a lot when the H-bomb was announced and the Soviets deported them to some terrible place in the mountains for almost a year. It has affected my mother dreadfully and I do not want anything like it to happen again.

Strauss   I understand, Edward, I understand. But in spite of Borden, I think we have never had a better opportunity to dislodge Oppenheimer and for you to take his place. I really do think this is a special moment. Honestly.

Teller   Borden perhaps told you I didn't believe him when he mentioned that possibility.

Strauss   I am quite serious. I have even spoken to the State Department, very informally you understand, about bringing your family out. I impressed on them your importance to us, and they thought it would be a possibility.

Teller (*quite moved*)   That would be the most wonderful thing. I am grateful to you for even thinking of it.

Strauss   If I can help, Edward, it will be my pleasure. And in the meantime, there's much we can do to keep you out of the limelight. So, shall we take things step by step, see how it goes? Is that okay?

Teller   For the time being, Yes. But what is Ike expecting?

Strauss   He's leaving it up to me. Oppenheimer might still resign, but I'm not sure I want a simple resignation. I want the kind of exposure that will destroy his influence but a trial? It's so messy.

Teller   If Ike wants a blank wall, then all that's needed is to remove his security clearance.

Strauss   It's been suspended already

Teller   Then what is needed for the future is to make it permanent. His colleagues won't be able to talk to him about what matters, and he won't be able to talk to them.

Strauss   Then a regular Security Board Hearing.

Teller   That's for recruits, surely?

Strauss (*thinking it through*)   It's been used to investigate staff security before. He'll appear, in camera, before a three-man board and both sides can call witnesses. It's without the publicity or the rules of evidence of a regular court, and we get to choose the board. It's—how shall I put it—much more flexible, don't you think? Yes, the more I think about it, the better I like it. I'll get a list of charges carefully drawn and confront him when he comes back from Europe.

Scene Nine

Strauss's *office, AEC* (*December 21, 1953*).

Strauss *confronts* **Oppenheimer**.

Strauss Robert, this is a truly painful task, and I can assure you this hearing is not what anyone wanted. However, we are faced with a very difficult problem over your security clearance.

Oppenheimer *is scanning the list of charges.*

Oppenheimer I am simply amazed looking through this, Lewis. It makes sweeping claims about espionage and my being a communist, and yet these claims seem to be based on the same information on my background that has been reviewed—what—four or five times, before, during, and since the war. You, yourself, were on the last board that cleared me only five years ago.

Strauss We do live in extraordinary times, Robert. Once the former government official who drew attention to your record had contacted the FBI, and they in turn had contacted the White House, there was no choice. The President had to act

Oppenheimer Then who is this official?

Strauss I can't say.

Oppenheimer I am not to be told who my accuser is?

Strauss In such cases we have to ensure anonymity.

Oppenheimer So I'm being accused—of treason—by an unnamed accuser. And this is twentieth-century America. Isn't this just the fascism we are meant to be fighting?

Strauss With McCarthy on the rampage, it is a difficult time even for the President himself. He can't act as he would like.

Oppenheimer But he seems to have been briefed by my enemies. The only new material in this sorry document are the charges about my obstructing the H-bomb development. They come directly from Teller.

Strauss Robert—

Oppenheimer Does Teller know who my accuser is? (*Pause*.) Have they gotten together, do you know?

Strauss I really can't say.

Oppenheimer You can't say. Does the President know that I only have six months to go before my consultancy ends?

Strauss He does.

Oppenheimer Then what does he want? To make an example of me? In six months I will be gone anyway.

Strauss The Executive Order he has issued limits the choices to resignation or a hearing.

Oppenheimer   Is he thinking of a criminal action, a trial?

Strauss   I don't know, honestly.

Oppenheimer   You don't know. Which means I could face a treason charge. Like the Rosenbergs.

Strauss   That would depend of course on how things emerge.

Oppenheimer   Well, what is there to do? Can I resign my contract?

Strauss   That's a possibility, Robert, yes. But it may not be the end of things.

Oppenheimer   What do you think?

Strauss   Well, it must be a personal decision.

Oppenheimer   And you won't help. I see. How long do I have to decide?

Strauss   By tomorrow.

Oppenheimer   Tomorrow! Oh, my God!

Strauss   And at the same time, I'm afraid we will have to remove all classified items from your home and office. You see, we've been waiting several weeks for your return from Europe.

Oppenheimer   I need to see my lawyer then—as soon as possible.

Strauss   Do you have a car? You can use mine if you wish.

Oppenheimer   That is kind. Thank you. Of course, if I resigned, it will be seen as an admission of guilt.

Strauss   It's a secret hearing, Robert.

Oppenheimer   But that counts for so little nowadays, doesn't it, Lewis?

Scene Ten

*Street outside the **Marks**' home.*

Two FBI agents are waiting in a car.

Agent 1   Here they come. (*A car draws up and people get out.*) Up the steps. Marks fumbles for his keys. We should pick them up from the inside any moment now.

The speaker in the car relays the voices and movement from the house.

Marks (*on distort*)   Well, hopefully some privacy here at least. A drink, Oppie?

Oppenheimer (*on distort*)   A straight bourbon.

Agent 1   Good reception. They don't seem to suspect anything.

Agent 2   It's the lawyer's house, for God's sake.

Oppenheimer (*on distort*) It was just so vindictive—so polite, but so vindictive. He was loving it. Jesus, I can't believe what's happening to me. Who is this unknown accuser?

Marks (*on distort*) Robert, what you're going to do, you're going back to Strauss and tell him to shove it. Tell him to sack you and then you'll go public. There will be armies of good people, the best people, who will back you.

Oppenheimer (*on distort*) I can't do that. This comes direct from the President. You want me to tell him to shove it?

Marks (*on distort*) It's come from Strauss for Christ's sake. Here's your bourbon.

Oppenheimer (*on distort*) Strauss is just his agent. No, grandstanding is out, Herb. You understand? This is not one of your segregation protests.

Marks (*on distort*) OK, OK. Well, it's going to be a long haul but we can explode every one of those charges. (*Pause.*) Oppie?

Opppenheimer Twelve years I've been involved in all this, and now I'm not considered fit to serve. Hell, I'm going to the bathroom. I need to think.

Oppenheimer *leaves the room and runs upstairs.*

A loud crash is heard from upstairs.

Agent 1 What's that?

Marks (*on distort, calling out*) Oppie, are you all right? Oppie?

Marks *is heard running upstairs and calling out.*

Agent 1 What's he doing?

Agent 2 Is he trying to kill himself?

Marks *is knocking on the bathroom door.*

Marks (*on distort*) Oppie! Oppie, are you all right? Oppie, can you hear me? Can you move at all?

Agent 1 Go call the office. They need to know. He is not a happy man.

Scene Eleven

Marks' *home.*

Oppenheimer *is recovering with* **Marks** *and his wife* **Ann**.

Oppenheimer Herb, I am sorry. It must have been very frightening for you. I suddenly felt dizzy, I guess I just fainted.

Marks You've had a real shock this afternoon. Strauss obviously milked the situation with maximum brutality.

Oppenheimer It's not that so much, it's the unknown accuser.

You know, as far back as I can remember, I've had this fear of something that would quite suddenly break into my life, striking at the root of my own world and leaving me to the consequences. And this is it. My beast in the jungle, it's here.

Marks   It's just a power-hungry bastard who will stop at nothing. It wouldn't surprise me if Strauss wasn't the mystery official and sent that letter to Hoover himself—truly.

Oppenheimer   You could be right. (*Pause.*) Anyway in a brief moment of clarity earlier, I made my decision. I intend to clear my name.

Scene Twelve

Teller*'s office* (*February 1954*).

Secretary   Dr. Teller, I have Admiral Strauss for you. Would you please scramble your phone?

Appropriate telephonic sound.

Teller   Lewis?

Strauss   Edward, this is a quick call before I disappear to Bikini for a couple of weeks—

Teller   For the Bravo test?

Strauss   For Bravo, right, and I'm staying on afterwards for your tests. You got my message about Roger Robb, our attorney for the hearing?

Teller   Yes. I'll be pleased to see him.

Strauss   He's a good man and knows this area from both sides. He's defended McCarthy's people and he's defended Reds as well.

Teller   He sounds an ideal match.

Strauss   Now the real reason for the call is a complaint I've had from Los Alamos. They say that Livermore's test failures have shaken the Army's confidence in the nuclear program.

Teller   They were our first two tests and on completely new concepts. We almost expected them to fail. What, and they want to close us down, I suppose.

Strauss   No, not closed down, put under Los Alamos's control.

Teller   So they're aiming directly at me?

Strauss   At you, and Ernest Lawrence, and me too.

Teller   That's Oppenheimer's handiwork.

Strauss   But Edward, I've dealt with it. I told them in no uncertain terms that I'm not even entertaining the idea. But he'll be there for your tests so I expect him to be back if anything goes wrong.

Teller   Oh, yes, I'm sure.

Strauss   We'll see each other at Bikini then. And in the meantime, enjoy yourself with Roger.

Scene Thirteen

Teller's *office* (*February 1954*).

Teller is with **Roger Robb**, *the AEC counsel.*

Teller   Mr. Robb, if you are coming to me hoping for proof absolute that Oppenheimer is a spy, then you may well be disappointed.

Robb   The crucial question for this board is whether he is a danger to national security.

Teller   Fine. But let me take you through a little history, see what you think.

No one questions that Oppenheimer was a brilliant wartime director at Los Alamos. As a result, in the past ten years he has controlled some thirty-five influential committees covering all areas of defence and security. He is perhaps the most influential scientist ever.

But throughout that time he has consistently opposed the development of the H-bomb. Firstly that was on moral grounds, that all we were creating was a weapon of mass genocide, but when it became clear we were in a race with the Russians and the President ordered a crash program, he argued that it wasn't technically feasible. When I proved it was, he switched to arguing that there weren't the facilities—but once again, we showed there was.

Robb   And you think this was a calculated plan?

Teller   I have difficulty in seeing it as anything else.

Robb   In their notes of their meeting with you, the FBI reported that you said that "numbers of people believe Oppenheimer opposed the H-bomb on direct orders from Moscow." Were you one of those people?

Teller   I am certainly one of those who thought his behaviour quite extraordinary and I also listened to the views of people more expert than me. For instance, the head of British intelligence firmly believes Oppenheimer is a Soviet agent—worse than Klaus Fuchs.

Robb   He told you this?

Teller   He told my colleague here, Luis Alvarez. You're seeing him?

Robb   Tomorrow. So Oppenheimer is dangerous?

Teller   On matters of judgment I think he is—very—and I would certainly say I can't trust him. He never has clear motives. For instance, a year ago he said to me, "Now we know the H-bomb works, we can use it to end the war in Korea." I was astounded and asked him how. And he replied by building a bomb in Korea, driving the enemy troops into a concentration nearby, then exploding the bomb.

Robb That is not credible.

Teller You ask Isidor Rabi. He is one of Oppenheimer's men and he will back what I told you. I would do anything to see him separated from any policy making and that's the view of Ernest Lawrence and a majority here on the West Coast.

Robb You are happy to express these views at the hearing?

Teller I shall welcome the opportunity.

Robb This is very useful. No, more than that—invaluable.

Teller I am glad. Mr. Robb, I do hope you will not underestimate Oppenheimer. He is very intelligent, has faced investigations already, and has proved himself very quick-witted and very slippery.

Robb Maybe so, but he's never been cross-examined by me before.

Scene Fourteen

Music cross-fade to original commentary of the 1952 mike test describing details of the explosion impact tests.

Scene Fourteen a

Conference hall (February 1954).

Fade the film soundtrack—fade up sound of public foyer at a busy scientific conference. **Teller** *is with* **Alvarez**.

Teller You tell me, Luis, you tell me what NBC will achieve by showing this film on national television.

Alvarez It's the public's show. They're paying for it, paying for us, and so far, after nine years, they've never seen what they're getting for their money.

Teller But it's truly terrifying, all these Norman Rockwell houses being torn apart, cars tossed around. It's one thing showing it at a scientific meeting like this, but the public will be horrified.

Alvarez Well, isn't it time for some reality?

Oppenheimer (*catching the others by surprise*) Edward, Luis. This is a pleasant surprise.

Alvarez Oppie.

Oppenheimer Such a long time since we last met. Are you both well? (*An awkward pause.*) Edward, I hope you are well?

Teller (*cold*)   Perfectly, Robert. Thank you.

Alvarez   Please forgive us but we are both due at a seminar.

Oppenheimer   No, of course, but Edward, perhaps we could have a word later.

Teller   It may suit your purposes to suggest that rational differences and a word or two are all that separates us, Robert, but that would simply be a lie.

The conversation nearby has stopped and there is an uncomfortable silence.

Alvarez   I think I should excuse myself. (*Looking for a reaction.*) Edward? (*He is ignored.*)

Oppenheimer   Is there somewhere we can speak in private?

Teller   There's an empty conference room over there.

Alvarez   I'll see you later then?

Oppenheimer   In here? (*A door shuts cutting out sounds from the foyer.*) Right, this is better.

Teller   So what do you want?

Oppenheimer   I am looking for your support.

Teller (*overlapping*)   You should make no mistake, Robert, our differences are deep, emotional, and personal. They always have been.

Oppenheimer   Even at the beginning?

Teller   Even then, right after Hiroshima.

Oppenheimer   When you argued that I tried to close Los Alamos down? Edward, it was dead on its feet, everyone was exhausted—except, of course, you. There had to be a pause while we all took stock.

Teller   A pause? Then why, after VJ Day, did you come to my office and, out of the blue, say—"with the war over, there is no reason to continue working on a hydrogen bomb."

Oppenheimer   Your memory is colouring things.

Teller   You think so? Well, a day or two later, you were in Washington telling Truman that you "had blood on your hands." You said that scientists were against not just the hydrogen bomb but any bomb, because it was against the dictates of their hearts. You can't deny that?

Oppenheimer   I was reflecting the mood amongst almost everyone I can think of at Los Alamos.

Teller   You were creating the mood and even then I thought it dangerous. If you had come out and warned that Hiroshima was not the end but only a beginning, everything would have been different. But you didn't, and because I disagreed, there were those who called me a criminal—

Oppenheimer Edward . . .

Teller Yes, a criminal, for working on the hydrogen bomb.

Oppenheimer Not a criminal, Edward, but it was difficult. You have always mistrusted the Russians, something which goes back to your years in Hungary. Can you blame the rest of us for not sharing those feelings and trying instead to negotiate with the Russians? And trying to set an example by deliberately not building this abomination of a weapon?

Teller That's so naïve. Look, once a new technology like fusion becomes possible, we simply cannot ignore it. Yet that is what you've done. (*Contemptuous*.) Setting an example.

Oppenheimer What if negotiations had succeeded?

Teller They would never have succeeded. You know something, Robert, the scientific community is remarkably homogeneous in its addiction, not just to science, but to liberal political judgments. And you, apparently, share these judgments, which are still touched by a sentimental view of communism. If we can negotiate with the Russians, people say, we can extract ourselves from this arms race. NEVER! I have lived in the shadow of the Russians for most of my life, and the lesson I have learned is—they do not compromise.

Oppenheimer You can't seriously believe that armed conflict with Russia is inevitable—that they will never negotiate.

Teller Yes, and yes to both questions.

Oppenheimer That is so hopeless.

Teller Unless—unless we argue from a position of strength, and our strength is, or was, our nuclear monopoly. But from 1945, instead of exploiting that superiority, you allowed it to erode to where they are most likely ahead of us. That is the crime you have allowed to happen. And that is why I and others despair of you.

Oppenheimer So what I did was treasonous?

Teller Treasonous . . . is a harsh word isn't it?

Oppenheimer That is what I am being accused of, espionage. My actions are not even mitigated by stupidity or need. They are those of someone betraying his country, Edward. And don't forget what they just did to the Rosenbergs.

Teller They were traitors in a way I have never associated with you.

Oppenheimer Even at your most angry, your most frustrated?

Teller No, no. It would never be that simple for you. It would never be "the Russians are right" or "the U.S. is right." Too simple. You could never be a traitor to a cause—or for a cause.

Oppenheimer To have you, of all people, come and say that at the hearing would mean a great deal to me. (*Pause*.) It is my loyalty and integrity which is at issue here, and to have the support of someone who disagrees with me so profoundly, dislikes me even, would mean a great deal. Please.

Teller   You are extraordinary. And what will that do to my testimony about your views? I think his judgment is disastrous but—he is disastrous with integrity?

Oppenheimer   Well, maybe that will be the nub of the hearing, Edward. But don't say any more at the moment. You obviously need to think about it, but would you let my lawyer know what you decide?

Scene Fifteen

An Air Force transport plane flies over (*back projection*).

Mix to:

Cabin of an Air Force transport plane (*March 1954*).

Teller *and* **Alvarez** *are playing poker.*

Teller   Another hand?

Alvarez   You deal. Did you go see Oppenheimer's lawyer?

Teller   It was like playing chess with my dog. Yes, I said, of course I'll say he isn't a traitor. But I'll also say that any traitor would be proud of the damage he has done. He soon realized I was a lost cause.

The intercom from the flight deck crackles into life.

Pilot   Dr. Teller, Dr. Alvarez, we are approaching Bikini and if you look out the port window, you can see the crater left by the Bravo shot two weeks ago. The island below is Namu and you can see that the tip has a large bite out of it. If you follow the arc of that out to sea, you can see the dark water which is filling the blast crater, and outcrops of coral. That crater is about 4 miles across and over a mile deep.

Alvarez   My God, Los Alamos has had a runaway.

Teller   The mike test produced 10.5 megatons with a crater—what—a mile across?

Alvarez   So this must have been fifteen, twenty megatons?

Teller   Certainly it must.

Alvarez   What price taking over Livermore now?

Teller   When I spoke to Strauss last night, he said he'd set up a special meeting with the Los Alamos people for soon after we arrive—including Isador Rabi. It should be interesting . . .

Pilot (*on the intercom*)   Will you gentlemen now buckle yourselves in.

Fade sound of aircraft.

Scene Sixteen

Seminar room, Bikini (March 1954).

Strauss *is addressing a group of scientists, including* **Teller, Alvarez,** *and* **Isidor Rabi**.

Strauss We have to be candid about what's happened here, gentlemen. At fifteen megatons, 1,000 times the yield of the Hiroshima bomb, Bravo is the biggest blast ever, and terrifying. A runaway. We were thirty miles away and still it felt like the heat from a furnace door. We talked of keeping the test results secret, but the shifting winds, which blew the radioactive cloud off course, ensured that was not an option. We have upwards of 200 locals on the Marshall Islands exposed to close on a fatal dose of radiation.

But worse is still to come. I've just heard from Washington. There was of all things a Japanese fishing boat—we think inside the restricted area, but we are not sure. They got back to port two days ago and the whole crew has radiation sickness. One, they think, will die. It's an international incident and there's nowhere to hide . . . So we have a lot to talk about.

Teller Lewis, this is devastating.

Rabi Oh, Edward—

Teller No, Rabi. This is a disaster which will have an impact on the attitudes to what we do for decades to come. It is bound to inhibit our activities. In the meantime, the Soviets, who are already very probably ahead of us, will be able to continue their development uninhibited—with all the consequences of that to our national security.

Rabi This was a test. You know, an experiment? Investigating the unknown?

Teller And producing fifteen megatons, not five, as you predicted, and with a radioactive cloud encircling the globe. You want us to discuss, nicely and politely, how we might limit the damage. No, what we should be discussing is how the arrogance of a monopolistic laboratory like Los Alamos can generate such sloppy weather forecasting and poor chemistry, such negligence in the first place.

There is a reaction around the room.

Rabi You call us arrogant. Edward, did you give an interview to a *Time* journalist, name of Clay Blair?

Pause.

Teller Yes, he came to see me. What is this about?

Rabi Well, it's in the latest edition and I've been wired a copy. It's an outrage.

Teller I haven't seen it, and I won't comment until I've read it.

Rabi Well, let me take you through it. It's the story of "two non-conforming scientists"—you and Ernest Lawrence—and how, against all the odds, you got the Presidential go-ahead for the H-bomb. Not one word about Los Alamos—which did all the work, remember—not one.

Teller   That's not what I told him. He must have got it from someone else.

Rabi   Oh, really? The article then gives all the credit for the mike test to you and to Livermore. A test Los Alamos mounted, for Christ sakes, after you had resigned, sulked, and made trouble for two years.

Teller   I agree it's an absolute travesty

Rabi   You agree? Then I can go and tell fifty angry Los Alamos scientists you will be writing to *Time* to put the record straight?

Teller   I certainly shall. However, Rabi, don't let this journalistic travesty disguise who did finally provide the solution to the thermonuclear ignition problem. I did.

Rabi   With others.

Teller   Oh, yes. And I was sulking, as you put it, because Oppenheimer gave my project to a man I could not possibly work with. Think of these things, then my bitterness when you try to take Livermore away from me should surprise you less.

Scene Seventeen

Base camp bar (April 1954).

The island's night sounds are barely audible above a jukebox playing Johnny Ray or Frankie Lane.

Strauss *is already at the bar when* **Teller** *joins him.*

Strauss   Edward. Are you here for the poker?

Teller   Not tonight, Lewis. I was hoping for a word with you.

Strauss   Right. A drink? I heard from Washington the hearing has started well.

Teller (*impatient*)   Lewis, that *Time* article. I never said those things and I want to know—

Strauss   Let me stop you. I've already told Rabi in so many words I'd encouraged young Clay Blair with his heroic approach, which played down Los Alamos's part.

Teller   You didn't just play down their part, you excluded them, and then exaggerated my role to the point of ridicule.

Strauss   Because your role is so crucial and has to be recognized.

Teller   You remember, I have a family which is as vulnerable—

Strauss   But, you see, things have moved on. Because your reputation is rising, the Soviets now see your mother and sister as valuable assets. They are probably safer than ever before.

Teller   Speculation. Lewis, don't try to pass this one off.

Strauss Look, Edward, our common purpose was something very clear between us from the beginning—that if this case against Oppenheimer is lost, then our whole atomic energy program will fall into the hands of left wingers. We will lose the race against the Russians, and there will be another even more devastating Pearl Harbor, a nuclear one. We have to prevent that at all costs. There is no greater cause to be fighting for, and everything we do has to be seen in that light.

Today in Washington, Oppenheimer is facing tough questions, new evidence about approaches he received from close communist friends. Roger is determined to break him. That is how it has to be.

Fade up newsroom.

News Reader 1 (*female*)   Worldwide, experts estimate the fallout from the Bravo test alone would lead to the birth of the least 1,800 children with birth defects, and every new bomb exploded will add to this harvest. Young growing children would also be affected . . .

Cross-fade between **Newsreader 1** *and* **Newsreader 2**.

News Reader 2   This week, Senator Joseph McCarthy will reveal that a key atomic figure had urged that the H-bomb not be built at all. This famous atomic scientist has been an active Communist Party member, and the leader of a Red cell including other noted atomic scientists . . .

Cross-fade between **Newsreader 2** *and* **Newsreader 1**.

News Reader 1   Dr. Robert Oppenheimer has been suspended by the Atomic Energy Commission at a special security review. The scientist is alleged to have communist ties and secret hearings have started during which the scientist is expected to face tough questioning over relationships with top communists. In the meantime he has been denied access to all secret data.

Fade **Newsreader 1**.

Scene Eighteen

Hearing room (April 14, 1954).

Oppenheimer *is being cross-examined by* **Roger Robb**.

Robb   Now, Dr. Oppenheimer, can we deal with the occasion in 1943 when, in what you describe as a casual conversation, your left-wing university friend Haakon Chevalier approached you about passing on secrets to the Russians?

Oppenheimer   Yes.

Robb   It was a passing remark at a social occasion.

Oppenheimer   In our kitchen, yes.

Robb Did Chevalier say anything to you about the use of microfilm or passing information to someone at the Soviet consulate?

Oppenheimer No, he did not.

Robb Or that he talked to any other scientist on the project but you about the matter?

Oppenheimer No.

Robb But some six months later, you decided to tell your security officer, Colonel Pash, about this casual meeting?

Oppenheimer Right.

Robb Just to remind you, that was September 12, 1943. I have both a recording and transcript of the interview here.

Oppenheimer (*increasingly perturbed*) Oh, you do.

Robb Did you mention Chevalier by name to Colonel Pash?

Oppenheimer No.

Robb Let us refer, then, to Chevalier as X. Did you tell Pash that X had approached three persons on the project?

Oppenheimer (*increasingly aware of* **Robb**'s *upper hand*) I am not clear—I am not clear whether I said there were three Xs or that X approached three people.

Robb Didn't you say that X had approached three people?

Oppenheimer Probably.

Robb Why did you do that, doctor?

Oppenheimer (*realizing the trap he is in*) Because I was an idiot.

Robb Is that your only explanation, doctor?

Oppenheimer I was reluctant to mention Chevalier.

Robb So why then would you tell him Chevalier had gone to see not just one but three people?

Oppenheimer I have no explanation for that, except the one I've just given.

Robb That you were an idiot. If he had gone to three people, that would have shown—

Oppenheimer —that he was deeply involved.

Robb Yes, and that it was not a casual conversation as you suggested earlier. Did you tell Pash that Chevalier mentioned microfilm and contacts in the Soviet Consulate?

Oppenheimer You have a record.

Robb Did you? (*No reply*.) Which would have shown definitely that he was not an innocent contact, and that there was a criminal conspiracy?

Oppenheimer That is right.

Robb And you knew that Pash would move heaven and earth to find out who X was, wouldn't he?

Oppenheimer Yes.

Robb And yet you wouldn't tell him, you deliberately obstructed him?

Oppenheimer That is true.

Robb So you would agree, wouldn't you, sir, that if the story you told Pash was true, it made things look very bad for Mr. Chevalier?

Oppenheimer For anyone involved.

Robb Including you?

Oppenheimer Right.

Robb Isn't it a fair statement to say, Dr. Oppenheimer, that you've told not one lie to Colonel Pash but a whole fabrication and tissue of lies?

Oppenheimer (*he is defeated*) Right.

Scene Nineteen

Washington Street (*April 14, 1954*).

Oppenheimer *and* **Marks** *are leaving the hearing.*

Oppenheimer A nightmare—no other word for it.

Marks Seriously, Oppie, this whole thing is a scandal.

Oppenheimer How could I be expected to remember the details of what I said eleven years ago?

Marks We should do what I said in the first place and tell them to shove it.

Oppenheimer It's too late for that . . .

Bethe (*approaching*) Oppie. Oppie.

Oppenheimer Hans! What a wonderful surprise. Herb, this is Hans Bethe. Hans, my lawyer, Herb Marks. (*They acknowledge each other.*) Are you in Washington for our show?

Bethe I am here for the Physical Society's get-together—my presidential year. Then I am coming to say my piece for you. So, tell me, how is it going?

Oppenheimer Terrible, quite terrible.

Marks They know our every move. Seems my house has been bugged. The board was hand-picked by Strauss. It's been a set-up from the beginning. Isn't that right, Oppie?

Oppenheimer Of course it has, but what do we do about it? He was right after all. I did lie.

Marks What? So that's it? Throw in the towel? He tricked you. You simply didn't remember the details of some schoolboy embellishments about microfilm and Soviet spies, stuff you invented to impress the security guy. That is all!

Oppenheimer Do you really think that is the way the board will see it? This afternoon, Herb, didn't even you, just for a moment, think, "What was he really up to? Am I being taken for a ride here?"

Marks Ah, nuts to that.

Oppenheimer Not just a tiny corner of doubt? All those Reds I brought to Los Alamos, my commie mistress during the war—

Marks Any thinking man dabbled in left-wing politics before the war, for God's sake.

Oppenheimer But that's such an easy let-out, don't you think?

Bethe Oppie, this is stupid. Herb is right. Next week, you have everyone who's anyone in science coming to speak for you. What, five, six Nobel Laureates, senior diplomats. After that, this afternoon will seem an irrelevance.

Oppenheimer They have important people coming to give evidence too.

Marks Oppie, there are only two, three at most who count. There's Ernest Lawrence—head and shoulders above the others—Luis Alvarez, and, of course, Teller. They are all worried men, worried sick they are going to lose control of their new lab at Livermore, and we have ways of getting to all of them. Isadore Rabi has had a serious talk with Lawrence already.

Scene Twenty

Washington hotel reception (April 27, 1954).

It is busy and **Teller** *is signing in.*

Receptionist Welcome to the Wardman Park, Dr. Teller. If I could have you register here.

Teller The hotel is busy tonight.

Receptionist It always is at this time of year. Will you be attending the Physical Society's dinner?

Teller They're here?

Receptionist This is the main hotel for their conference this year.

Teller Oh, my God. No, I won't be going to the dinner.

Receptionist Very good. I also have two messages here for you. The first is from a Mr. Robb confirming his meeting with you at nine, and this one from Dr. Alvarez asking if you could—

Alvarez (*calling*) Edward.

Alvarez approaches across reception.

Teller Here he is. Would you believe this, Luis? Why would they put us here of all places?

Alvarez (*confidentially*) Edward. We have a huge problem. Ernest Lawrence isn't coming.

Teller You mean he isn't going to testify?

Alvarez That's right.

Teller Why?

Alvarez He says he's too ill, but look, let's go up to your room. There's just so much to tell. It's a disaster, Edward, a real disaster. And we're on our own.

End of Act One.

Act Two

Scenes Twenty-One to Twenty-Eight inclusive take place in the twenty-four hours between early evening on April 27, 1954 and early evening on April 28, 1954.

Scene Twenty-One

Teller's *hotel room.*

He is with **Alvarez**.

Alvarez   God, where do I begin? Everything is going wrong.

Teller   Why the hell isn't Lawrence coming?

Alvarez   He called two days ago when he got back from the lab directors' meeting. He was in a real state. He announced that he wouldn't testify, and that I shouldn't either. He said people had convinced him that Livermore would be greatly harmed if he testified—

Teller   He was being blackmailed.

Alvarez   Yup, no doubt.

Teller   By who?

Alvarez   He wouldn't say but my guess is Isidor Rabi.

Teller   Rabi was at the meeting?

Alvarez   He was and as an old friend of Ike's he's the only person with the clout to rattle Lawrence. Anyway the upshot was that Ernest called Strauss and told him he wasn't coming.

Teller   What did he say to Strauss?

Alvarez   I guess what he said to me—that his colitis was real bad and that he must avoid any stress. He even told me he'd got two guys in to look at the blood in his toilet bowl, so I guess he told Strauss that as well. He said when Strauss realized he wasn't changing his mind, Strauss called him a coward and slammed the phone on him.

Teller   But then you're not testifying either?

Alverez   Lawrence told me not to, yes. But then I had—

Teller   That's wonderful. Wonderful! So where does that leave the rest of us?

Alverez   Edward, shut up. Yes, he did tell me not to testify, and I did call Strauss and say I wasn't coming. He gave me hell as well. But as a parting shot be warned me that if I didn't show up, I would be unable to look myself in the mirror for the rest of my life. And that made me think for myself for once—and so I booked myself on the night flight, and here I am.

Teller Oh, thank God for that. Luis, I am sorry. But Ernest is a coward and completely thoughtless. He knows perfectly well how exposed his withdrawal makes the rest of us. And now that the hearing has become public, every physicist in this hotel knows about Oppenheimer's plight. And they know that Luis Alvarez and Edward Teller have more than a little to do with it.

Alvarez Are you thinking of backing out as well?

Teller While we've been talking, yes. But I can't.

Alvarez Why not?

Teller Two years ago, when I was just so angry at Oppenheimer's obstructiveness, I talked to the FBI and I spoke my mind. I even hinted he was working for Moscow. Robb and the board have a record of that meeting. If I was to back away from what I said then, it would do serious damage to our credibility . . . I am trapped.

Alvarez Well, let's go down to the conference. Hans Bethe is giving his presidential address and he's sure to say something about the hearing.

Scene Twenty-Two

Hotel dining hall.

Hans Bethe *is addressing several hundred dinner guests.* **Teller** *and* **Alvarez** *are at the back of the hall looking on.*

Bethe What disturbs us all so much in this case is that anyone could seriously doubt the loyalty of a leader with Oppenheimer's record of devotion.

Sounds of agreement from the audience.

But they do.

Now Oppie isn't always right, but if advisers whose strong convictions are not shared by the administration are dubbed disloyal, then honest differences of opinion, which are fundamental to democratic rule, will soon be replaced by a totalitarian conformity.

Hear hears and fragmented applause from the audience.

As the great Huey Long said when he was asked if communism was coming to America, "Sure communism is coming to America, but here we call it anti-communism."

Loud applause.

Alvarez Look Edward. Over there. It's Oppenheimer.

The applause breaks into cheers as the audience catches sight of him.

Bethe That greeting says everything. Oppie has come straight from an exhausting day at the hearing but would just like to say a few words.

Oppenheimer (*speaking quietly*)   Well, just a few. Such a welcome is always deeply moving and, at this time, doubly so. Hans's speech, of which I only caught the end, must, in these strange times, have taken some courage, and I am truly grateful. Thank you, Hans, and thank you, all, for your support.

There is more applause and loud cheers.

Alvarez   I think we are best out of here, Edward. Let's go eat. In the lobby—five minutes?

As they leave the hall, the cheering and clapping continue as **Oppenheimer** *leaves the platform.*

Scene Twenty-Three

Hotel corridor.

Teller *is humming to himself, arrives at his room, and unlocks it.*

Rabi   I saw you at the back of the hall, Edward.

Teller   Isadore Rabi. So you're following me.

Rabi   Just to say one thing. Lawrence isn't coming because he now realizes that, just as Hans was saying, it is no crime for an advisor to be wrong, whether from ignorance or for moral reasons.

Teller   And you no doubt impressed on him that you would move heaven and earth to shut Livermore if he did come.

Rabi   Livermore isn't as important to Lawrence as it is to you, Edward. It's your baby, isn't it? I hope I've made myself clear.

Teller   Oh, yes. Now let me go on my way.

Rabi   Have a good evening, Edward.

Scene Twenty-Four

Hotel lobby.

It is thronging with crowds from the conference dinner.

Alvarez   We're too late. The dinner is over.

Teller   Is there another way out?

Alvarez   Let's take the elevator to the basement.

Bethe   Edward. Edward.

From some distance away, **Hans Bethe** *accompanied by his wife,* **Rose**, *is trying to reach* **Teller**.

Teller This is the worst. It's Hans and Rose Bethe.

Bethe (*approaching*) Edward, Luis, they told me you were here.

Teller Hans, Rose. Yes. We missed the dinner so we're just going to find something to eat.

Bethe Can you spare a few moments? Please.

Teller If it is about the hearing—

Rose It will only take a short while. Will you come back to our room? Luis, will you forgive us?

Alvarez Of course. Edward, I'll go see the concierge, see what he suggests, and you can follow.

Teller Fine. I'll see you later. Now, Hans. Which floor are you on?

Scene Twenty-Five

The **Bethes'** *hotel room.*

Teller, **Bethe**, *and* **Rose** *arrive in the room.*

Teller Before we start, Hans, I know what I intend to do.

Bethe We're old friends, Edward, and there are things we can say to one another that others cannot.

Rose Please. We have your interests at heart as much as Oppie's.

Teller All right. I shall listen to you, Rose. And Hans—as old friends.

Bethe Then let me speak honestly. For years now, you have been carrying on a private war against Oppenheimer. It has infected everything in our atomic program and it has now led to this outrage, this hearing. It has to stop. If you testify in support of the charges against Oppie, which everyone realizes are so much of your making, the damage you'll do will be irreversible.

Teller You're not suggesting that this private war, as you call it, is all my fault, are you?

Bethe I think everyone, Fermi, myself, even Oppenheimer, understands how frustrated you have been over the H-bomb, and how it must have seemed as if Oppie was deliberately stalling you. But for you, Edward, it has become deeply personal and that has distorted your judgment.

Rose These things have changed you.

Teller Hans, you say you can see how it must have "seemed" as if Oppie was stalling the program. You don't think he actually was? Even though it took a Presidential order to get the H-bomb development going?

Bethe He had other choices, and, admit it, even after the Presidential order, every calculation made showed that it wouldn't work. And if we are to talk about stalling things, have you ever thought how much *you* have delayed things?

Teller How do you mean?

Bethe When I arrived back in Los Alamos in '50 there was one crucial question everyone was trying to answer—how to contain the energy from the initiating atomic explosion for that tiny millisecond necessary to set the fusion reaction going. And almost everyone who came to work on the problem came to you and said, "What about compressing the reaction in some way?" But no, you had done your sums, and you went on dismissing the idea. And yet what was the crucial element in your final solution?

Teller Yes, compression played a role but there were other factors.

Bethe You wouldn't listen, Edward, you were so embattled in your thinking. Now you accuse Oppenheimer of delays, but how much did your own "blinkered" thinking delay things, Edward? Three years? Four years?

Teller You are blaming me for not providing the solution to order?

Bethe You were completely paranoid. When Fermi, your friend, who suggested the whole project to you, when he came to help and kept getting negative results, you even saw his efforts as sabotage. Everyone was your enemy. Everyone was one of Oppie's men and that was that. You had lost your bearings.

There is a knock at door.

Rose Let me get that. (*Opens door.*)

Bethe Oppie.

Oppenheimer I'm going back to Georgetown now, Hans. I so appreciated this evening, it was a real boost. (*He sees* **Teller**.) Oh, Edward.

Teller Robert, my two old friends here are blaming me for not providing the solution to the H-bomb ignition problem to order. Instead they are saying I was at least as responsible for delays as you, that I was paranoid and had lost my bearings.

Oppenheimer Well, I think that's a discussion you don't need me to join. Hans, once again—

Teller Well, they are wrong and I shall tell you why. Because I did eventually find a way to fire a thermonuclear reaction, and no one else did. So fortunately we had the H-bomb first. But what would have happened if we had not and the Soviets had produced an H-bomb? An even bigger blast—twenty, fifty megatons?

Rose Why should anything have happened? We had enough firepower with our fission bombs to act as a deterrent, so why should we need anything bigger?

Bethe Rose is right, and that is an argument that is as true today as it was in 1950.

Teller Rose, things are just not like that. Take Bravo, a weapon capable of obliterating whole cities. If there had been a Soviet weapon like Bravo and we didn't have one, the questions would really have started, wouldn't they? And the answer? We had moral scruples and tried to set the Soviets a good example by not building one.

Rose That is a ridiculous scenario.

Teller No, Rose, it isn't, Is it, Robert? This is exactly what your committee advised the President when he was deciding on a crash program. You argued that the H-bomb should never be produced, that here was a unique opportunity for providing, by example, some limitations on the totality of war. You called it a threat to humanity.

Oppenheimer I don't think big bombs are the answer to anything, and nor did the committee. Frankly, to hear people like General LeMay talk about "nuking" North Korea with such weapons is not only sickening but politically absurd.

Rose You were developing a weapon which was so vast, so imprecise, that it has no military use and can only be used against civilian populations—for genocide.

Oppenheimer Rose is right.

Rose That is what you created, Edward, an instrument of genocide, and I have nothing but admiration for Robert and the others who had the courage to confront its total immorality.

Teller You say developing such a weapon, Rose, but you are making no distinction between developing and using a weapon. There is all the moral difference in the world between developing a weapon to maintain peace from a position of strength, and developing one with every intention of employing it. You know of Genghis Khan?

Rose Of course.

Teller He had the intention. He descended on Hungary and killed 90 per cent of our population. He didn't need nuclear weapons to carry out his genocide. The limitation is not in the ability but in the intention. There has been reason to fear at any time.

Rose And now, because of your device, there is reason to fear *all the time*.

Oppenheimer Exactly. And you believe we have to maintain our defensive superiority whatever the cost. Even though with new technology, there is every chance it will be used.

Teller We have no choice but to continue to explore and develop whatever is possible. Our greatest protection is an illusion of overwhelming power. Hans knows that.

Oppenheimer And so the Soviets and the West become like two scorpions in a bottle, each threatening each other, each capable of destroying one another. An ever more unstable spiral, increasingly costly, increasingly without reason. Can't you see that without negotiation, searching for common interests with our enemy, we are bound to end in disaster?

Teller If something is possible, it is out of our power to prevent it. And sure enough, the Soviets have created their own super-bomb. That is why I despaired of the delays caused by your simplified romantic approach to such issues—

Rose   Simplified and romantic, because he allowed morality into consideration?

Teller   Because at a critical time with the Russians, he renounced the H-bomb because it was the most powerful. The half megaton bombs he was building were apparently moral. Five megaton H-bombs were not. That decision had all the moral force of the girl who wants to get a little pregnant. You can have a bomb which is a little better but no more. That is the practical outcome of his morality. And meanwhile the Russians, an amoral power, have the H-bomb and are ready to use it. The risk you have taken with our national security, Robert, is truly frightening, and yet because I fought your unreasoned morality, I have been a victim of one setback after another. And that goes back to—

Oppenheimer   1942, I guess, when I appointed Hans here as head of theory at Los Alamos.

Teller   Exactly, Hans, who I had actually persuaded to come to Los Alamos.

Bethe   Oppie didn't make that decision alone. He took advice, in particular from Rabi.

Teller   Rabi thought I spent too much time on impractical pursuits.

Bethe   And he was right. You've great gifts, a wonderful instinct for physics. I owe my best work to an idea you gave me. But you're a dreamer, Edward, and you're unreliable.

Teller   It was a failing I could have corrected.

Oppenheimer   But, can't you see, that at such a critical time I couldn't have taken that risk?

Teller   So don't I have even some justification for the anger I feel?

Oppenheimer   Of course you do, but Edward, that was all twelve, thirteen years ago and if anything your bitterness now is even more intense.

Teller   Because I haven't forgotten what happened?

Bethe   And because of what you're involved in now, this obscene persecution.

Teller   Why obscene? Is the great Oppenheimer above having his actions questioned?

Oppenheimer   How much do you know of what's been happening at this hearing?

Teller   A certain amount.

Oppenheimer   Did you know that immediately before the hearing, Roger Robb spent a whole week briefing the board, and yet my lawyer wasn't even allowed to talk to them?

Bethe   And did you know that his lawyer has been denied documents on security grounds that are being made available to Robb?

Teller   He didn't apply for security clearance. Strauss told me.

Oppenheimer Strauss is lying. He applied a good two months before the hearing began, and he's still waiting for clearance. Time after time the board is considering material we haven't even seen. We've been blindfolded, Edward. There is nothing that Strauss and his people will not do.

Teller You think Strauss has a monopoly of these tactics. Ernest Lawrence isn't coming because he has been threatened, blackmailed. It's Washington hardball, and it's tough.

Bethe And you are part of it. This hearing is one the Soviets would be proud of themselves, don't you think?

Teller You think I want all this, that I am to blame? Robert Oppenheimer, he's the man who is to blame.

Oppenheimer God, Edward, you are so difficult to like.

Teller You never even tried. At Los Alamos you had your own little clique, you surrounded yourself with ex-students, all leftists and dubious at best. And for the rest of us, we just had to admire the great man from afar.

Oppenheimer Throughout the war I had a weekly meeting with you! No one but you had that privilege.

Teller (*incensed*) And that was just to stop me rocking the boat. Then we had to watch when you took your stricken conscience for a walk. Or admire your carefully chosen pictures, the Indian rugs, and cigarettes you smoked, the quotes from Sanskrit so subtly expressing your beautiful conscience.

Bethe Edward, that's enough!

Teller Why? Why is it enough?

Bethe You will end up doing nothing but damage. Please, both of you, stop.

Oppenheimer Well, I have long overstayed my welcome. Thank you both as I said when I arrived, this evening was a marvelous tonic, really. Edward, I have no idea what to say to you.

Bethe *goes to the door with him.*

Oppenheimer One thing. You were at the dinner tonight. You experienced the strength of feeling there. Do consider the consequences of what you do, not on me but on yourself.

Oppenheimer *leaves.*

Teller I shall go and find Luis. Rose, it is always a pleasure to see you. I am so sad about how things are.

Rose Please, Edward, stay a few moments more. Please. (**Bethe** *joins them.*) Edward, this is consuming you, and you know it's so sad to see you like this, particularly for old friends.

Teller Why particularly for old friends?

Rose   Old friends know how much you have changed. Do you remember our trip to the West Coast in the summer of '38? Back then you were full of life, enthusiastic, generous—truly a lovely man. Now, few people who have known you these past years would talk of you like that. As I've listened to you, I've been asking myself why, after all these years, your bitterness is so intense? And it made me think of one evening on that trip when we stopped over in Estes Park. You'd been climbing with Hans, and after supper we sat talking about ourselves.

Teller   Rose, I think I know where this is leading and I . . .

Rose   Please let me finish, please, this is so important. For the first time, you told us of your problems at school, how when you eventually went at the age of eight you could debate the existence of free will but couldn't tie your shoelaces.

Teller   There can hardly be a gifted child alive who hasn't experienced something similar.

Rose   And you became deeply unpopular didn't you, Edward? That's what you told us. You were serious minded, without a sense of humor or any of the social graces that might have eased your path, and you knew everything. You thought your classmates lacked a proper enthusiasm for learning and you told them so. Your teachers were sometimes wrong and you corrected them—and they resented you for it. You were teased, you were bullied. For seven, eight years, you were lonely, friendless, miserable. By your own admission you were a social outcast, Edward.

Teller   It wasn't half as bad as you're making out.

Rose   But it didn't stop there, did it? Years later when you and Hans went as postgraduates to Fermi's lab in Rome, he saw you bullied mercilessly by the others there, including Rabi. Hans told me you almost apologized for being alive.

Teller   Do you have to go on?

Rose   No. But Edward, please don't dismiss what we are saying—those setbacks and rejections over the H-bomb must have played on those old wounds, and seriously but unjustifiably colored your view of the man you hold responsible, Oppenheimer. You have the future of a remarkable man very much in your hands. And as Oppie pointed out, you could also do untold damage to yourself.

Teller (*perplexed*)   Rose, you think I don't know that?

Scene Twenty-Six

Alvarez's *hotel room.*

Teller *is with* **Alvarez**.

Alvarez   Edward, we simply misjudged the strength of feeling here.

Teller   No, for me, Luis, it goes much deeper. I feel that I've arrived at my present confusion with all the assurance of a sleepwalker. Sure, I was expecting the rapturous greeting given to Oppenheimer. But I certainly wasn't expecting a deeply disturbing onslaught by two good friends, nor having Oppenheimer describe how he's been treated at the hearing.

So now I have absolutely no idea how I should testify, or what I say to Robb in a few minutes. He will obviously expect me to repeat the damning comments I made when we last met. But now I'm not even sure they are justified. I'm in total confusion and if I don't go now I shall be late and that—

Alvarez Edward, you can't talk to Robb in this state of mind. Sit down and for God's sake let's try and clarify things. You say it's the power of your emotional response to Oppenheimer that Rose and Hans called into question?

Teller And the way it has influenced my judgment of him. Yes.

Alvarez So did they manage to convince you of where you might have been wrong about him?

Teller Certainly they made me examine how paranoid I had been.

Alvarez But is there anything, anything they said which shakes your belief in the disastrous quality of his decision-making? (*Pause.*) I'm talking about his judgment, nothing else.

Teller No, there isn't. I still firmly believe that his judgment has been seriously flawed all along.

Alvarez Then that's what you say to Robb. Never mind the whys and wherefores of what he has done, whether he is loyal or disloyal, moral or immoral, just stick to how you see the outcome of his actions.

Scene Twenty-Seven

Teller's *hotel room.*

Teller *is with* **Roger Robb**.

Teller So tell me, how is the hearing going, Mr. Robb?

Robb Pretty well, I think. The main thing is that the board has formed a pretty bad impression of Oppenheimer—almost from the beginning. But now we've moved on to the H-bomb for the last day or two and so I wanted a word about tomorrow. Cutting to the chase, can I ask if you will be testifying that Oppenheimer is a security risk?

Teller No, I don't believe that he is.

Robb That's not what you said to me two months ago, Dr. Teller.

Teller I've given it a great deal of thought since then, Mr. Robb. What I said then was that I didn't trust his judgment, but now it's clear to me that you cannot treat someone as a security risk because of the advice they give.

Robb You did more than raise the question of his judgment. What has happened, Dr. Teller?

Teller Nothing has happened, Mr. Robb. However, Borden's original letter is so extreme it taints everything. In just testifying against Oppenheimer, I am virtually accusing him of being a spy. Feelings are running high and now with Lawrence becoming unavailable, I stand very much exposed and am exceedingly nervous about it.

Robb You're not as exposed as you might think. Look, this is something I would never be allowed to do in a court of law, but, here, read this. (*Document rustle.*) It's part of my cross-examination of Oppenheimer a few days ago. (*Pause.*) We unearthed an old Presto disc of Oppenheimer being interviewed by security in mid-1943. In it he talks about being approached by one of his left-wing university friends, Haakon Chevalier.

Teller I know Chevalier.

Robb So we set a simple test—have him tell us what happened, then compare this version with what he said on the disc. And sure enough there were big differences. See, here.

Teller You ask "Did you tell Pash the truth?" and his reply, "No."

Robb This was a big discrepancy.

Teller And then you go on. "Why did you do that, doctor?" and he replies, "Because I was an idiot." I can hardly believe that. Why is he doing it?

Robb To protect his brother, we think, but then who else, what else?

Teller It is amazing, but it has no direct relevance to my testimony.

Robb It shows your testimony would not be alone.

Teller But I have only ever concerned myself with the quality of his opinions and his judgment.

Robb No, Dr. Teller, you've said more than that—both to me and to the FBI. You have given us both a clear picture of how Oppenheimer's changing reasons over the years for opposing the H-bomb made a calculated pattern by which to stall the whole program. Much worse than a matter of opinion and judgment. And you've hinted at an involvement with Moscow, and mentioned British intelligence's view that Oppenheimer was a bigger spy than Klaus Fuchs. Now all this material is already before the board as evidence, so it would be confusing, to say the least, if you were to say you now felt differently. I'm sure you understand what I'm saying.

Teller You're threatening me with a perjury action.

Robb I'm simply reminding you of our agreement the last time we met and how very serious it will be for the nation's weapons program if Oppenheimer comes through with his clearance intact. We have to make our case as strongly as possible to leave the board in no doubt.

Teller That is obvious. What is not so obvious is exactly how far you expect me to go. So shall we be blunt?

Robb Bluntly, I want to hear you clearly state that you think Oppenheimer is a risk to this country's security. Once I hear that, I shall move on, leaving the board to savor your opinion.

Teller Will the board ask me questions?

Robb They might, particularly the chairman, Gordon Gray, but they usually leave me to do their badgering for them.

Teller Mr. Robb, my testimony will remain secret, won't it?

Robb Absolutely. Your testimony will never be made public. No need to worry on that score.

Scene Twenty-Eight

The hearing room.

Robb *is examining* **Teller** *in front of an audience including* **Oppenheimer**.

Robb Dr. Teller, is it your intention to suggest that Dr. Oppenheimer is disloyal to the United States?

Teller No, it is not. I have always assumed that he is loyal to this country. I think it would be presumptuous on my part to try to analyze his motives.

Robb Do you or do you not believe that Dr. Oppenheimer is a security risk?

Teller At times Dr. Oppenheimer has acted in a way which for me is exceedingly hard to understand. I thoroughly disagreed with him in numerous issues and his actions frankly appeared to me confused and overly complicated. To this extent, I would like to see the vital interests of this country in hands which I understand better, and therefore trust more.

Robb Very good. One question I should have asked you before, Dr. Teller, are you an American citizen?

Teller (*relieved*) I am.

Robb When were you naturalized?

Gray Mr. Robb.

Robb Yes, Mr. Gray.

Gray I am sorry to interrupt but I want to return to the security issue. Dr. Teller, can I remind you of the question this board has to answer—whether it will, or will not, endanger the common defense and security to grant clearance to Dr. Oppenheimer.

Teller (*pushed further than expected*) If it is a question of wisdom and judgment, as demonstrated by actions since 1945, then I would say one would be wiser not to grant clearance. May I limit myself to these comments?

Gray Thank you very much, doctor. That is all for this afternoon, gentlemen. My thanks, Dr. Teller. Can I just remind you that these proceedings are confidential and ask that you respect that.

Teller I certainly shall.

Gray You are excused. We will recess until 9:30 tomorrow.

General conversation starts up. **Robb** *comes across to* **Teller**.

Robb My thanks, too, Dr. Teller.

Teller Good. Well, excuse me. I just want a word with Oppenheimer—(**Teller** *finds his way across to* **Oppenheimer**.) Excuse me—Robert, I am sorry.

Pause.

Oppenheimer After what you've just said, I don't know what you mean.

Scene Twenty-Nine

Teller's *office* (*April 29, 1954*).

Teller *is with* **Strauss**.

Strauss Edward, you surpassed yourself. You were considered, mature, just the approach to be expected from Oppenheimer's successor. And he shook your hand, Robb tells me.

Teller Yes.

Strauss Which shows that even he saw how reasoned you were.

Teller I apologized.

Strauss Apologized. For what?

Teller I had done what was expected of me. I had given the board the lever they needed to find against him. What remains are the consequences, and they are frightening for both of us. Lewis, the passion, the anger Alvarez and I experienced in those few hours yesterday was frightening. Frightening because of what it says about the future. First there will be speculation. Who was behind his fall? Was it the Air Force? Was it you, Lewis, or Ernest Lawrence—or me?

There were things that Oppenheimer told me about the conduct of the trial which, particularly hearing them from him, I think, are—shaming.

Strauss Oppenheimer is not only a danger but he is arrogant, vain, a truly vile person. I have had the deepest dislike for him ever since we first met. The contempt he showed me then—I offered him the job at Princeton and he didn't deign to contact me for five months—me, his benefactor. And then he made a fool of me in front of a congressional committee. I have never forgotten that and never will. When this hearing is over, I want to bring criminal proceedings against him for treason.

Teller   Maybe, but right now I can't share the hatred you feel. The scientist on the board asked me whether I thought the hearing would create a schism among scientists. I said it would but his question made me think he too had been touched by the passions and sense of betrayal out there.

Strauss   It will all dissipate soon enough, and we can concentrate on other matters like speeding up the release of your family. There's only Borden to come. Oppie will know who his tormentor is at last.

Scene Thirty

Hearing room (April 30, 1954).

Borden *is appearing as a witness.* **Marks** *is with* **Oppenheimer**.

Gray   Would the witness please give his full name?

Borden   My name is William Liscum Borden.

Court business continues.

Oppenheimer   What the hell is Borden doing here?

Marks   There's your 'beast in the jungle'

Gray   Were you the executive director of the Joint Committee on Atomic Energy in 1953?

Borden   Yes, sir, I was.

Oppenheimer   Until Ike fired him.

Marks   This is absurd, we have to stop this.

Gray   Mr. Borden, you have a copy of the letter you sent to Mr. Hoover?

Borden   I have it in front of me, sir.

Marks   Mr. Chairman, As the board knows, we have never seen this letter which provoked these proceedings, and we are deeply concerned that introducing it at this late stage could raise completely new issues.

Gray   He will be reading it for the benefit of all of us, Mr. Marks.

Marks   You see, the thing that struck me at once was the third clause on page four: "More probably than not he has since been functioning as an espionage agent." That issue has simply not been dealt with here.

Gray   I will have something to say about this when he has finished reading, Mr. Marks. So will the witness proceed.

Borden Dear Mr. Hoover, the purpose of this letter is to state my view based on years of study that Robert Oppenheimer is a serious risk to the security of this country, and that more probably than not he is an agent of the Soviet Union.

This opinion is based on the following factors: his pre-war activities, his entry into government service, his behavior during the war, and lastly his conduct following the war especially regarding the H-bomb.

One. Between 1929 and 1942, more probably than not, Dr. Robert Oppenheimer was a sufficiently hardened communist that he either volunteered espionage evidence to the Soviets or complied with their request.

Borden *continues under the following dialogue*:

Indeed in singling out atomic weapons research as his specialty he acted under Soviet instructions.

He was contributing substantial sums to the Communist Party.

His wife and younger brother were Communist Party members.

His mistress was a member of the Communist Party.

Marks (*whispers*) Oppie, I can't believe they took this man seriously.

Oppenheimer (*whispers*) Let's listen.

Fade up **Borden** *then cross-fade his last line with*:

Borden Three. He vigorously supported the H-bomb research program until the Japanese surrender, since when he personally urged senior researchers in this field to desist.

Borden *continues under the following dialogue*:

Four. From mid-1946 through January 1950, he was instrumental in effectively suspending H-bomb development.

Five. From 1950, he has worked tirelessly to retard the U.S. H-bomb program.

Marks (*whispers*) Oppie, this is like Teller actually wrote this letter.

Oppenheimer (*whispers*) Does that surprise you?

Marks (*whispers*) It's the fact it's so obvious that surprises me. If this ever gets out, Teller will have all hell to pay.

Fade up **Borden**.

Borden . . . atomic energy, intelligence, and diplomatic policy.

So these are the conclusions I have painfully crystallized. That is the end of the letter, sir.

Gray Thank you. The board has come to a view with respect to this letter—namely that after three weeks of testimony, the board has no evidence at all before it that Dr. Oppenheimer has been functioning as an espionage agent or acting under Soviet directive. So therefore we will reach no judgment on these issues. Mr. Robb, your witness.

Marks (*whispering*)   We are turning them round, Oppie. I do think we are winning.

Scene Thirty-One

Fade up music and **Newsreader 1**.

Newsreader 1   The findings of the security panel, investigating "Father of the A-bomb" Robert Oppenheimer, are published today. By a two votes to one majority, Dr. Oppenheimer has been found guilty on twenty-one of the twenty-four charges against him, and his top-level security clearance has been revoked by the Atomic Energy Commission . . .

Cross-fade between **Newsreader 1** *and* **Newsreader 2**.

Newsreader 2   At the government's bomb laboratory at Los Alamos, 199 scientists have signed a resolution condemning the findings of the security board investigating Dr. Robert Oppenheimer, and they are on strike until further notice . . .

Cross-fade between **Newsreader 2** *and* **Newsreader 1**.

Newsreader 1   A senior government scientist has described the country's nuclear research as at a standstill . . .

Fade **Newsreader 1**.

Scene Thirty-Two

Teller'*s house* (*June 14, 1954*).

Teller *is on the phone to* **Alvarez**.

Alvarez   This is a real blow, Edward. Strauss has just phoned to tell me that the commissioners are going to publish the transcript of the hearing.

Teller   They can't. The board chairman gave every witness a personal assurance that the proceedings were confidential.

Alvarez   There's been a security breach, Lewis said. One of the commissioners, Zuckert I think, was taking a copy home for the weekend and left it on a train.

Teller   Our trains must be littered with lost secret documents. Was it stolen?

Alvarez   No, they found it quickly, but because there was time for it to be copied, they feel they must publish the whole thing.

Teller   Oh, that's outrageous. It sounds absolutely like a put-up job. Luis, forgive me. I'm going to call Strauss.

Alvarez   OK. Get back to me.

Teller I will.

Fade down.

Scene Thirty-Three

Teller's *office. Later* (*June 14, 1954*).

Teller *is on the phone to* **Strauss**.

Teller Lewis, this is an outrage. This release is being engineered on the flimsiest of pretexts, and yet you know what effect the release will have, not just on me, but on others.

Strauss You are right, it is a cover-up but we have no choice. We're still bugging Oppenheimer and we've learnt that he has organized for the *Times* to publish selected parts of the transcript favorable to Oppenheimer early next week.

Teller Can't you just stop them?

Strauss They're breaking no law unless they publish classified material.

Teller If I'd known this was a possibility, Lewis, I would never have testified in the way I did. Now I am to be revealed to the world as the Judas, as the one scientist who accused Oppenheimer of being a risk to security. And you must have known this was possible.

Strauss I am truly sorry it's happened.

Teller When will it be published?

Strauss Tomorrow.

Teller Tomorrow! You've known about this all along.

Strauss We're determined to beat the *Times* to it.

Teller It's a crazy decision, Lewis, crazy. For some short-term political end, you are destroying everything that's been achieved in that hearing.

Strauss It's done, Edward. I can't stop it.

Teller You could, but you won't. You're now going to release a document containing enough poison to feed feuds for generations.

Strauss Edward, give me this much credit. I have been striving not just to remove Oppenheimer but to replace him with you. I wouldn't have anything damaging happen to you if it had been avoidable.

Teller It's published tomorrow, and I am due in Los Alamos at the weekend for a reunion?

Strauss You mustn't go.

Teller Mici is on her way now.

Strauss You can't go. Anything could happen. If you go, I won't be responsible for what happens.

Teller Responsibility doesn't seem to be one of your strong points, Lewis. (*Hangs up.*)

Scene Thirty-Four

Teller's *office, Los Alamos.*

Mici (*on distort*) Edward you must do nothing that can be seen as running away. We must face them.

Teller Here at Los Alamos?

Mici Absolutely at Los Alamos. And you must have that journalist come. No doubt about it. Will other people from Livermore be there?

Teller Luis will be there and maybe others. I don't know.

Mici Be sure they are with us and that we stay together. It is absolutely the best thing to brave this out. If not, it will shadow us forever.

Scene Thirty-Five

Teller's *room, Los Alamos* (*late June 1954*).

Teller *and* **Mici** *are being photographed. From the terrace below come the sounds of a picnic—conversation, laughter, music some of the time.*

Teller How many people are down there, Mici? Can you look?

Mici *goes to the window.*

Mici I would guess forty—forty to fifty.

Teller You recognize anyone? Any friends?

Mici All I can see are Los Alamos people, the Bradburys, Carson and Fay Marks.

Teller I thought Luis would be here by now. Are there none of the Chicago people—the Allisons, people like that?

Mici Not that I can see.

Teller Oh, this is awful. Let me look.

Mici Don't come to the window. You don't want to be seen.

Knock at the door.

Teller Come in. (*The door opens.*) Luis, thank goodness.

Alvarez Edward, Mici, I'm so sorry I'm late. Of all the things, we had to—

Teller   Who did you see down there?

Alvarez   How do you mean?

Teller   Friends. Were there friends down there?

Alvarez   None that were obvious. It seemed to be all Los Alamos people.

Mici (*from the window*)   I can see the Critchfields, and there's someone else I can't see properly—

Alvarez   The sooner we get down there the better. I was one of the last to arrive and we're in danger of making an entry after everyone is seated.

Mici   Yes it is, it's the Christys. They are sitting right below us.

Teller   Well, thank goodness for that—at least one friend. You know Bob Christy, Luis?

Alvarez   By reputation.

Teller   We shared a house with them in Chicago just after the war. Good, lively family.

Mici   People are looking up in this direction.

Alvarez   They know a crew from *Life* magazine is here.

A single person outside sings "Why are we waiting?" There are sniggers and laughter which build.

Teller   Oh God, Mici, this is madness. We can't go down.

Mici   We have to go. There's no choice. Everyone knows we are here.

Alvarez   Seriously, Edward, this is rubbing salt into the wound. If we're going we must go now.

Teller   All right.

Mici   There's a table close to the entrance. When we appear, Edward, don't go across to anyone, and don't show off. We just go to the table and sit down quietly.

Scene Thirty-Six

Los Alamos terrace (*late June 1954*).

The **Tellers'** *party arrives. A healthy buzz of conversation.*

Mici   Luis, if as soon as we sit down you go and fetch us a drink—

Rabi   There he is!

The buzz of conversation subsides.

Teller   There's Bob Christy. I'm going across to see him.

Mici   No, don't do that.

Teller It'll show I've got at least one friend here.

Mici Edward.

Teller Bob, it's good to see you. It must be more than a year now. (*There is no reaction from* **Christy**.) Bob?

Christy I think I need a refill. Can I get one for anyone else?

Teller Bob, will you not shake my hand?

Christy No, I will not.

Teller *staggers against the table, upsetting drinks, as if about to collapse. The surrounding picnickers react.*

Alvarez Edward, are you all right?

Mici Edward?

Alvarez Look, come and sit down.

Teller I think I caught my foot. We must go back now.

A slow handclap starts and slowly builds.

Mici Edward, we must stay here. We have to face this. We must go and sit down.

Teller We go back—now. Please, Luis, don't follow us. We'll come back.

Scene Thirty-Seven

Teller*'s room.*

The sound of the picnic in the distance. **Teller** *and* **Mici** *enter.*

Teller Mici, I can't grasp what has just happened out there.

Mici They are stupid, stupid people. You must take a moment, collect your thoughts and then we'll go out and face them. After all, how can they insult us any more?

Teller *is absorbed in contemplation.*

Teller You know, I am godfather to one of the Christy children. How can they forget that? I can't remember ever having a cross word with them, all the time we were in Chicago.

Mici Edward, they are stupid, they are like sheep and we must face them.

Teller It's like a shunning by some religious group. They are driving us out.

Mici And you are their best allies talking like this.

Teller We have been driven from Europe, from our families, and now we are being excluded—excluded by our own kind here. I've been dreading this. Oh God, Mizcika, what have I done? What have I done?

Teller *weeps uncontrollably.* **Mici** *tries to comfort him. Fade up music gradually.*

Scene Thirty-Eight

The setup is the same as for Scene One.

Teller *is being interviewed by a* **Journalist** *who is setting up a small recorder.*

Journalist   Robert Cowan. Interview with Dr. Teller for the *Christian Science Monitor*. January 15, 1955. (*Addressing* **Teller**.) We were talking about the result of the hearing. How has that affected you?

Teller   It has affected me profoundly. It has affected my wife profoundly. I never wanted Oppenheimer handled in that way and what has hurt me has been how many of my friends have dropped me and are very angry with me. My entire life was among physicists, but now, wherever I go, I have no idea how I will be greeted.

Journalist   They show their anger?

Teller   I have been cut dead more times than I can count. I am a leper at social gatherings, people walk away from me in the street, occasionally they spit on me. This is the saddest time of my life. But enough. I still have much. I still have Livermore and the government still needs me. I have new friends, friends in the Air Force.

Journalist   But they are not the same as the old ones.

Teller   The camaraderie of physics, the company of like minds, that world is closed to me now as finally and completely as if I had been found guilty of an awful crime.

Journalist   Perhaps in time—

Teller   It is finished. I have to stop regretting and embrace what I do have. I am quitting the appeasers and joining the fascists.

Journalist   Is that what you want me to write, Dr. Teller?

Teller   Now that Oppenheimer has gone and with all that has happened, there's no reason now to compromise. We shall be working to ensure our supremacy over the Russians. We shall be striving to maintain peace through strength. Everything is now quite clear.

Fade up final music.

The end.

Setting

1959–68

Original Live Theatre Production

RFK: The Journey to Justice by Murray Horwitz and Jonathan Estrin was originally commissioned and produced by L.A. Theatre Works, with generous support from the DeBartolo Performing Arts Center at the University of Notre Dame, the Clarice Smith Performing Arts Center at the University of Maryland, Stanford Lively Arts at Stanford University, and the Modlin Center for the Arts at the University of Richmond. Following an L.A. Theatre Works national tour, it was recorded before a live audience at the Skirball Cultural Center, Los Angeles in March 2010. It was directed by John Rubinstein. The cast was as follows:

Burke Marshall/Others	Michael Leydon Campbell
John F. Kennedy/Others	Philip Casnoff
Robert F. Kennedy	Henry Clarke
Byron White/Others	Kyle Colerider-Krugh
Martin Luther King, Jr.	Kevin Daniels
Harris Wofford/Others	Ross Hellwig
John Seigenthaler/Others	Thomas Vincent Kelly
Coretta Scott King/Others	Sheilynn Wactor
Louis Martin/Others	John Wesley

Producing Director Notes

Susan Loewenberg

When we received the offer to create an original L.A. Theatre Works docudrama from four of our outstanding and longtime presenters, the University of Notre Dame, Stanford, the University of Maryland, and the University of Richmond, we were elated and then challenged by the formidable task of choosing just the right subject. Despite the many ideas offered by our staff and the writers and academics we consulted, one subject kept coming back to me, perhaps because it also haunted me. I had unfinished business with Robert Kennedy.

As a graduate student in the history department at UCLA, I was, in 1968, taking a seminar on biography, taught by the late Fawn Brodie, whose biographies of Thomas Jefferson, Joseph Smith, and Richard Nixon, among others, were both well known and controversial, informed as they were by psychoanalytic theory and concepts.

For my seminar paper, I had chosen Robert Kennedy as my subject, and the intent of the paper was "to examine the major forces that have shaped Robert Kennedy's personality and determined his pattern of behavior." In short, under the influence of my professor, I had set myself the goal of "psychoanalyzing" RFK. Leaving aside the merits of this method as well as the merits or shortcomings of the paper, here is what happened.

It is June 4, 1968. I am sitting in front of the television, watching the post-presidential primary election party in the ballroom of the Ambassador Hotel in downtown Los Angeles. Robert Kennedy is giving a rousing victory speech and I am putting the finishing touches to my paper. I am literally on the last page. A little after midnight, as I am writing the final paragraph, sleepy yet exhilarated, Kennedy's aides decide to take him through the kitchen and we see them leaving the ballroom. I can hear the local anchor announcing the entourage's movements as they enter the kitchen. Then I watched in horror as chaos and confusion erupted on the screen and learned that the person I had intimately come to know had been gunned down. I struggled over the next few days to find an ending to the paper, but nothing seemed right. I had lost my objectivity, and I was in despair over the senselessness of his death. I ended the paper with this sentence: "But with the death of his brother John, the spotlight turned on him, and drawn to it like a moth to a flame, he didn't have a chance."

History and my own maturity have tempered those sentiments and given me a less simplistic perspective, as will this play.

Following Robert F. Kennedy's Path to Justice

Elizabeth Bennett, Dramaturg and Researcher

In the spring of 1963, U.S. Attorney General Robert F. Kennedy, concerned about rising racial tensions in the North and South, and looking for fresh ideas on how to cope with civil rights problems, convened two meetings with African-American writer James Baldwin. Baldwin had been sharply critical of President John F. Kennedy for not being more forceful about the civil rights struggle gripping the United States. At the conclusion of the first meeting (held at Kennedy's home in Virginia), Kennedy asked Baldwin to put together some of his "best people in New York" to "talk this whole thing over." The group that met with Kennedy at his New York City apartment included Baldwin and his actor brother David, Pulitzer Prize-winning playwright Lorraine Hansberry, singers Harry Belafonte and Lena Horne, psychologist Dr. Kenneth B. Clark, consul to the Gandhi Society Clarence B. Jones, and Freedom Rider Jerome Smith. The result was unexpected for both sides. Kennedy—publicly tight-lipped about the meeting—expressed privately his shock that his brother's administration wasn't lauded by blacks for its efforts, who told him that if this is the best he could do, then the best was not enough. Kennedy was humiliated by the group's desperate laughter and surprised by so much anger. "We were a little shocked by the extent of his naïveté," James Baldwin explained afterwards. Baldwin noted that he and his friends left the meeting convinced that Kennedy didn't understand the full extent of the growing racial struggles in the North.

From this footnote to history comes the play that you will read. L.A. Theatre Works Producing Director Susan Loewenberg remembers hearing about the Baldwin–Kennedy meeting, whose cast of characters sounded like it could have been dreamed up by a Hollywood producer posing a "what if" scenario. Loewenberg wondered about what happened within the walls of the Kennedy apartment. She also wondered about the dramatic possibilities to be found in the story of "Bobby" Kennedy, the scrawny seventh child of Joseph P. Kennedy and Rose Fitzgerald Kennedy, who grew up to be a fierce football end, staunch protector of his adored older brother John, and a combative criminal justice prosecutor, Attorney General, New York State Senator, and presidential candidate. The possibility of exploring the co-existing dualities of RFK's persona—the Attorney General who ordered the wiretapping of Martin Luther King Jr.'s phones alongside the grim-faced, much-moved visitor who talked to children on visits to homes of the Appalachian poor—was too good to pass up.

The role of hero of the civil rights movement is not one that Robert Kennedy intended to take on. His initial ambivalence—he and his brother courted black voters in 1960 as a way of helping to shore up JFK's presidential election bid —has been largely forgotten over time and in light of his later achievements. But the ensuing eight years—chronicled in our play—contained a series of incidents, growing relationships, and social changes that put RFK at the forefront of the fight for civil rights. He was a man with a strong sense of right and wrong, both morally and legally. Deeply moved by the injustices he saw through the multiple arrests of Martin Luther King on trumped-up charges, the humiliations suffered by black students trying to get an education, and the lack of employment and business opportunities for blacks, RFK's strides towards achieving equality began with legislative measures, eventually expanding his concerns beyond black–white issues to fundamental issues such as workers' rights and poverty—issues that went beyond race.

It's strangely appropriate that Loewenberg located writers for the RFK play as the fortieth anniversary of RFK's shocking assassination approached, through a chance meeting at a screening of *RFK Remembered*, the film commissioned by the Kennedy family after RFK's death and shown at the 1968 Democratic National Convention. Loewenberg connected with an old friend, actor/writer/director Murray Horwitz, and they discussed the project. Horwitz—who had been a supporter of Eugene McCarthy in the 1968 campaign—recalled the continuing devotion and excitement expressed by anyone who worked with RFK. In short time, Horwitz and writing partner/TV producer and writer Jonathan Estrin were engulfed in reading RFK's eloquent speeches, numerous Kennedy biographies, period newspaper articles and editorials, and transcripts of Senate hearings. In the RFK files at the John F. Kennedy Presidential Library in Boston copies of telegrams, drafts of campaign flyers and speeches, hate mail letters, and itineraries from RFK's many fact-finding tours were found. Robert Drew's 1963 documentary *Crisis: Behind a Presidential Commitment*, which follows RFK and Governor George Wallace through the days leading up to the integration of the University of Alabama, depicts the atmosphere of the Attorney General's office, the tension of the time and situation, and gave the writers a first-hand view of how the Kennedy brothers interacted with each other.

Perhaps more valuable than the historical records are the personal accounts of RFK's humor, hard work, and faith in justice. A number of RFK's confidantes and staff gave interviews to Horwitz and Estrin—interviews that provided enormously helpful character details and went beyond the historical record of the personal journey of RFK. Journalist John Seigenthaler—RFK's administrative aide whose Southern drawl and humor comes across in news clips and accounts of the era—first met Kennedy in 1957 and remained close with him to the end—despite having tried to convince his friend not to run for president. Seigenthaler's insight into the solitary, internal changes undergone by RFK after the President's assassination helped guide the writers as they explored RFK's emergence from his brother's shadow. Frank Mankiewicz—who worked as RFK's press secretary during his years in the Senate and later went on to become CEO of NPR—told the writers exactly what happened on a horrible night in April 1968 when RFK faced an urban crowd in Indianapolis that had not yet heard that Martin Luther King Jr. had been shot and killed. Also on board to provide comments and relevant historical material was presidential biographer and columnist Richard Reeves. These and many other firsthand, eyewitness accounts helped Horwitz and Estrin dramatize the complexity of RFK's personality and his struggle for civil rights and other causes.

The play you'll read is the result of the extensive research and exploration described above. But this is not a time piece depicting frozen moments. Kennedy's achievements—at the time so controversial and groundbreaking—have become part of the fabric of American life. But had Kennedy not taken a gutsy, hard-nosed view toward legislative innovations, and later a heartfelt approach to the construction of social and economic development programs, many Americans wouldn't have enjoyed the rights and prosperity of the last forty years. As we remember the age of Barack Obama, it's well worth looking back at the complexities of one of the men who indirectly made it possible for Obama to sit where he did. And to contemplate the possibilities of what else might have been, had RFK been President himself.

Father Ted Hesburgh Interview Highlights (February 2010)

Susan Loewenberg It is my great privilege to be sitting with Father Ted Hesburgh in his office on the campus of the University of Notre Dame in South Bend Indiana. Father Hesburgh served as Notre Dame's President for thirty-five years, from 1952 to 1987, the longest tenure in the university's history. He's a priest of the congregation of the Holy Cross, and has been a major figure in the Catholic church and US politics for the past fifty years. Father Hesburgh served on the United States Civil Rights Commission from its inception in 1957, working closely with Presidents Eisenhower, Kennedy, Johnson, and Nixon, until stepping down in 1972. Father Hesburgh, welcome to L.A. Theatre Works and thanks for being with us.

Could you tell us please how you came to be nominated to the Civil Rights Commission? You were a charter member when it was created in 1957.

Father Ted Hesburgh Well, I remember being in Vienna at the meeting of the International Atomic Energy Agency, and I was walking from the meeting back to my hotel, and I noticed this new *Time* magazine. I picked it off the rack and bought it, waiting for the light to change, and I was so fascinated that as I flipped through it, I saw the announcement of the US Commission on Civil Rights. I've been involved in civil rights for a long time and I said well that's a great commission and maybe I'll be on it! And sure enough, about three weeks later back in the States on a Sunday afternoon, I got a call from the White House and the president's assistant said President Eisenhower would like to know if you would accept a commission on the US Commission on Civil Rights. And I said it's something I've been deeply interested in and I thought we could make a contribution. In fact, we changed the face of America.

Susan Loewenberg I was just about to ask you about the mission of the Civil Rights Commission and how did you carry out that mission in the infancy of the Commission?

Father Ted Hesburgh Well, it was very simple. We only had one power: the power of subpoena. We could subpoena anyone to come and testify under oath. We had all our meetings across the land in federal courtrooms, and the only place that would take us throughout the South, because they wouldn't give us a room anywhere else. But we had multiple meetings north, south, east, west, and after two years we came up with a strong report. And following that, the President reinstated the Commission for another year and it continued being recommissioned every year after that.

Susan Loewenberg How would you contrast the efforts and efficacy of the Civil Rights Commission under the Eisenhower administration versus the Kennedy administration?

Father Ted Hesburgh Well, it was a field that was very hot politically and it was a field that desperately needed new legislation. Because as a matter of fact, most blacks were second-class citizens in America. They had problems voting in some places and are getting unemployment, buying houses, and schools were mainly segregated throughout the South by law. Backed up by the Supreme Court Plessy v. Ferguson. And we had to break through all of those barriers to get decent human rights for all blacks in America. And the commission could only recommend it, but since we were a Presidential Commission, our report went directly to the President of the United States. And after our first two years, we came up with such a strong report that Eisenhower invited the Commission down to the White House. We met with him to discuss the recommendations of the Commission, and he said he was surprised that we came up with such strong recommendations about voting, education, and employment. It caught his attention and we were then recommissioned and they continued it over the next ten years that I was on it.

Susan Loewenberg   And how were the recommendations that you gave the Kennedy administration received?

Father Ted Hesburgh   Well, they were in a bit of a spot; I have to try to interpret their mind, although I didn't discuss this with Jack or Bobby directly. But the simple fact was that he [Kennedy] won by a very small margin. And there was no question about Jack's knowledge about this problem. He gave a lecture here at Notre Dame which is one of the best statements of the problem in America and what we should do about it in the way of creating new laws . . .

He knew exactly what needed to be done, but they had such a slim margin in the election that I think they decided to solidify their situation first. And my guess is that Jack decided if he could get reelected, then he's going to come out strongly for a new law on civil rights. Unfortunately, he never had that chance.

Susan Loewenberg   So you're saying that had he lived, in his second term he would have been more proactive.

Father Ted Hesburgh   Oh, no question about it. Because he knew exactly what needed to be done. But he had such a thin margin in the election, and he had such a weak base in a way, but he was President. Then he got caught up, of course, in the Cuban crisis and many other things. And I think we were—while they did put a law before the Congress, it wasn't anywhere near as strong as the law we were recommending.

Susan Loewenberg   What were some landmark events during your tenure on the Civil Rights Commission that played a significant role in turning the tide of public opinion—on issues like voting rights and segregation?

Father Ted Hesburgh   Well, we came out early on with a strong report, even though we only covered the questions of voting and employment and education, but when that didn't get much recognition from the President and the Congress— they all got a copy of the report of course and it went in the bottom drawer. So then we got a little bit angry, and our next report covered the whole field—not just education and employment and housing, but also administration of justice, public accommodations and all of the other things that were the fabric under which blacks didn't have a fair square in America.

Susan Loewenberg What outside events were occurring during this time that increased your ability to be effective?

Father Ted Hesburgh Well, the big one of course was the assassination of Martin Luther King and of course the assassination of President Kennedy and Bobby Kennedy. It got through to the people of America and to the Congress that this problem needed a solution. I have to say that the solution came when Lyndon Johnson inherited the last year of Jack's four years. And when Lyndon became President, he thought I'll only have this job for a year what can I do to get into the history books? And the one thing you could do is take up this problem which we had going all the way back to slavery ... the largest and oldest problem in American life was segregation of blacks. And he came out with the law that came out of our report, covering all of these points. And it was a very strong law. And he hammered it through Congress as only he could do. I don't think any president since him could have possibly gotten that law through.

Notes

RFK: The Journey to Justice was written as a radio play, to be performed before a live audience. Thus, it may be performed as such, or as a kind of reader's theater, or staged as a conventional play, with appropriate adjustments (but not changing the text of the play).

At certain points, characters in the play relate previous conversations, and we hear from those speakers. We have chosen to set off those speeches in quotation marks, in the expectation that the staging and/or audio production will similarly set off those speeches.

The characters appear very often in public settings (speeches, press conferences, hearings, etc.) at which they would normally be amplified by a variety of public address systems. We have indicated these points by the direction "OVER P.A." next to the character's initial speech in each scene. The kind and quality of reverb, room tone, etc., is a matter for stage direction and/or audio production, but it is crucial that, for example, a speech at a political convention sound different from a testimony at a Congressional hearing.

There are telephone conversations between onstage characters and offstage ones. In such cases, we have indicated that one character speaks INTO PHONE (i.e., "live" and unfiltered), and the second voice is heard through a PHONE FILTER (i.e., just as the onstage character would be hearing it).

We have capitalized the phrase "civil rights" when it refers to aspects of the Civil Rights Movement and its adherents.

We have indicated where scene transitions appear, and where sound effects do not make those transitions and the passage of time clear. The stage director and/or audio producer may use a variety of production techniques to achieve these transitions and denote the passage of time where needed.

Cast Breakdown

Actor 1 (black male): Harry Belafonte, Louis Martin, Jerome Smith, Cesar Chavez, Black Man, Earl Graves.

Actor 2 (white male): Byron White, Governor Vandiver, Sargent Shriver, John Seigenthaler, Earl Long, Clancy Lake, Nicholas Katzenbach, Businessman #2, Industry Representative, Official, White Farmer, Dr. Coles, Union Official #2, Chief Churchill, Douglas Edwards.

Actor 3 (black female): Coretta King, Secretary, Diane Nash, Black Woman Leader, Mrs. Olivarez, Liberal Woman, Child, Marian Wright, Myrlie Evers, Dolores Huerta, Female Riot Victim, Woman Campaign Aide.

Actor 4 (black male): Martin Luther King, Daddy King.

Actor 5 (white male): Robert F. Kennedy.

Actor 6 (white male): John F. Kennedy, Senator Eastland, Dean, Mr. Cruit, Lyndon Johnson, Nelson Rockefeller, Senator Murphy, Sheriff Galyen, Union Official #1, Frank Mankiewicz.

Actor 7 (white male): Harris Wofford, Senator Keating, Burke Marshall, Governor Patterson, J. Edgar Hoover, Governor Barnett, Southern Talk Radio Host, Teddy Kennedy, Businessman #1, Peter Edelman, Senator, Dr. Wheeler, Commission Spokesman, News Anchor, Senate Committee Chairman.

Ensemble: Reporters.

Act One

A suite in the Waldorf-Astoria Hotel.

SFX: Door slam.

JFK   Goddamn, Jackie Robinson wouldn't have his goddamn picture taken with me.

RFK   Jack, calm down.

JFK   This is your fault, Bobby. Is there any ice in this goddamn hotel room?

RFK   I'm just trying to get you the Negro vote. The ice is over there.

JFK   He turned me down—in front of the whole goddamn NAACP dinner.

RFK   It was only the reception and he didn't turn you down.

SFX: Ice cubes tossed into glasses, liquid pouring.

The brothers are enjoying their characteristic bantering.

JFK   Do I have a picture with him?

RFK   He's for Humphrey, the "civil rights hero."

JFK   Of 1948. Ancient history. And when I beat Humphrey, who will Jackie Robinson back? Goddamn Richard Nixon!

RFK   Jack, a ballplayer can't be the only way to get the Negro vote.

JFK   Hire someone to work on this, Bobby. You know what Eleanor Roosevelt said to me?

Imitating her.

"You have no record. The Negroes don't know you. You should be Stevenson's Vice-President. Grow and learn. *Mature.*"

RFK   Jack, we'll wipe the floor with Stevenson.

JFK   Johnson's the real problem. He'll have lots of endorsements.

RFK   So what? We're gonna get the delegates.

JFK   Lyndon's crafty, Bobby. Don't let that shitheel accent fool you.

RFK   We have our own friends with southern accents. We can go head-to-head with him down there. But how do we go for the Negro vote without pissing off the South? We need some help. Who do we know?

JFK   Or who can we get to?

Scene transition: **Harry Belafonte***'s apartment, NYC.*

RFK   My brother and I would like to thank you for seeing us on such short notice, Mr. Belafonte.

Harry Belafonte What can I do for you, gentlemen?

RFK We know you're for Stevenson, and that's fine, but my brother is going to beat him and get the nomination. So, we'd like to ask you two favors.

Harry Belafonte And those would be?

JFK Can you tell us how Jackie Robinson can even think of supporting Richard Nixon?

Harry Belafonte May I speak frankly?

RFK We will with you.

Harry Belafonte Well, I can understand how some Negroes wouldn't choose you among the Democrats. You're an unknown, without friends and acquaintances in the community, and you don't have a record of sympathy with the cause of Civil Rights.

JFK But Richard Milhous Nixon?

Harry Belafonte I agree with you. If you get the nomination, I'd support you over him.

RFK Well, when that happens, that'll bring up the second favor. Would you consider organizing some Negro stars for my brother—to offset Robinson?

Harry Belafonte You ought to make a relationship with Reverend Martin Luther King.

JFK The bus boycott fellow. We were thinking more . . . Sammy Davis Jr. Someone with . . . universal appeal.

Harry Belafonte You asked for my opinion . . .

RFK How can King help my brother?

Harry Belafonte The Civil Rights cause is growing. Forget me and forget Jackie Robinson. Join the cause, join King, and you'll have an alliance that can make the difference.

A Kennedy campaign office in a primary state.

SFX: Ringing telephones, general office hubbub, muffled conversations.

Harris Wofford Thank you for the job, Mr. Kennedy.

RFK I like first names. Call me Bob. Frankly, we need to find some ways into the Negro community, and I was impressed by your contacts there.

We really don't know much about this whole thing, Harris. I haven't known many Negroes in my life. So, basically, the strategy's up to you. Tell us where we stand and go to it.

Harris Wofford Well, the Negro leadership and rank and file have no . . . feeling for the Senator.

RFK   He's a very pleasant fellow . . . That was a joke, Harris. Why don't they care for him?

Harris Wofford   Well, his legislative record; his support of white southerners who are . . . frankly, segregationist; and . . . the attacks by Jackie Robinson.

RFK   I'll start rooting for the Dodgers. Is there a bright side to this? Can we fix it?

Harris Wofford   Appoint a Civil Rights adviser.

RFK   That would be you, Mr. Wofford.

Harris Wofford   I mean, appoint a Negro as well. Hold some conferences and meetings—various groups—and individuals like Martin Luther King.

RFK (*arch*)   Did Harry Belafonte send you?

Harris Wofford   What?

RFK   Never mind. Go on.

Harris Wofford   But the biggest thing you could do would be if the Senator supported a strong civil rights plank.

RFK   Go draft one.

Harris Wofford   How strong do you want it to be?

RFK   . . . Just strong enough to get my brother the Negro vote.

SFX: Office sounds out. Scene transition: Kennedy family apartment, NYC.

JFK   I hope it's not too little too late, Bobby. The convention's in three weeks.

RFK   Jack, everybody says King's the guy. It's kind of now or never.

SFX: Door buzzer.

JFK   Be still, my heart!

RFK   I'll get it.

SFX: Door opening.

Throughout the scene, they are all a bit uncomfortable, and **King** *is particularly formal.*

RFK   Dr. King, good afternoon. Please come in.

Martin Luther King   Mr. Kennedy.

RFK   Dr. King, this is Senator Kennedy. Senator, Dr. King.

JFK   Doctor, or do you prefer Reverend?

Martin Luther King   I answer to either, Senator.

JFK   Thank you for taking the time to meet.

Martin Luther King Harris Wofford is very persuasive, and I recall Harry Belafonte having mentioned you.

JFK Yes, well . . . do sit down.

Scene transition: Lobby of the apartment building.

Coretta King What's he like, Martin?

Martin Luther King He's kind of formal.

Coretta King Were you impressed?

Martin Luther King Well, Coretta, it's hard to believe that's the man who's going to lead us to a New Frontier.

Coretta King But will he be helpful to the cause?

Martin Luther King I don't know. They sure don't have a deep understanding of civil rights—either of them.

Scene transition: Kennedy family apartment.

JFK Bobby, I find it hard to believe that's the guy who's going to lead the Negro race to the promised land.

RFK The question is, can he deliver their votes? And can we get him to back us?

Scene transition: Democratic National Convention, L.A.

SFX: Convention sounds.

Music: "Happy Days Are Here Again," convention band. Fade under:

JFK (*over P.A.*) I accept your nomination, with a full and grateful heart, and with only one obligation—to lead our Party back to victory and our Nation back to greatness. I am grateful, too, for our platform.

The Rights of Man, the civil and economic rights essential to the human dignity of all men, are indeed our goal. This is a platform on which I can run with enthusiasm and conviction.

Scene transition: Ebenezer Baptist Church, Atlanta.

SFX: Applause. Cross-fade to smaller crowd sounds including "Amen," "Yes, Reverend," organ, etc.

Martin Luther King We have a determination to be free in this day and age. This is an idea whose time has come. We want to be free everywhere. Free at last, free at last.

Scene transition: Kennedy campaign headquarters, Washington.

SFX: Busy campaign office sounds.

Harris Wofford (*irritated*) Why can't I call it the "Office of Civil Rights"? After all, Bob, that's what it is.

Act One   123

Byron White   Because it's inflammatory, Harris.

Harris Wofford   To whom?

Byron White   Marginal white voters.

Harris Wofford   Racists. Bob, you siding with Whizzer here? You courting the racist vote now?

RFK   I'm courting every vote. Look, Whizzer, what if Harris keeps that name . . . but he agrees not to use the phrase "Civil Rights" in that Harlem conference of his?

Harris Wofford   That's the only event of ours you've promised the Senator will appear at.

Byron White   Fine with me.

RFK   Harris? . . . C'mon, get on the team here.

Harris Wofford   . . . Then what will we call this conference on civil rights?

RFK (*triumphant*)   The Democratic National Conference on Constitutional Rights.

Louis Martin *enters.*

Louis Martin   Hi, Bob. Am I interrupting?

RFK   Louis, welcome aboard. Fellas, Louis Martin, fresh from Chicago. Louis, you know Harris—

Harris Wofford   Hi, Louis.

RFK   —and this is Byron White, one of our campaign chairmen.

Byron White   Call me Whizzer, please. Thanks for that advice on dealing with the Negro newspapers.

Louis Martin   If you hadn't greased them, there'd have been the devil to pay. You're carrying some heavy baggage with that Texan on the ticket.

RFK   Well, we have another problem besides Lyndon. Since Jackie Robinson's stumping for Nixon, the next best endorsement we're after is Adam Clayton Powell—

Louis Martin   And he's asking . . . ?

Byron White   300,000—in advance—to buy his nationwide organization for turning out the Negro vote.

Louis Martin   No offense, but that's the white man's price. And there *is* no nationwide organization. That goes right into his pocket. Want me to negotiate?

RFK   Sure. What's his support *worth*?

Louis Martin   Ten speeches on behalf of the Senator, 5,000 per, payable *after* each speech.

RFK   Let's get all of our horses out on the track. Who else besides Powell?

Byron White Sammy Davis Jr.?

RFK C'mon, he's married to a white woman.

Louis Martin Martin Luther King?

RFK Christ, this is like a broken record. We already tried that. No go.

Louis Martin Well, it's not really in King's interest to endorse anybody . . .

Byron White His father and some other Baptist ministers are endorsing Nixon.

Louis Martin . . . but maybe we can get him to make a statement that sounds favorable.

RFK Harris, what would it take to get that?

Harris Wofford Well, he might say something about the Senator's commitment to civil rights if . . . the Senator did something dramatic that would justify it.

RFK Harris, may I remind you that—at the risk of pissing off the entire South—he endorsed *your* goddamn plank in the party platform! I think that was plenty dramatic.

Gentlemen, this meeting is over.

Scene transition: A satellite Kennedy campaign office in Washington.

SFX: Less busy campaign office sounds.

Harris Wofford Louis, we have a situation. Dr. King and thirty-five students have been arrested for sitting-in at a lunch counter in Atlanta.

Louis Martin Terrible timing.

Harris Wofford It gets worse.

Louis Martin You ever bring *good* news?

Harris Wofford The students all got released, but King's been hit with a trumped up charge—violation of parole on an old traffic misdemeanor. It's bullshit, but they've sentenced him to four months hard labor.

Louis Martin Jesus Christ. A chain gang?

SFX: Office sounds out.

Scene transition: A hotel room on the campaign trail.

JFK (*into phone*) Shit. Two weeks before the election! Do we jump in or not?

RFK (*phone filter*) There are more risks than rewards, Jack. But doing nothing is not a good option. Nixon's guys could very easily take the moral high ground here.

JFK So, we get him freed?

RFK (*phone filter*) But quietly, and without provoking a backlash.

JFK Who do we know?

RFK (*phone filter*)   . . . The Governor, Vandiver.

JFK   Well, let's make sure this goddamn thing doesn't get out of hand.

Scene transition: A satellite Kennedy campaign office in Washington.

SFX: Campaign office sounds.

Harris Wofford (*into phone*)   Mrs. King, please—try to calm down.

Coretta King (*phone filter*)   Harris, they're going to kill him! I know they're going to kill him!

Harris Wofford   Coretta, we'll do everything we can. I'll call you back.

SFX: Phone hanging up.

She's five months pregnant.

Louis Martin   Why don't we call Sarge Shriver? See if he can get the Senator to at least make a phone call to her.

SFX: Office sounds out.

Scene transition: A hotel room on the campaign trail.

JFK (*into phone*)   Bobby, I just got off the phone with Governor Vandiver.

RFK (*phone filter*)   What did he say? . . .

Gov. Vandiver   "Senator, you know I support you. I want you to win. Only thing is, I could use a little cover. I can't do anything publicly—I'm sure you understand."

RFK (*phone filter*)   Ah, yes—one can't risk losing the all-important redneck vote.

I'm sure the good governor had a solution.

JFK   He knows someone who knows the judge who sent King to the rockpile. He'll get back to us. I have to go, Bob.

SFX: Phone hanging up. Knock on door.

JFK   Come in.

Sargent Shriver   Senator, you have a minute?

JFK   Sure, Sarge. What's on your mind?

Sargent Shriver   I've been thinking about poor Mrs. King—her husband in jail and all . . .

JFK   Sarge, it's too risky. The campaign can't get involved . . .

Sargent Shriver   No, nothing official. I was thinking . . . Maybe you should just pick up the phone and talk to her.

Scene transition: Kennedy campaign HQ.

SFX: Office sounds.

Harris Wofford You wanted to see us, Bob?

RFK You two bomb throwers know what you've done by instigating that call? Do you know that three southern governors told us if Jack supported Jimmy Hoffa or Nikita Khrushchev or Martin Luther King they'd throw their states to Nixon? This election is razor close and you probably just lost it for us.

Harris Wofford It was just a call to his wife.

RFK You're both in the deep freeze. Your Civil Rights section isn't going to do another goddamn thing in this campaign.

Louis Martin Bob, for Chrissake—he was refused bail and sent to a chain gang for driving with an out-of-state license.

RFK How could they do that? You can't deny bail on a misdemeanor.

Louis Martin Try not being white in Georgia . . . And Jackie Robinson's urging Nixon to publicly blame the whole thing on the Democrats . . . *who are running things down there.*

RFK Goddammit . . . Get me John Seigenthaler. Tell him I need to see him.

SFX: Office sounds out.

Scene transition: **RFK***'s private office, Kennedy campaign HQ.*

RFK John, maybe I should be the lightning rod. Maybe I should call this judge and take the heat off Jack.

John Seigenthaler (*southern accent*) I've already got enough southern pols angry about the call to Mrs. King. Stay out of this, Bob. Let it die down.

RFK Okay. I will. Okay.

SFX: Phone rings.

JFK (*phone filter*) Hi, Bobby. Vandiver called back.

RFK Hold on, Jack.

(*To* **Seigenthaler**.) John, I need to take this.

SFX: Office sounds briefly, as door opens and closes.

Jack, he worked it out with the judge?

JFK (*phone filter*) The judge needs political cover too. He's willing to release King, but he has to be able to say he only did it after being called by me . . . or you.

RFK Oh . . . Okay, give me the good jurist's number.

JFK (*phone filter*) All you have to say is your name and he'll let him go.

RFK Not exactly a fucking profile in courage, Jack.

JFK (*phone filter*)   That's very—what's the word?—funny, Bobby.

Scene transition: Kennedy campaign HQ.

SFX: Campaign office sounds.

RFK   Good morning, John, Harris, Louis.

John Seigenthaler   Bob, guess what that crazy old Georgia judge says. He's claiming you called to insist King be granted bail! Don't worry, I put out a denial.

RFK   . . . Well, you'd better retract it.

John Seigenthaler   What? You did call him? Why?

RFK (*lying convincingly*)   . . . It was disgraceful. It just burned me up. The more I thought about the injustice, the more I thought what a sonofabitch he was. So I gave him a lecture on the constitutional right to make bail.

Louis Martin   Good for you, Bob.

RFK   He was screwing up my brother's campaign and making this country look ridiculous . . . So, what's on for today? Did King endorse us when he got out?

Louis Martin   He said he was "very grateful" to the Senator—

RFK   Close, but no cigar.

Harris Wofford   But his father's influential, and he's publicly switched from Nixon. He said . . .

Daddy King   "I had expected to vote against Senator Kennedy because of his religion. But now he can be my President, Catholic or whatever he is. He has the moral courage to stand up for what is right. I've got a suitcase full of votes, and I'm going to dump them in his lap."

RFK   In spite of Jack being Catholic? That was a hell of a bigoted statement, don't you think?

Imagine Martin Luther King having a bigot for a father . . . (*Grinning.*) Well, as my brother always says, "We all have fathers don't we?" . . . So King the elder is a big deal?

Harris Wofford   Especially among Baptist ministers.

RFK   . . . So, how do we make something out of this?

Harris Wofford   You mean we're no longer in Siberia?

RFK   Don't put away your long johns, fellas. No more freelancing. We need to reach Negro voters with this without creating a white backlash.

Louis Martin   Let's print a pamphlet. Mass distribution to Negro churches on the last Sunday before the election. Nothing that could leak to the white press.

RFK (*liking the idea*)   Nice . . . Whose name'll be on it?

Louis Martin   We'll set up a dummy committee of preachers to protect the campaign. No statements from Kennedy spokesmen. Just the King family and other preachers talking about the call to Coretta.

RFK   Nothing about my call to the judge.

Louis Martin   No. And I think we title the pamphlet: "No Comment—Nixon Versus a Candidate with Heart, Senator Kennedy."

Scene transition: Radio newsroom.

SFX: Teletype machine under:

Douglas Edwards (*newscaster*)   This is Douglas Edwards in New York. It was a squeaker, but when the electoral votes are counted, John Fitzgerald Kennedy will be the next President of the United States.

In one of the closest elections in history, Senator Kennedy dominated the ethnic vote. He captured a stunning 70 percent of Negro voters, almost doubling pollsters' predictions.

Scene transition: A private hotel dining room, Washington.

SFX: Cutlery on plates; coffee cups.

JFK   You haven't touched your eggs.

RFK   The subject ruined my appetite.

JFK (*selling*)   I need someone I can trust, Bobby, someone who can handle Hoover, keep J. Edgar in line, keep him off my back. You're the best blocker I've ever known.

RFK (*not buying*)   Jack, I'm known as your enforcer. People will raise holy hell if you make me your Attorney General. *The New York Times* already did when you floated the idea.

JFK   The southern Senators all support you.

RFK   They liked me from the Rackets Committee when I stuck it to the unions. But they'll turn on you when your A.G. has to do something about civil rights. And if it's me, it'll be worse for you.

JFK   I hate all this civil rights pressure. Couldn't appoint Bill Fulbright to anything because he voted segregationist. Christ, he's from Arkansas! How the hell else could he get elected?

RFK   I'd rather be a college president, or go to work for Dad, learn the business. You need someone who *wants* this job. I can't say I stay up nights worrying about civil rights.

JFK   Well, get someone on board who does. It's not the only thing you'll have to deal with. Besides, Dad is pushing for this. He says you're the one most like him.

RFK   Is that a compliment?

JFK   If this administration is going to give the country leadership, it has to have leaders. I need you.

Scene transition: A Senate hearing room.

SFX: Gavel bangs.

Senator Keating (*over P.A.*)   Mr. Kennedy, quite frankly, I would like to hear a firmer commitment from you on this subject.

RFK (*over P.A.*)   Senator Keating, my philosophy is that we have to move vigorously in the field of civil rights. I do not think this is a matter that can be solved overnight, however. I think there has to be understanding and tolerance on all sides.

Senator Keating   You supported the eloquent Democratic platform. If confirmed as Attorney General, would you seek new legislation to enforce it?

RFK   I would await my instructions and guidance from President-elect Kennedy.

Senator Keating   Which means what exactly?

RFK   I think I've answered that question.

Scene transition: the Attorney General's office, Dept. of Justice, Washington.

SFX: Subdued ambience of the A.G.'s large, private office.

Byron White   The southern Senators really laid off you, Bob. They didn't even ask you about school desegregation.

RFK   Well, they know we're not going to do anything radical.

Byron White   Which brings us to your last appointment . . . Who do you want to head your Civil Rights Division?

RFK   Harris Wofford's the obvious choice. I mean, he helped write the civil rights plank . . .

Byron White   I sense less than enthusiasm.

RFK   Very perceptive, Whizzer. I don't want an activist telling me what to do on this. What do you think of Burke Marshall?

Byron White   He's more your style, Bob. Negotiate rather than litigate.

RFK   And he doesn't have close friendships within the Civil Rights Movement. Martin Luther King is already "recommending" people for jobs in the administration.

Byron White   If it's Burke Marshall, before he says yes, he'll want to know how you'll want him to play things.

RFK   Appoint and elect. Put good people on the bench and register Negro voters so politicians will have to treat them right to get elected down there.

Byron White   Will we be able to get him past the Judiciary Committee?

RFK   I still have a friend or two.

Scene transition: Office of **Senator Eastland**.

SFX: Subdued office sounds.

Senator Eastland (*bantering with a political bedfellow*)   Ah, Mr. Kennedy, so nice to see you. Are you here to discuss appointing my dear friend Harold Cox to the Federal District Court?

RFK (*also bantering*)   Senator Eastland, I have Burke Marshall outside who is going to be the head of our Civil Rights Division. I thought you'd like to meet him. He's going to put Negroes in your white schools in Mississippi.

Senator Eastland   Well, then, I guess I don't want to see him.

RFK   C'mon, Jim. See him for a minute.

Senator Eastland   Bob, as a favor to you and your brother, I won't hold up his appointment, but I'm going to vote against him. I'd vote against Jesus Christ if he was up for that position. Now, before he comes in, let's discuss your appointing my Mr. Cox.

Scene transition: An auditorium in the North.

Martin Luther King (*over P.A.*)   The new administration has the opportunity to be the first in 100 years of American history to adopt a radically new approach to the question of civil rights. It must begin with the firm conviction that the principle is no longer in doubt. The day is past for tolerating vicious and inhuman opposition on a subject which determines the lives of 22 million Americans.

SFX: Mild applause.

Scene transition: The Attorney General's office.

SFX: Door slams.

RFK   Jesus Christ!

John Seigenthaler   Have a nice visit with the President?

RFK   Everyone's twisting his arm, John. The goddamn Civil Rights Commission "recommended" he appoint a White House Assistant on Civil Rights.

And you know who he already picked?

Burke Marshall   Are we going to find this amusing?

RFK   Goddamn Harris Wofford!

The two aides laugh.

Okay, it is a little ironic. And he's making all sorts of "suggestions."

John Seigenthaler   Like what?

RFK   "Increase minority hiring." Hell, we're already working on that. Burke, how many Negro lawyers did we find in the Justice Department?

Burke Marshall   Only ten.

RFK   Out of a thousand. And I've already told the President I'm contacting law schools to get their best Negro graduates. Oh, he also got the President to name a Committee on Equal Employment. And you won't believe who's heading that.

John Seigenthaler   J. Edgar Hoover.

RFK   Almost as funny—Lyndon Johnson. And I have to be a member and watch while he screws it up.

Burke Marshall   I thought you didn't want to be saddled with all the civil rights responsibility.

RFK   Burke, once I'm given the ball, it's my job to move it downfield. I want guys who can follow the play, not a bunch of grandstanding amateurs. Too many people are getting involved. Either we're going to have just one administration position on this, or we're going to fumble the ball.

Minimum legislation, maximum executive action.

Secretary (*on speaker phone*)   Mr. Hoover's returning your call.

RFK   Thank you, tell him I'll be right there.

Explaining to his aides.

The Committee is charged with removing "every trace of discrimination." So . . . ,

SFX: Phone being picked up.

RFK (*into phone*)   Mr. Hoover, always a pleasure. The thing I wanted to ask you, J. Edgar, is if you could tell me how many Negro agents there are in the F.B.I?

J. Edgar Hoover (*phone filter*)   Mr. Kennedy, it would be discriminatory to catalogue our employees by race, creed, or color.

RFK   Well, that's very commendable, but the President's Committee on Equal Employment would like to know how many Negroes you have.

J. Edgar Hoover (*phone filter*)   Five.

RFK   I see. Would your chauffeur and your office boy be included in that number?

J. Edgar Hoover (*phone filter*)   . . . Their title is "Special Agent."

RFK   Ah, well then. And that's five out of how many?

J. Edgar Hoover (*phone filter*)   Agents? Five thousand.

RFK   Well, I want you to start hiring more.

J. Edgar Hoover (*phone filter*)   Mr. Kennedy, certainly you're not suggesting that we lower our standards—

RFK   No, I'm sure you can find qualified candidates. After all, the F.B.I. always gets its man, doesn't it?

Please report your progress to me.

SFX: Phone hanging up. All laugh.

Scene transition: The A.G.'s office, a few days later.

SFX: Door opens and closes.

Louis Martin   You wanted to see me, Bob.

RFK   How are things at the DNC, Louis? You like being number two there?

Louis Martin   Everything's fine. You called me over to chit chat?

RFK   Well, we're dealing with Cuba, we're dealing with the Russians, communist guerrillas in Laos, proxy wars in Africa—I thought a lighthearted conversation about civil rights would be a relief.

Louis Martin   I'm not laughing.

RFK   The President is going to hold a mass meeting of Civil Rights leaders.

Louis Martin   That sounds like a good idea.

RFK   But he's not going to invite Martin Luther King.

Louis Martin   Is this the lighthearted part?

RFK   It's important for us to stay independent, not too identified with him. And we can't risk a disagreement in a very public setting. So I wanted to pick your brain, hear your thoughts about how to play it.

Louis Martin   Well, you could invite him to an "off the record" secret meeting. If he agreed, and then kept it out of the papers, that would be a reassuring sign about how he operates. If he doesn't, better to find out sooner than later, and you can limit the damage easier from a secret meeting than a public one.

RFK   Nice. Okay, go ahead. Set it up.

Scene transition: A private dining room in the Mayflower Hotel, Washington.

SFX: Cutlery, tableware, Muzak, etc.

Martin Luther King   You know, Mr. Kennedy, this is my first time inside the Mayflower Hotel.

RFK   Yes, well, I thought a private dining room would give us more of a chance to talk.

Martin Luther King   And with a buffet, there are no Negro waiters.

RFK   No anybody.

An awkward silence.

Reverend, did you ever play football?

Martin Luther King   . . . I was more of a basketball man.

Pause.

RFK Well, do you follow sports?

Martin Luther King Not really.

Pause.

Mr. Kennedy, has the President given any thought to that new cabinet position—Secretary of Integration?

RFK Well, he received your recommendation about that . . . The Bay of Pigs has had him somewhat preoccupied . . . Dr. King, we have a strategy on civil rights. It's centered on voting. We've been filing suits in the South to stop them from harassing or discouraging Negro registrants.

That's where we have the most authority. But we have to fly low for political reasons.

Martin Luther King I understand your concerns, but the future lies in fundamental change, Mr. Kennedy, and you have great power at your disposal.

RFK Actually, Dr. King, under the Constitution, the federal government has *little* power to intervene with states in school desegregation or police brutality cases. My point is simply that it won't help if you push too hard or too fast.

Martin Luther King . . . We can step up our registration work in tandem with your lawsuits, but voting is not the only avenue for progress toward Negro rights—sit-ins, mass boycotts, and, yes, legislation can also make contributions . . . And for all your lawsuits so far, there are still, sadly, many instances of voter registration workers being harassed—and much worse.

SFX: Pen on paper.

RFK Here are the numbers of two of my top people—Burke Marshall and John Seigenthaler. You can call them any time, day or night . . . And if you have time right now, let's go to the White House.

Martin Luther King I thought the President didn't have time to see me.

RFK I have a feeling he might be able to squeeze you in.

Scene transition: The Oval Office in the White House.

RFK I don't think you exactly charmed him, Jack.

JFK He was more relaxed than last time.

RFK Great. At this rate, he'll give you a smile by the end of your second term. Look, the important thing is that he understands and he'll play ball.

JFK I hope you're right.

RFK In the meantime, you could get those Civil Rights Commission do-gooders off my ass. They're getting in the way.

JFK They were here before both of us, Bobby.

RFK (*sarcastic*) And they've accomplished so much. Jack, they're going over old ground. I'm already investigating the exact same violations.

JFK My reining them in would look *swell* politically . . .

RFK Jack, they're going to keep hounding us about new civil rights legislation.

JFK You can handle them—all of them, Bobby.

Scene transition: The A.G.'s office.

Burke Marshall Going into the lion's den for your first major speech?

RFK Burke, I'm not going to learn anything by making a civil rights speech in New York. We need to see how our position is going to play.

Scene transition: An auditorium at the University of Georgia.

Dean (*southern accent*) (*over P.A.*) And with that, ladies and gentlemen, I give you the University of Georgia's Law Day speaker, our new Attorney General, Robert F. Kennedy.

SFX: Mild applause.

RFK (*over P.A.*) Southerners have a special respect for candor and plain talk. So, I must tell you our policies in the field of civil rights.

We are maintaining the orders of the courts—nothing more or less. And if any one of you were in my position you would do likewise, for it would be required by your oath of office. You might not want to do it, you might not like to do it, but you would do it.

I happen to believe that the 1954 Supreme Court desegregation decision was right. But my belief does not matter—it is the law. Some of you may believe the decision was wrong. That does not matter. It is the law. And we both respect the law.

You may ask: Will we enforce the civil rights statutes. The answer is: Yes, we will. We can and will do no less.

SFX: Thunderous applause. Fade under:

Scene transition: Offstage in the auditorium.

Burke Marshall I got to hand it to you, Bob. I thought they'd tar and feather you.

RFK Frankly, so did I. Who'd have thought they'd go for it? I guess that means we'll be able to handle this issue.

SFX: Applause out.

Scene transition: The A.G.'s office.

RFK (*annoyed*) Freedom Riders? Burke, what the hell is a Freedom Rider?

Burke Marshall It was James Farmer's idea. A bunch of Negroes and whites riding Greyhound buses from here to New Orleans. They mean to stop along the way and integrate all the bus stations. You know, *Boynton* vs. *Virginia*.

RFK   Jesus Christ. Couldn't they fly?

John Seigenthaler   Any white women?

Burke Marshall   Yep.

John Seigenthaler   Oh, great. Black men and white women. You know where the bus stations are in those towns—and who hangs around in 'em? There's gonna be—

Burke Marshall   Already is, John. Anniston, Alabama—mob firebombed the bus, slashed the tires, and blocked the doors. Happy Mother's Day, by the way.

RFK   Did they get out?

Burke Marshall   Just barely. There was an undercover cop on the bus—probably to keep an eye on the Riders, but he ended up drawing his gun and getting them out of there—not before they got beat up quite a bit.

RFK   A state cop? Good, we can say the state handled it. Let's try to keep the lid on this.

Burke Marshall   Too late. UPI sent out a wirephoto of the burning bus. Pretty spectacular. Here, take a look.

RFK   Jesus. We've got to control this.

Burke Marshall   I don't think we can. John, turn on the radio—they've been running bulletins.

News Anchor (*V.O., radio filter*)   . . . on to Birmingham, where they were attacked inside the bus station by a vicious mob, armed with clubs, chains, and lead pipes. News reporter Clancy Lake, of station WAPI, was filing this live report when the mob attacked *him*.

SFX: Through yet another audio filter, mob charging, attacking, smashing car windows (i.e., one radio broadcast within another), as we hear:

Clancy Lake (*V.O., southern accent, radio filter*)   . . . seemingly indiscriminate violence on whites as well as Negroes. I can see a press photographer being beaten—oh, my! I just—wait a minute, I—Hey! I'm a reporter, I—

SFX: Mob sounds stop abruptly.

News Anchor   That was reporter Clancy Lake, reporting from Birming—

SFX: Radio being switched off.

RFK   These Freedom Riders are not helping us . . .

Burke Marshall   Bob—

RFK   . . . they're messing up the strategy.

Burke Marshall   Bob, it's not *their* strategy.

RFK   What do they expect? Federal troops every time someone gets on a goddamn bus?

Pause.

John, I want you to go down there. Talk to both sides. You've got a southern accent.

John Seigenthaler   Y'all noticed?

RFK   And you tell those Riders . . . we're concerned about them.

Scene transition: The Oval Office.

JFK   Bobby, these Freedom Rides haven't stopped. You've got to block for me on this. I'm going to Europe this week. I'm meeting Khruschchev, for God's sake. We're going to look terrible overseas. We've got to stop this.

SFX: Intercom button being pushed.

Get me Harris Wofford.

RFK   I'll handle it, Jack. I'm talking to Governor Patterson—when he deigns to call me back.

Secretary (*filter*)   Mr. Wofford on line one.

SFX: Phone being picked up.

JFK   Hello.

Harris Wofford (*phone filter*)   Mr. President.

JFK   Harris, you've got to call this bus thing off.

Harris Wofford (*phone filter*)   Mr. President, I can't—I don't have anything to do with this.

JFK   Well, they're your friends, and they're taking matters into their own hands.

Harris Wofford (*phone filter*)   Mr. President, they're pouring into Birmingham. I have no control—

JFK   I'm telling you to stop them! Get them off those damn buses!

SFX: Phone being slammed down.

"Pouring." He said more Freedom Riders are *pouring* into Birmingham.

RFK   And you should also know that King's announced he's going to join them. I sent Seigenthaler down there.

JFK (*cheerfully*)   Tell him I said—good luck.

Scene transition: Office of **Gov. Patterson**.

Gov. Patterson   You tell Bob we can handle this just fine, Mr. Seigenthaler. It can't look like I haven't got the spine to stand up to the goddamn niggers!

John Seigenthaler   Governor Patterson—

Gov. Patterson   We don't need federal troops in Alabama . . .

John Seigenthaler   I certainly hope not, sir.

Gov. Patterson   We can protect everybody—even these sumbitches.

John Seigenthaler   Yes, sir—

Gov. Patterson   If that bus wants to go to Montgomery, I'll see that it gets there . . . Of course, that's assuming you can actually get it to leave.

Scene transition: The A.G.'s office.

SFX: Bus engine through phone filter.

Mr. Cruit (*phone filter*)   Mr. Kennedy I am not tryin' to be difficult, no sir, I'm not.

RFK   I don't understand, Mr. Cruit. You're the supervisor of the Greyhound Bus Company down there in Birmingham, are you not?

Mr. Cruit (*phone filter*)   Yes, sir, I am. But the drivers refuse to drive.

RFK   Well, do *you* know how to drive a bus?

Mr. Cruit (*phone filter*)   No, I'm an administrator. These buses cost $45,000, and amateurs can't handle them.

RFK (*exasperated*)   Well, surely *somebody* in the damn bus company can drive a bus, can't they? I think you should—had better be getting in touch with Mr. Greyhound, or whoever Greyhound is . . . I am—the government is going to be very much upset if this group does not get to continue their trip.

Scene transition: A radio playing somewhere in Montgomery.

SFX: Audio playback of **RFK**'s *last line through phone and radio filters:*

RFK (*phone and radio filter*)   I am—the government is going to be very much upset if this group does not get to continue their trip.

Southern Talk Radio Host (*radio filter*)   You heard 'im, folks. That's the Attorney General of the United States, Bobby Kennedy, an' you heard him on tape! Now he's not merely protecting these so-called Freedom Riders—he's in league with 'em! These outside agitators! Now, when that bus gets here to Montgomery, it's our sacred duty . . .

Scene transition: A street near the Montgomery bus terminal.

SFX: Screams, beatings, riot sounds.

John Seigenthaler   Hey, you! Get your hands off her! For God's sake, stop that! Leave that girl alone!

Female Riot Victim   Mister, you get on outta here. This ain't your fight. You gonna get yourself killed.

John Seigenthaler   I said leave that girl alone! My name is John Seigenthaler. I'm a federal agent. I—

SFX: Loud thud of **Seigenthaler** *getting cracked on the head with a pipe and moaning.*

Scene transition: The A.G.'s office.

SFX: Out.

Burke Marshall   Bob, it was awful. And there wasn't a cop in sight.

RFK   How's Seigenthaler?

Burke Marshall   He's smashed up pretty bad. They left him there—bleeding. He was out for about a half hour.

RFK   Jesus.

Burke Marshall   And now the Riders and all the Negroes are holed up in a church. Dr. King is in there with them. There's a mob gathering outside.

RFK   For God's sake—

Burke Marshall   And I'm afraid our friend the governor's double-crossed us.

RFK   What?

Burke Marshall   He's keeping the mob back, but he won't let the Negroes leave the church. They're trapped in there—and so is King.

RFK   For Christ's sake, "the flower of white southern manhood"! Who the hell are these people?

Burke Marshall   They're Americans, Bob. Most of them voted for your brother.

RFK   Yes. Well. *They're* the enemy now. Not the Freedom Riders. Tell Seigenthaler I'll call him in the hospital. You make sure they take good care of him!

SFX: Intercom buzzes, button being pushed.

Yes?

Secretary   It's Governor Patterson on three.

SFX: Phone being picked up.

RFK (*into phone*)   Governor—

Gov. Patterson (*phone filter*)   Well, now you got what you wanted, Bob! You got yourself a fight, and martial law, and all this violence, just like you wanted!

RFK   Governor, I'm trying to prevent violence! Now, if you'll just—when are you going to let those people out of that church, and go on to Mississippi?

Gov. Patterson (*phone filter*)   I'll let 'em all go except that Martin King. I can't guarantee his safety.

RFK   Wait a minute—you've got the National Guard out there, and you can't guarantee his safety?

Gov. Patterson (*phone filter*)   No, sir, I can't.

RFK   I don't believe that, Governor. Have General Graham call me. I want to hear a general tell me he can't protect Martin Luther King.

Gov. Patterson (*phone filter*)   Goddamn it, Bob, that's not the point! I can't let him go. Damn it, I supported your brother! You're destroying us politically.

RFK   It's more important for the people in that church to survive physically than for us to survive politically.

Gov. Patterson (*phone filter*)   It's gonna be on you, Bob. Not on your brother, on *you*!

SFX: **Patterson**'s *phone being slammed down,* **RFK**'s *phone hanging up.*

RFK (*mission accomplished*)   Well, Jack's got the blocking he wanted.

Scene transition: Same, a few days later.

SFX: Buzzer.

RFK   Rosemary, did you get through to the jail?

Secretary (*over intercom*)   They said they're getting him, Mr. Kennedy.

Burke Marshall   Bob, they shouldn't call 'em "Freedom Rides," anymore. They should call 'em "A Guided Tour of Southern Jails." But at least there hasn't been any violence in Jackson. And they've granted the bail you wanted. But the city didn't really have a choice. The jails are overflowing.

SFX: Buzzer.

Secretary (*over intercom*)   Dr. King is on the line.

SFX: Phone being picked up.

RFK   Hello, Dr. King.

Martin Luther King (*phone filter*)   Mr. Kennedy, can you hear me?

RFK   Yes. How are you doing? Are you all right?

Martin Luther King (*phone filter*)   Well, I'll admit I've been better. But I'm among friends—lots of them.

RFK   Well, I wanted you to know that we've arranged bail so you and your friends can go home.

Martin Luther King (*phone filter*)   I appreciate that, Mr. Kennedy, but we will refuse to accept bail.

RFK   What? Why? This wasn't easy . . .

Martin Luther King (*phone filter*)   Our conscience tells us the law is wrong and we must resist, but we have a moral obligation to accept the penalty.

RFK That is not going to have the slightest effect on the government's actions. Your staying in jail is not going to have the slightest effect on me.

Martin Luther King (*phone filter*) Perhaps you'd be affected if students came down here by the hundreds—by the hundreds of thousands.

RFK (*angry*) The country belongs to you as much as to me. We can disagree, but don't make statements that sound like threats. That's not the way to deal with us.

Martin Luther King (*phone filter*) (*backing off.*) I'm deeply appreciative of what the administration is doing. I see a ray of hope, but I feel the need of being free *now*.

RFK Well, if you and the others in jail want to get out, we can get you out.

Martin Luther King (*phone filter*) There is a social revolution going on, and frankly I'm not sure you understand what we're doing. Thank you, but we'll stay.

SFX: Phone hanging up.

RFK Remind me not to buy any fucking Harry Belafonte records.

Burke Marshall Maybe we could give them one of the things they want, Bob. We could file a request with the Interstate Commerce Commission to desegregate travel facilities . . .

RFK How soon could we get it, Burke?

Burke Marshall If you keep after them, maybe a few months.

RFK King and his pals won't sit still that long . . . How can we manage this?

Burke Marshall Bob, it's not just a political situation that we can manage. It's bigger than that.

RFK I'm the Attorney General of the United States. I have to enforce the law, and when I do I'm going to cross *somebody*.

One day it's Martin Luther King, one day it's Governor Patterson. Fine. Nobody owns the Department of Justice.

Scene transition: Same, some weeks later.

Diane Nash Mr. Kennedy, thank you for taking the time to see our Committee.

RFK Well, the Freedom Rides have certainly . . . had an effect. And you know I've always . . . tried to support—

Diane Nash We're here to talk to you about that support. We need additional help, protection, enforcement, and legislation.

RFK Miss Nash, frankly, the Freedom Rides are no longer productive. You can accomplish more for civil rights by registering more Negro voters.

Diane Nash Dr. King would like the President to take a moral stand, issue a second Emancipation Proclamation.

RFK Miss Nash, I have told Dr. King that registration will ultimately be more effective than confrontations.

Diane Nash Mr. Kennedy, it seems we have . . . philosophical differences.

RFK But we have the same goals.

If you agree to move in this direction, I think I can get some foundation grants for a Voter Education Project . . . Such an entity could easily be run by you and your colleagues . . .

Gauging their reactions.

And I'll do everything I can to see you're supported and protected.

Diane Nash Mr. Kennedy, are you trying to buy us off? With respect, it's not your responsibility to tell us how to honor our constitutional rights. It's your job to protect us when we do.

RFK You have an opportunity to do something larger than making headlines. You could truly alter the politics of the South forever.

Diane Nash And you could have your cake and eat it too—no more embarrassing confrontations or political backlash either.

RFK Miss Nash, we can help you and your colleagues achieve the rights and freedoms you want. The direct action *you* prefer can only go so far. Political power comes from votes, and rights come from political power. You can have jails filled with Freedom Riders, or jails filled with white southern officials who obstruct voting rights.

Diane Nash We look forward to the latter.

Scene transition: The Oval Office.

JFK So, no more Freedom Rides?

RFK For the moment. But, Jack, you're likely to hear from your ever-so-helpful Civil Rights Commission.

JFK Oh? And what will they be telling me?

RFK That I forced them to cancel their hearings on violations of voting rights in Louisiana.

JFK Jesus, if they made race an issue there, our guy would lose in New Orleans.

RFK They're going to kill *all* the southern moderates. Governor Long was helping them, by the way. Know what he told them?

Earl Long "You're here to help niggers vote. And I'm for you because they're my niggers and I want their votes. Now I'm gonna get my state registrar to give you the records you need. But, after you talk to him, remember *you never talked to me.*"

JFK Well, you have to admire his eloquence. But they did call off the hearings?

RFK Not with a smile.

JFK And our fingerprints won't be on this?

RFK No, I said they could tell the press anything they wanted, but to remember . . . *they never talked to me.*

Scene transition: The A.G.'s office.

Burke Marshall We're in a bit of a quandary, Bob. These voter registration drives are being met with violence, just like the Freedom Rides were.

RFK Yes, Dr. King sent me a telegram . . .

Martin Luther King "There is an apparent reign of terror that is going on unaddressed by the Justice Department. There have been the brutal beatings of volunteers John Hardy and Bob Moses, the murder of Herbert Lee, and uncounted perversions of justice . . ."

RFK "Unaddressed"? What does he want me to do? The federal government is not the police, and he knows it. That authority rests with the states.

Burke Marshall True, but try telling that to someone whose kid just got shot.

RFK So, obey the Constitution and be dammed for it?

Burke Marshall Or . . . radically change the balance of federal power—God knows where that might lead.

RFK Well, I really wouldn't mind my brother as a dictator, but we might get a sonofabitch later . . . What about those cases he mentioned, Burke?

Burke Marshall We tried to intervene in the Hardy case, but guess which federal judge rebuffed us?

RFK (*pointedly*) Harold Cox was the price I paid for Senator Eastland considering making Thurgood Marshall the second Negro ever on the circuit court.

Burke Marshall That's a helluva price, Bob. We can't have it both ways. We promised the Civil Rights workers protection, and now we tell 'em our hands are tied.

SFX: Door opens and closes.

John Seigenthaler Sorry to bother you, Bob, but I thought you ought to know.

RFK Ought to know what, John?

John Seigenthaler That telegram from Dr. King? He just leaked it to the press.

RFK Goddamn him! What the hell is his game? If he wants to piss me off, he's just accomplished it!

Secretary (*over intercom*) Mr. Attorney General, it's J. Edgar Hoover on line two.

RFK   Thank you. Excuse me, fellas.

SFX: Door opens and closes. Telephone being picked up.

Mr. Director.

J. Edgar Hoover (*phone filter*)   Mr. Kennedy, I know you'll thank me for sparing you a lot of trouble. We now have very strong evidence that a certain Stanley Levison, an, uh, intimate of Dr. King—whom I know you've been speaking with frequently—this Mr. Levison is a secret member of the Communist Party.

RFK   I see.

J. Edgar Hoover (*phone filter*)   Now I know how strongly you have fought the communist conspiracy—your work on Senator McCarthy's staff and all the rest of it—and I'm sure your brother would want to know that this civil rights agenda you're pursuing with Dr. King is infiltrated with communists. I'd hate to see *anything* compromise the administration—

RFK   Well, that's certainly . . . troubling information.

J. Edgar Hoover (*phone filter*)   Of course, I'll bring this to the President's attention directly.

RFK   Well, I appreciate that, Mr. Hoover, but I'm the Attorney General. I'll tell him. Thanks so much.

SFX: Buttons being pushed, switching lines.

Evelyn, is the President there?

Pause.

Jack, Hoover's up to his old tricks.

JFK (*phone filter*)   What now, Bobby?

RFK   Nothing much. Just that King's staff is lousy with commies.

JFK (*phone filter*)   How many is "lousy"?

RFK   One.

JFK (*phone filter*)   One's enough. Do you trust what he's saying?

RFK   I don't trust either one of them.

JFK (*phone filter*)   Hoover's unpredictable . . . but so is King.

RFK   Yes, I agree. But given the choice, I'd go with the guy who doesn't wear a dress.

JFK (*phone filter*)   But what if Hoover's right?

RFK   . . . Okay. I'll have Seigenthaler pass the word to Dr. King to ditch this guy.

Scene transition: The same, months later.

RFK Dr. King, I have to admit, I'd never even heard of Albany, Georgia before.

Martin Luther King (*phone filter*) I can't say I recommend it, Mr. Kennedy. Not in August, anyway.

RFK I'm hearing rumors that you intend to disobey a federal restraining order—

Martin Luther King (*phone filter*) Issued by a recently appointed segregationist judge. He ruled that protest marches denied *white* people equal protection by taking police out of *their* neighborhoods. I am told that it's illegal.

RFK Nonetheless, it's a federal order.

Martin Luther King (*phone filter*) I feel impelled to march.

RFK (*re Hoover's accusation*) . . . Who's advising you on this?

Martin Luther King (*phone filter*) The SCLC and our attorneys. Why do you ask?

RFK . . . Just curious. Whether you agree with him or not, if you disobey the judge, it's open season for all the southern governors who're praying for any excuse to ignore desegregation orders.

Martin Luther King (*phone filter*) The whole point of the movement is to rise up against blatantly unconstitutional laws. Someone will always find a way to make protest seem unreasonable. We're tired, very tired. We are sick of it.

RFK Nonetheless, you can't afford to risk the goodwill of federal courts where your cause is generally winning. You can question and challenge the laws, *but don't disobey the rule of law*. It will destroy your credibility.

Martin Luther King (*phone filter*) And undermine your position? . . . You have created some of these problems by appointing segregationist judges.

RFK No matter who issued it, if you march in defiance of this order, you'll go to jail for contempt of court—not for fighting segregation.

Martin Luther King (*phone filter*) . . . Very well. We will not march—until we get it overturned.

Scene transition: The same, a couple of months later.

Gov. Barnett (*phone filter*) Bob, I need some cover here. How 'bout all your marshals pull their guns on me, and I got no choice?

RFK Governor Barnett, the idea is simply to enforce the law and integrate the University of Mississippi. This is not—

Gov. Barnett (*phone filter*) Wait! I got it—we'll tell everybody we're gonna have a big ol' confrontation Monday. Then you can enroll him on Sunday, an' I'll say you did it behind my back.

RFK Governor . . .

Gov. Barnett (*phone filter*) Now, don't you worry—we'll keep everything under control.

He chuckles.

After all, the Civil War ended a long time ago.

Scene transition: The Oval Office.

SFX: Teargas cannisters exploding, crowds chanting ("2-1-4-3/We hate Kennedy!" and "Ask us what we say/It's the hell with Bobby K.!"), general rioting, gunshots—all through phone filter. Continue under **Katzenbach** *only:*

Nicholas Katzenbach (*phone filter*)   Bob, can you hear me?

RFK (*into phone*)   Nick, hold on.

(To JFK.) Jack, it's Nick Katzenbach. It sounds like a war down there.

Nicholas Katzenbach (*phone filter*)   It's bad, Bob. A full-scale riot. They've started shooting at us. They're yelling about lynching James Meredith!

RFK (*into phone*)   Nick, we're all here—the President's here, too. We've federalized the National Guard. They're on their way.

Nicholas Katzenbach (*phone filter*)   How soon will they be here? It's like the Alamo.

RFK (*gallows humor*)   Well, you know what happened to those guys.

Pause.

Nick, they'll be there soon.

SFX: Phone hanging up, riot sounds out.

How soon, Jack? You have that damn general on the phone?

JFK   Bobby, please.

(*Into phone.*) Where's the goddamn Army, General?

Pause.

I don't care! I want to know where they are! Why aren't they moving?

RFK   Our men are going to be killed. And they're going to lynch that student.

JFK (*into phone*)   Damn it, General! Two people are dead already! Get your men there!

SFX: Phone slamming down.

I haven't had such an interesting time since the Bay of Pigs.

RFK   I'm sorry, Jack. I let you down. All that son of a bitch Barnett wanted was a violent confrontation, and he got it. I fell for it. I should have seen it.

Scene transition: A television studio.

Douglas Edwards (*filter*)   To this commentator, the Kennedy administration should count itself lucky that its blunders at Ole Miss only cost two lives. If the Army had shown up just a few minutes later, the mob would have overwhelmed the Attorney General's federal marshals. It can be fairly argued that Governor Barnett had every chance to keep order, and did not. But the plain fact is that the Department of Justice is trying to do a balancing act—and failing. It is no wonder that Martin Luther King and other Negroes are beginning to feel like pawns in a white man's game.

Scene transition: The A.G.'s office, a month later.

Louis Martin   Not bad for an off-year election.

RFK   Louis, we needed this. We haven't had a win around here in quite a while.

Louis Martin   The party in power *always* loses some Senate seats, but we actually picked up four . . . thanks to Civil Rights.

RFK   Come on, Louis. Spread the credit around a *little*—

Louis Martin   Think about it Bob: Pennsylvania? California? You think we would've won the Negro vote if you hadn't done what you did?

RFK   All I did was do my job. And it cost us votes in the South.

Louis Martin   Forget the South—the President can win without 'em. We just proved it. Now we gotta play it up big: a White House Conference on Civil Rights—*all* the Negro leaders—

RFK   Louis, slow down. Even northern whites are still ambivalent—

Louis Martin   Lose the Negro vote at your peril, Bob. You can't hold us forever with promises. Your brother said he'd integrate housing with the stroke of a pen. What you need, ink?

RFK   No, but we do need something, you're right.

Louis Martin   It's got to be legislation, Bob, or the GOP's gonna outflank you. They'll say they've got a Civil Rights Bill, and you don't.

RFK (*thinking aloud*)   If we start outlawing segregation in restaurants and movie theaters and hotels—it's too much, Louis, too soon . . . And I don't want anything to interfere with the voter registration drive . . . (*Then, an idea:*) But maybe . . . legislation *about* voting rights . . . I think the President could get behind that.

Louis Martin   Better be a helluva bill.

RFK   But it won't get public support if things don't stay calm.

Scene transition: The same, some months later.

Burke Marshall   Bob, Birmingham's the toughest town in the South. This is Armageddon. King's making a full-scale assault: lunch counters, fitting rooms, drinking fountains.

And he's betting that you and the President are going to stand by him.

RFK Burke, for God's sake, call King and tell him this is not the time. They just had an election there, for Christ's sake. Tell him to give the new mayor some time. Tell him we're calling some people.

Scene transition: A radio plays.

SFX: Teletype machine.

News Anchor And in Birmingham, Alabama, today, Sheriff Bull Connor has arrested hundreds of demonstrators, including Dr. Martin Luther King. The standoff between Civil Rights advocates and the city turned violent, as blasts from fire hoses were directed at the demonstrators.

Scene transition: The A.G.'s office.

SFX: Out.

RFK Jesus, Burke, have you read this thing that King wrote?

Burke Marshall "Letter From a Birmingham Jail?" Yes, I have.

RFK It sounds like he's criticizing my brother and me.

Martin Luther King "I have almost reached the regrettable conclusion that the Negro's great stumbling block is not the Ku Klux Klanner, but the white moderate, who is more devoted to 'order' than to justice; who paternalistically believes he can set the timetable for another man's freedom."

RFK Jail is like a pulpit to him. Burke, I want you to go down there. Arrange bail. Get them out.

Burke Marshall Bob, they don't want out. Their whole point is to accept the penalty, fill the jails, and bring the city to its knees. King says that unlike the segregationists, they expect to be punished. They respect the rule of law.

RFK That's all very noble, but it's not how things work in the real world. He should work with us. How can staying in jail advance his cause?

Martin Luther King "We will reach the goal of freedom in Birmingham and all over the nation, because the goal of America is freedom. Our destiny is tied up with America's destiny."

Scene transition: The White House.

SFX: Press conference sounds.

JFK I'm gratified to note the progress in the efforts by white and Negro citizens to end an ugly situation in Birmingham, Alabama. The Birmingham agreement to desegregate public accommodations and end discriminatory hiring practices is a fair and just accord.

Reporters Mr. President! Mr. President . . .

Burke Marshall (*aside to* **RFK**) You have to hand it to them, Bob. They won. No more segregation in Birmingham—who'd have thought it?

Scene transition: The Oval Office.

SFX: Out.

JFK   Right in Dad's apartment?

RFK (*angry*)   Yes! They weren't even civil. You could've heard them in Central Park. And these were prominent people. God, I'm so pissed off.

JFK   I thought *you* invited *them*!

RFK   I did! I asked James Baldwin to get them all together, and they attacked me. It was a disaster.

JFK   Jesus, in Dad's apartment . . . Who all was there?

RFK   Belafonte, Lena Horne, Kenneth Clark, that playwright, Miss Hansberry . . . I just told them I wanted their advice.

JFK   About all this Negro anger?

RFK   Yes—despite all we've done on civil rights. I told them we're concerned about the Muslims and the extremists causing real trouble . . .

Jerome Smith (*shouting*)   "You don't have no idea what trouble is!"

RFK   This fellow Smith—one of the Freedom Riders—just started shouting at me all of a sudden . . .

Jerome Smith   "Because I'm close to the moment where I'm ready to take up a gun. It's gonna be some folks who've had it with nonviolence. And when *I* pull the trigger, kiss it goodbye!"

JFK   Didn't any of the others—

RFK   No, they piled on! They told me I was naive.

JFK   Well, I've always said you lack a certain *savoir-faire*—

RFK   Goddamit, Jack, this was serious. He said he wouldn't fight for his country . . .

Jerome Smith   "Not in a million years! Never! I don't identify with a country where people are beaten."

Pause.

"Man, I've had enough of this shit. Just sitting here makes me wanna vomit."

JFK   My God, Bobby—

RFK   Then they started to walk out. Belafonte apologized, said he couldn't say anything.

JFK   Jesus.

RFK   Jack, they don't know anything, they don't understand anything. One of them said *you* should walk the Negro students into the University of Alabama yourself, and

I laughed. And then I talked about some of the liberal judges we've appointed, and *they* laughed . . . It was a disaster.

Pause.

You know what one of them said to me?

JFK   What?

RFK   "Would you trade places with me?"

There is a pause. Then:

Scene transition: The A.G.'s office.

Louis Martin   Geez, Bob, you've been a holy terror this week. You okay?

RFK   I'm fine, Louis.

Louis Martin   Yeah, well, you tore Lyndon Johnson a new asshole at that meeting.

RFK   It's a committee on equal employment, and he doesn't *mention* Negro hiring.

Louis Martin   Y'know, you're beautiful when you're mad. What did those people *say* to you up there in your father's apartment?

RFK   Nothing. It's just—maybe I'd feel differently about this country if I'd been born a Negro.

Louis Martin (*sardonic*)   Well, you wouldn't have seen as much of it.

RFK   In any case, you got what you wanted. We're introducing a Civil Rights Bill.

Louis Martin   Ah, the sweet sound of legislation.

RFK   Integrated public accommodations—hotels, restaurants, stores, movie theaters—

Louis Martin   Will I be able to sue?

RFK   Yes. But under the Commerce Clause, not for equal protection.

Louis Martin   But, Bob, the real issue—

RFK   This is what I think can get passed. Now, Louis, as you suggested: I want you to get real leaders in here—Civil Rights folks, businessmen, politicians, newspapers. We need them to lobby for us, and we need to know what *they're* thinking.

Louis Martin   And Dr. King?

RFK   Save him for last. We don't want people to think he's driving this.

Scene transition: The Oval Office.

Archival audio tape of George Wallace:

Wallace   Now, therefore, I, George C. Wallace, as Governor of the State of Alabama, have by my action raised issues between the central government and the sovereign state of Alabama. . .

*Archival audio fade (on **JFK**'s cue, below) Under:*

JFK   What horseshit. Turn down the volume. "Standing in the schoolhouse door." Bobby, this isn't going to be like Ole Miss is it?

RFK   No, I don't think so. It'll be Katzenbach entering the building—not the two students. They'll register later. We've nationalized the Guard in advance. It won't be the Alamo this time.

JFK   And Wallace won't double-cross us?

RFK   I think the governor knows he's licked. We're letting him have his show.

Archival audio up:

Wallace   . . . do hereby denounce and forbid this illegal and unwarranted action by the central government.

Archival audio fades, continues under:

RFK   Well, he's left you no choice.

JFK   What?

RFK   He's on national television. So you've got to make that TV address tonight. Let's get the writers together.

JFK   You're the only one who thinks I should speak.

RFK   It's going on out there, Jack, this change—all over the country. It's primarily a moral issue, and now this guy's made a speech on TV, full of some shit about his sovereign state. We've got to grab this back.

JFK (*pauses, listening to **Wallace**; then:*)   You're right.

Pause.

Jesus, he looks worse on camera than Nixon.

Scene transition: The Oval Office, that evening.

Archival audio out.

Douglas Edwards   Ladies and gentlemen, the President of the United States.

JFK   Good evening my fellow citizens. This afternoon, following a series of threats and defiant statements, two clearly qualified young Alabama residents who happened to have been born Negro were admitted peacefully on the campus of the University of Alabama.

We are confronted primarily with a moral issue. It is as old as the scriptures and is as clear as the American Constitution.

The heart of the question is whether we are going to treat our fellow Americans as we want to be treated. If an American, because his skin is dark, cannot enjoy the full and free life which all of us want, then who among us would be content to have the color of his skin changed and stand in his place?

Martin Luther King   Dear Mr. President, I have just listened to your speech to the nation. It was one of the most eloquent, profound, and unequivocal pleas for justice and the freedom of all men ever made by any President. You spoke passionately to the moral issues . . .

Myrlie Evers   Dear Mr. President. I just want you to know that my husband, Medgar Evers, telephoned me right after listening to your speech. He said it was the most important speech he'd ever heard. He told me he was coming right home after the meeting, and he did. The gunman shot him as he was getting out of the car, and he bled to death in the arms of me and the children.

Scene transition: The A.G.'s office.

RFK   Louis, every four days, the President asks me if we're doing the right thing. Even before we introduce it, this Civil Rights Bill is causing problems. Everyone knows what's wrong with it and just how to fix it, too.

Louis Martin   Has my citizens' lobby helped?

RFK   Well, yes, Congress is feeling some pressure. But there are still minefields all over. I'm thinking of cutting the public accommodations section. It covers damn near every business. It'll lose us every southern senator.

Louis Martin (*suddenly personal*)   Bob, there's a restaurant near my home. The manager refuses to serve blacks. If he shuts the door on my daughter, I'm going to want to shoot him. Now, I'm a nice man who wouldn't shoot anyone, but if *I* feel that way, just imagine how the angry young black people feel.

RFK   . . . Well, I guess that section can stay in for now.

Louis Martin   With all the leaders you convened, you should've invited Dr. King.

RFK   That'd be seen like having Karl Marx coming to the White House.

Louis Martin   Bob, if they do this march on Washington, King's gonna be out front making demands. Somebody's gonna have to meet with him.

Scene transition: The same, some weeks later.

Martin Luther King   The President was too busy to meet with us?

RFK   Pressing global issues . . . And he's chasing votes for the Civil Rights Bill.

Martin Luther King   We share his concern . . . And we're going to lend our bodies and voices to his call for true equality.

RFK   Dr. King, a march would be counter-productive. Discreet persuasion will win over Congress, not a noisy public rally.

Diane Nash   Mr. Kennedy, this is our moment. If you'll forgive me, we shall not be moved.

RFK   Miss Nash, right-wing extremists are waiting for an excuse for violence. The Klan could come, and the Nazis. It could be a bloodbath.

Diane Nash It could be a classic display to the world of our First Amendment.

RFK (*exasperated*) This is the bill you wanted! You could create a Congressional backlash. The timing is terrible, gentlemen—and Miss Nash.

Martin Luther King It is in the great tradition of American protest. The timing always seems wrong to those who would be affected by change. With all respect, this is not the first instance when you have found the movement ill-timed.

RFK . . . At least call off the sit-in in the Congressional galleries. Restrict yourselves to the Mall.

Martin Luther King . . . I think the other organizers can be persuaded to do that.

Scene transition: The same.

J. Edgar Hoover (*phone filter*) Mr. Kennedy.

RFK Mr. Hoover, to what do I owe the pleasure?

J. Edgar Hoover (*phone filter*) I know you dispatched Mr. Seigenthaler to try to dissuade Mr. King from having further contact with that commie, Levison, but we know that they're still in touch.

RFK You are a font of information.

J. Edgar Hoover (*phone filter*) You'd be surprised what I know, Mr. Kennedy.

RFK And how do you know that Mr. Levison is a communist, exactly?

J. Edgar Hoover (*phone filter*) Providing you with explicit details would compromise the special agent who has deeply penetrated the American Communist Party.

RFK That's very graphic, J. Edgar, but not very forthcoming.

J. Edgar Hoover (*phone filter*) You'll just have to trust me on this one.

Scene transition: The same, some days later.

Martin Luther King Mr. Attorney General—

RFK Call me Bob—after all, we've been through a lot together. Thanks for coming a little earlier than the others.

Martin Luther King I thought you were going to ask me to stop them from criticizing the President at the march, but Mr. Marshall just took me aside and repeated the accusations Mr. Seigenthaler had made against my adviser Mr. Levison.

RFK You continue to seek his counsel.

Martin Luther King He's a trusted friend of the movement. It's my Christian and pastoral duty not to turn my back on a friend.

RFK (*firm*) The President is about to put his whole political life on the line for this Civil Rights Bill. He cannot be made vulnerable to charges of communist associations.

Martin Luther King   This is all hearsay. Unless you can show me proof—

RFK   Unfortunately, that's classified. You have to get rid of him. If they shoot you down, they shoot us down too.

Martin Luther King   "They"? Who is "they"?

RFK   . . . I assume you know you're under very close surveillance.

Scene transition: The Oval Office.

JFK   Is King going to do the right thing?

RFK   I wouldn't bet on it, Jack. Meanwhile, what about this march?

JFK   They don't strike me as very organized. We better make sure it comes off well. I don't want any problem or embarrassments: nobody pees on the Washington Monument.

RFK   I'll arrange for portable toilets.

JFK   And it better be interracial.

RFK   I'll contact the unions, white clergy. You want me to close the bars and the liquor stores?

JFK   Good idea, just to be safe. What if the speeches get out of hand?

RFK   We'll have someone ready to pull the plug on the P.A. system. Don't worry. You want to bring in Daley's guy who staged all the parades in Chicago?

JFK   No, he'd screw up a two-car funeral. I feel safer if you handle it . . . What are you going to do about King?

RFK   If he's naive and foolish enough to keep contacting Levison, I may have to let Hoover put a wiretap on him.

JFK   Jesus, if it got out . . . We need his support for the Civil Rights Bill, and to hold onto the black vote.

RFK   Yes, but I have to protect us from charges of being soft on communism. So let's wear a belt and suspenders. If he's clean, we're wrong—and if he's not, we're covered.

Pause.

Jack, I care more about you than him, or any piece of legislation.

Scene transition: The Lincoln Memorial.

SFX: Crowd noise.

Martin Luther King (*over P.A.*)   . . . We will be able to speed up that day when all of God's children, black men and white men, Jews and Gentiles, Protestants and Catholics, will be able to join hands and sing in the words of the old Negro spiritual: Free at last! Free at last! Thank God Almighty, we are free at last!

SFX: Cheering and applause.

Scene transition: A Senate hearing room.

SFX: Gavel bang.

Senate Committee Chairman (*over P.A.*)   The Committee will come to order. Mr. Attorney General, before the recess, you were telling us about the need for a Civil Rights Bill.

RFK (*over P.A.*)   Yes, the United States is dominated by white people, politically and economically. The question is whether we, in this position of dominance, are going to have not the charity but the wisdom to stop penalizing our fellow citizens whose only fault or sin is that they were born. That, Mr. Chairman, is why Congress should enact this bill.

SFX: Gavel bang.

Senate Committee Chairman (*over P.A.*)   The Chair recognizes the distinguished Senator from Mississippi, Senator Eastland.

Senator Eastland (*over P.A.*)   Mr. Kennedy what you are proposing is a tragic usurpation of the sacred concept of states' rights.

RFK (*over P.A.*)   States' rights, as our forefathers conceived it, was a protection of the rights of the individual citizen. Those who preach most frequently about states' rights today are not seeking the protection of the individual, but his exploitation. The time is long past when we should permit the noble concept of states' rights to be betrayed and corrupted into a slogan to hide the bald denial of American rights, of civil rights, and of human rights.

Scene transition: The Oval Office.

JFK   Bobby, you were great at the hearing.

RFK   We're a long way from getting it passed. Even Lyndon's deal-making may not be enough.

JFK   I think this thing's become more important to you than fighting organized crime.

RFK   It's been kind of unavoidable.

JFK   Either way, it puts your heart in your voice.

RFK   Maybe. But they're tying you to me, blaming my moves on "the Kennedy brothers." That'll kill you in the South when you run next year . . . Maybe I ought to resign and let you run unencumbered by me.

JFK   Forget it. I'm proud you're my brother, and you're doing a damn fine job. Besides, the polls say I'm gaining more voters than I'm losing because of this stand. So, keep on pushing this. You care about it—and it's helping me. Bobby, we're in this together, all the way to the end.

Archival audio: Tape of Erich Leinsdorf announcing JFK assassination:

Leinsdorf Ladies and gentlemen, we have a press report over the wires—we hope that it is unconfirmed, but we have to doubt it—that the President of the United States has been the victim of an assassination. We will play the funeral march from Beethoven's Third Symphony.

Music: Beethoven's Third Symphony, second movement. Swell as **RFK** *steps forward in a circle of light. He stands for a moment, alone. Music and light fade out.*

End of Act One.

Act Two

Music: Beethoven's Third Symphony, second movement.

Spotlight up on **RFK** *standing alone. Other lights up on a group of his friends and advisors.*

Music: Slowly fade out under:

Nicholas Katzenbach   Bob seems completely lost. I'm worried. He hasn't slept in days.

Burke Marshall   I know. He soldiered through as long as there were "arrangements" to deal with, but ever since then . . . He's a ghost of himself.

Louis Martin   I'm really concerned about him. I'm not sure that jumping back into politics is the best thing right now.

Burke Marshall   It's in his blood. He'll adjust to it in time.

Louis Martin   I'm not sure there *is* much time. Everything's changed. It's a new game. If he can't play, maybe it'd be better for Bob to resign.

John Seigenthaler   And I don't know if he *can* adjust. I've never seen anyone with less resilience.

Louis Martin   I know, he looks terrible. His clothes just hang off of him.

John Seigenthaler   And he's always wearing his brother's overcoat—it's—

Nicholas Katzenbach   It's sad: And you know what it is? The dream may've died, too . . . and he's trying to figure out how to keep it alive.

Scene transition: Hickory Hill, **RFK***'s home in Virginia.*

Seigenthaler *goes to* **RFK**, *who is holding a book.*

John Seigenthaler   Hey, Bob . . . You want to go for a walk?

RFK   . . . No.

John Seigenthaler   You want something to eat?

RFK   No, thanks.

John Seigenthaler   You want me to leave you alone?

RFK (*after a pause*)   I've been reading about the ancient Greeks, John, and some of the classic tragedies.

Pause.

Kind of obvious, huh?

John Seigenthaler   Well, anything that helps.

RFK Listen to this. It's Edith Hamilton: "tragedy is pain transmuted into exaltation by the alchemy of poetry." Do you believe that?

John Seigenthaler More importantly, do you?

RFK I don't know . . . Hard to imagine exaltation . . . And here's Aeschylus: "In agony, learn wisdom! Pain and error are steps on the ladder of knowledge." . . . Wisdom, knowledge—helluva price to pay . . .

From another place on the stage, not addressing **RFK**, **Martin Luther King** *adds* . . .

Martin Luther King Unmerited suffering is redemptive. And even if physical death is the price, it is the price paid to free the soul of our nation, and to free our children from a permanent spiritual death.

Back to scene.

RFK The Greeks believed that "men are not made for safe havens. The fullness of life is in the hazards of life."

John Seigenthaler That mean you want to go for a walk?

RFK . . . Yeah, I think I ought to.

Scene transition: The A.G.'s office.

Burke Marshall Now that you're back, Bob, you've got to think of your future. Secretary of State, Vice President—Johnson will give you whatever you want.

RFK My brother twisted my arm to take this job. I can't leave it until the Civil Rights Bill is passed. Lyndon's right for once: it *is* Jack's legacy.

Burke Marshall . . . There's a lot of you in it, too.

RFK I have to get this done for him, Burke. Besides, there's so much left to do—for Negroes, for everyone who's not getting a decent break.

Burke Marshall Lots of ways to accomplish those things.

RFK Yes, but we've only got 'til the election. After that, it'll be all Lyndon. And he's more interested in politics than he is in anything else.

Burke Marshall So, what are you going to do?

RFK Right now, I'm going back down South to make the case for that bill.

Burke Marshall Back to the lion's den?

Scene transition: A university auditorium in the South.

SFX: Crowd noise.

RFK (*over P.A.*) How many of us would like it if we were in the Negro's situation? A law to end this continuous insult is long overdue.

SFX: Cheering and applause.

Scene transition: The A.G.'s office.

SFX: Door opening and closing.

Burke Marshall   How'd your meeting go? Can I start to call you Mr. Vice President? . . . Bob, are you going to get the nod? What did the President say?

RFK   He didn't "say" anything—he read from a piece of paper.

Burke Marshall   He read you a written statement? I thought passing the Civil Rights Act made you bosom buddies. So what was this "statement"?

RFK   Well, Burke, let's just say I ought to think about getting another job.

Burke Marshall   What? Are you kidding?

RFK   I'm afraid not.

Burke Marshall   Leave government? . . . You'd hate being a college president.

RFK   There's always astronaut . . . Ah, what the hell, we could start our own country.

Scene transition: The Oval Office.

RFK   President Johnson, all these places—Harlem, Watts, the Chicago South Side—they're riots waiting to happen. This summer was just the beginning. We have to—

LBJ   Yes, I read your memo. I'm not saying it's not a problem, Bob, but we're facing a *lot* of problems—

RFK   I really think you need to address this in the strongest possible terms, and right away.

LBJ   Well, first let's get through this election. Then let's pass that Voting Rights Act. Hell, we've lost the South anyhow—

RFK   The South was easy compared to what we face in the North. We can pass a law to ensure the vote in Alabama, but we can't pass a law to get a fellow a job in Cleveland.

LBJ   I can't wave a magic wand and do it, either. I know how strongly you feel about this, Bob, so why don't you bring this up with some of the other cabinet members—some time after November.

RFK   . . . Speaking of November—here's another memo for you.

SFX: Paper rustling.

LBJ   What's this?

RFK   My resignation, Mr. President. I'm running for the Senate from New York.

Scene transition: **RFK** *outdoor campaign rally, upstate NY.*

Johnson City is the shoe manufacturing capital of New York State, and everybody here should vote for me. After all, I have eight children, and they need a lot of shoes . . .

SFX: Crowd cheering wildly.

Fade and continue under:

Louis Martin   Geez, Bob. Look at these crowds you're getting. Listen to 'em.

RFK   They're not for me. They're for him.

Louis Martin   They love you!

RFK   Don't you understand? They're for him.

Louis Martin   Bob, enough. You've got to stop. Goddamit, get a hold of yourself. You're real, you're alive, they love you, and your brother's dead.

SFX: Crowd noise continues under:

Myrlie Evers (*over P.A.*)   My name is Myrlie Evers. I'm from Mississippi, so I can't vote for Robert Kennedy. But I sure can urge you in New York to vote for this man who has done more for the Negroes throughout this country than any other single individual.

SFX: Crowd cheers out.

Scene transition: **RFK**'s *Senate office.*

RFK   I've been in the Senate for three weeks already. What's the big deal, Teddy?

Teddy Kennedy   I waited sixteen months before I made my first Senate speech. Some wait for years.

RFK   I get bored quickly. It takes too long to get things done here.

Teddy Kennedy   But you shouldn't have walked out on Javits and Wayne Morse while they were debating the final wording of that resolution.

RFK   They were splitting hairs over adverbs.

Teddy Kennedy   It didn't win you any friends to say: "Hell, why don't you just flip a coin?"

RFK   I want to get things done, not make friends.

SFX: Intercom buzzer.

Secretary   Senator, Governor Rockefeller is on line one.

Teddy Kennedy   Speaking of not making friends . . .

SFX: Phone picking up.

RFK   Hello, Governor Rockefeller. You wanted to speak with me?

Nelson Rockefeller (*phone filter*)   How can you have thirteen New York counties declared part of Appalachia?

RFK   It seemed to be the best way to get them aid under the Appalachia Redevelopment Program.

Nelson Rockefeller (*phone filter*)   New York is not like Appalachia! I'll object to this legislation.

RFK   Are you embarrassed by poor white people? You don't want $29 million for roads, vocational schools, and hospitals? You want to lose the southwestern counties next election? Go ahead. Object.

Scene transition: The same, some months later.

Teddy Kennedy   Bobby, I don't understand it. Five days after the Voting Rights Act gets signed, all of Watts explodes. All this violence—

RFK   It's not about the right to vote, Teddy. These people have no hope.

Teddy Kennedy   And then that sonofabitch Eisenhower goes on TV and practically blames it on you and Jack—"creating a policy of lawlessness."

RFK (*sarcastic*)   I wonder who was moving his mouth for him.

Pause.

Well, I'm not going to let it stand.

Teddy Kennedy (*mock sympathy*)   Aw, he's an old man.

Pause, then for real.

Go get 'im, Bob.

Scene transition: An auditorium in New York.

RFK (*over P.A.*)   There is no point in telling Negroes to obey the law. It has almost always been used against them. The problems of the ghetto will yield only to fundamental change—to better education and housing and job opportunities. It is one thing to assure a man the legal right to eat in a restaurant; it is another to assure he can earn the money to eat there . . . I also believe that Civil Rights leaders, by focusing on the South, have neglected the problems in the North and West.

Scene transition: Press conference in L.A.

SFX: Press conference sounds.

Martin Luther King   I came to Los Angeles to walk the streets of Watts, where thirty-five people have been killed, over a thousand injured and nearly 4,000 arrested. I have called on Mayor Yorty to investigate the apparent police brutality and convene a civilian review board to oversee the police department—all to no avail.

I find the white leadership of Los Angeles displaying a blind intransigence and ignorance of the tremendous social forces which are at work here.

Scene transition: The U.S. Senate chamber.

SFX: Out.

RFK (*with reverb of Senate chamber*)   This Senate needs to pass the War on Poverty Act. I have witnessed what happened in Watts. I have witnessed what happened in Harlem.

Almost every major city has seen terrible outbreaks of violence. Who are the rioters? Why do they riot? The riots were caused, more than anything else, by the terrible frustration and alienation of the young Negroes of the impoverished ghettos. The typical rioter was seventeen, from a fatherless home, unemployed, out of school, without any hope for the future. We simply must do more to see that people get off welfare, off the streets and into decent, productive jobs, and that every American shall have the same opportunities to make a life for himself and his children—and the same opportunity to share in the government of his city and his state and country.

Scene transition: **RFK**'s *office, NYC.*

Black Woman Leader   I think I speak on behalf of most of the Civil Rights organizations in thanking you for your eloquent speech in the Senate this week.

RFK   You're welcome, but I think you and your colleagues haven't provided leadership in the North. The northern problems are problems of everyday living—jobs, education, and housing. Sit-ins can't change the fact that adults are illiterate. Marches don't create jobs. So a lot of demagogues have assumed positions of leadership.

Black Woman Leader   I'm so sorry you see it that way.

RFK   Believe me, so am I.

Scene transition: A midtown restaurant, NYC.

SFX: Restaurant sounds (including Muzak).

Businessman 1   Senator, the afternoon I walk into my board of directors and tell them Bob Kennedy took me to lunch, and he thinks we should put a factory in Bedford-Stuyvesant, that is the day they'll have me committed.

RFK (*countering*)   Well, you can tell your board that I can offer some nice tax incentives.

Pause.

Gentlemen, Bed-Stuy is one of the poorest parts of New York City, and we can make a real difference. This pilot program will create jobs by partnering your industries with government and community leaders. There's nothing like it anywhere in the country. Your companies should be part of it.

Businessman 2   Senator, with all respect—A: there's no profit in community development. B: the unions will not cooperate. C: we can't deal with black militants and their climate of violence.

RFK   We can't denounce extremists who reject our system if we don't prove that system capable of helping people make better lives . . . (*The pragmatist:*) And I'll take care of the unions.

SFX: Out.

Scene transition: **RFK***'s office, NYC.*

Liberal Woman   Bob, all of us in the progressive movement know about these meetings you're having with big businessmen. You're putting too much trust in them. They're only motivated by profit. They don't give a good goddamn about about our social goals.

RFK   We have to show it can be done—not just more programs—but new kinds of systems for jobs and education, and health and housing. This is about the future of urban life. Either you're in or you're out.

Scene transition: A commercial airliner en route to California.

SFX: Interior of a jetliner in flight.

RFK   Edelman, now why the hell am I dragging my ass all the way out to California?

Peter Edelman   Labor Subcommittee hearings. You agreed to go.

RFK   Remind me, Peter.

Peter Edelman   There's a new effort to organize farmworkers, led by a man named Cesar Chavez. Their wages and conditions stink. Walter Reuther wants to help them. He knows the TV cameras will be there if you attend the hearings. It'll give them a national spotlight.

SFX: Out.

Scene transition: A Senate subcommittee hearing in an auditorium in Delano, CA.

SFX: A gavel bangs.

RFK (*over P.A.*)   Can I just ask a question? How much does it cost for a worker to pick a head of lettuce? I don't mean the supermarket price because we got that from Senator Murphy.

Industry Representative (*over P.A.*)   Senator, the cutting and trimming and packing would cost, oh, half a penny a head.

RFK   And Senator Murphy, how much did you buy that head of lettuce for?

Senator Murphy   33 cents, Bob.

RFK   Well, I'd like to find out—we'd all like to find out—where that other thirty-two half-cents went. I think we're in the wrong business.

SFX: Laughter and a gavel bangs.

Mrs. Olivarez (*over P.A.*)   I have some check stubs where it shows we earned only five or six dollars in a whole day of work. Are we not protected by the law? If agriculture is California's most vital industry, how come we have such low wages?

How come we work under such bad conditions? How come we can't have a union? Do not our children deserve a better chance for their future?

SFX: A gavel bangs.

RFK (*over P.A.*)   Sheriff, when you arrested those picketers when they were just walking along, what did you arrest them for?

Sheriff Galyen (*over P.A.*)   If I have reason to believe there's going to be a riot—if somebody tells me there's going to be trouble, it's my duty to stop it.

RFK   Who told you there was going to be a riot?

Sheriff Galyen   The new men working out in the field said: "If you don't get those strikers out of here, we're going to cut their hearts out." So rather than let them get cut, we removed the cause.

RFK   On the say-so of the strike breakers? Sheriff, this is a most interesting concept. How can you arrest somebody if they haven't violated the law?

Sheriff Galyen   They're gettin' ready to violate the law.

Senator (*saving the* **Sheriff** *from further embarrassment*)   Gentlemen, we will recess for lunch now.

RFK   Can I suggest that during lunch the sheriff might want to read the Constitution of the United States.

SFX: Applause. A gavel bangs.

Scene transition: A parking lot outside the building.

Dolores Huerta   Senator, I know you have things to do during the recess, but I wanted you to meet Cesar Chavez. Cesar, Senator Kennedy.

Cesar Chavez   Thank you, Dolores. And thank you for coming all this way, Senator.

RFK   Please call me Bob.

Cesar Chavez   It was a pleasure to watch you in there, but maybe you shouldn't go so far. I'm afraid it'll get you in trouble.

RFK   From what I've heard about your work, you're the one putting himself on the line. Doesn't the real danger lie in moving too slowly? . . . I only have two questions. What do you want? And how can I help you?

Scene transition: A television studio.

Douglas Edwards   Senator Kennedy, it seems that your version of civil rights is expanding. I'm sure our viewers would like to know: aren't you afraid that you may be too far ahead of the American people on this issue?

RFK   Well, if I am, the country seems to be catching up with me pretty quickly. Here it is 1966, and I was invited to speak at the Universities of Mississippi and Alabama. Just a few years ago, my name was considered a curse word there.

Douglas Edwards   What did you tell those audiences?

RFK   That America is changing, the world is changing, and that we will no longer find answers in old dogmas or outworn slogans, or by fighting old battles against old enemies. I told them the real struggle has moved on.

Douglas Edwards   And you've been carrying that message around the globe. Frankly, I was impressed by your speech in South Africa, at the University of Cape Town. Let's listen.

Audio: Playback of recording of **Actor 1**:

RFK (*over P.A.*)   Few will have the greatness to bend history itself; but each of us can work to change a small portion of events and in the total of all those acts will be written the history of this generation.

Each time a man stands up for an ideal, or acts to improve the lot of others, or strikes out against injustice, he sends forth a tiny ripple of hope, and those ripples build a current which can sweep down the mightiest walls of oppression and resistance.

Douglas Edwards   Do you see yourself as the leader in connecting politics overseas to the issues of justice in America?

RFK   Well, I'm hardly alone. There are others who have been speaking out on these issues for some time.

From another place on the stage:

Martin Luther King (*over P.A.*)   Over the past two years, many have questioned me: "Why are you speaking about the Vietnam War? Peace and Civil Rights don't mix." When we formed the Southern Christian Leadership Conference, we chose as our motto: "To save the soul of America." We were convinced that we could not limit our vision to certain rights for black people. All over the globe men are revolting against old systems of exploitation and oppression, and out of the wounds of a frail world, new systems of equality and justice are being born. We are confronted with the fierce urgency of now. We must find new ways to speak for peace in Vietnam and justice throughout the developing world, a world that borders on our doors. If we do not act, we shall surely be dragged down the long, dark, and shameful corridors of time reserved for those who possess power without compassion, might without morality, and strength without sight.

Scene transition: A hearing room in the Federal Building, Jackson, MS.

Peter Edelman   Jesus, Bob, look at all the network cameras.

RFK   Peter, these guys follow me everywhere. But dragging them to Mississippi to cover poverty—that's kind of fun.

Peter Edelman   You're putting economic justice on the six o'clock news.

SFX: A gavel bangs.

RFK (*over P.A.*)   There is no state or local welfare here, is that correct?

Official (*over P.A.*)   That is correct, sir.

RFK   So poor people depend on food stamps. And how many people in this state get food stamps?

Official   Around 470,000.

RFK   That would be one-fourth of all Mississipians. And how much do these food stamps cost?

Official   Two dollars per head a month.

RFK   And what if someone doesn't have two dollars?

Official   Senator, there's nobody in Mississippi who can't raise two dollars a month.

SFX: A gavel bangs.

Black Man (*over P.A.*)   I can't remember the last time I had one dollar in my pocket. Right now, I got just two pennies on me. Even if them food stamps was just fifty cents, no way I could raise it.

SFX: A gavel bangs.

Marian Wright (*over P.A.*)   There are people going around begging down in the Delta, because they have insufficient food. Contrary to what some people believe, these people aren't poor because they're too lazy to work.

SFX: A gavel bangs.

Scene transition: The lobby of the Federal Building Jackson.

RFK   Peter, I want to do more than just sit and listen. I wonder if those cameras would follow me out into the countryside?

Peter Edelman   You said they follow you everywhere. But Bob, I've been out there—it's pretty rough. Kids with swollen bellies, open sores. It's like a third-world country out there.

RFK   Well, then, I want to make sure the whole country sees it.

Scene transition: A shanty town on the Mississippi Delta.

Douglas Edwards   The Senate subcommittee's work has not only elicited testimony from some of the nation's most impoverished people, it has also exposed scenes of human suffering among the most emotional that this reporter has ever witnessed. New York Senator Robert Kennedy, in particular, has taken his investigations into the very shacks and shanties where some of the poorest people live.

RFK   What's your name?

Child   Pearl.

RFK   How old are you, Pearl?

Child   Eight.

RFK When did you last eat? How many meals do you eat each day?

Child Mostly, only once a day, and we already ate what we gonna get.

RFK What did you eat?

Child Some butterbeans.

RFK Well, how about yesterday, what did you eat then?

Child Bread and butterbeans.

RFK And the day before that?

Child Just bread.

Douglas Edwards But our cameras were not able to capture a scene almost devastating in its poignancy. In one shack, the Senator found a malnourished child, playing listlessly with a few grains of rice on the floor. He picked him up and sat down on a dirty bed, rubbing the child's swollen belly, whispering quietly, caressing, trying to get some response from the child—but the child never looked up or moved. Robert Kennedy sat there with tears streaming down his cheeks. Later, he had this to say:

RFK How can a country like this allow it? Americans spend three billion dollars each year taking care of dogs.

You'd think we could do more for children.

Douglas Edwards As a parent himself, Mr. Kennedy seemed to relate to these children and their parents.

RFK What do you say when your child here wants more to eat and it isn't there?

White Farmer (*southern accent*) That there isn't any more . . . I try to be calm when I speak, and sometimes I'll say tomorrow will be here soon—with some food, and sometimes I'll hold the little one tight, and she'll feed off that, you know—the closeness.

RFK . . . I'm sorry. We can do better in this country. We will—we ought to . . . (*With emphasis.*) We will—we ought to.

Scene transition: **RFK***'s Senate office.*

Dr. Coles Senator, we've done all we can do.

RFK It's not enough, Dr. Coles. Americans are starving, and that's unacceptable.

Dr. Wheeler (*southern accent*) Well, you *did* get the Agriculture Department to send some emergency food down South—

RFK A drop in the bucket, Dr. Wheeler. People have to know about your work in Mississippi with malnourished children—

Dr. Coles We've already presented our findings to quite a few officials.

Act Two   167

RFK   But you've been largely ignored. In Washington, presenting your findings is the beginning, not the end.

Dr. Coles   But our findings speak for themselves.

RFK   Not to the American people. I think they'd like to know what you've found. Dr. Wheeler, *you* should tell the story.

Dr. Wheeler   And why would that be, Senator?

RFK   Because as a southerner, you'll be harder to dismiss than a Yankee being critical.

Dr. Wheeler   So we're turning science into show business?

RFK   We're getting those children the help they need. Now, I'll set up a televised Senate hearing. You'll tell your story to the nation. But you need to do it differently this time.

Dr. Wheeler   With music?

RFK   No—with pictures. But in some of those photos you showed me, the children look fat.

Dr. Coles   They're overweight, but they're malnourished because their families only have cheap food.

RFK   I know, but perception matters in politics. Show the *scrawny* children.

Dr. Coles   Isn't that taking advantage of them?

RFK   Poor people don't have many ways of making their voices heard. Senators hear a lot of issues. They have to decide which ones matter most. These hearings will be on the news—and maybe people will write to their Senators and ask them to do something about this. I expect we'll get through this struggle, and I expect that if we do, those children and many others will eat better than before.

Scene transition: A Senate hearing room.

Peter Edelman   Bob, be careful. You don't need to piss this guy off.

RFK   The whole Congress is too careful, Peter. I want to get something *done*. I need to call attention to these issues. Give me those labor statistics.

Peter Edelman   Issues are one thing, Bob. This is slaughtering sacred cows—Democratic ones.

SFX: A gavel bangs.

Union Official #1 (*over P.A.*)   Senator, I'm proud to say that the AFL-CIO's four-year program to abolish discrimination in eighteen building trades unions is 99 percent successful.

SFX: Papers rustling.

RFK (*over P.A.*)   Well, Mr. Haggerty, according to these official Labor Department statistics, in Houston, for example, of the 8,164 journeymen in eleven construction unions, this says only sixty were Negroes. That doesn't seem to me to be "99 percent successful."

SFX: A gavel bangs.

RFK (*over P.A.*)   Let me get this straight, Mr. Schoemann. You say the reason there are only twenty-one Negroes in your Plumbers and Pipefitters local is that they lack motivation and skills?

Union Official #2 (*over P.A.*)   We can't take a boy that can't read, and a boy that's a high school dropout. We have certain minimum standards.

RFK   Well, I would think there are more than twenty-one Negro boys in all of Cincinnati who can read.

Scene transition: A television studio.

News Anchor   New York Senator Robert Kennedy appeared in Detroit today, at the same time that speculation has been growing about his possibly challenging Lyndon Johnson in the 1968 Presidential primaries.

Senator Kennedy has dismissed such conjecture, but his speech certainly had national overtones.

RFK (*over P.A.*)   Let us be clear at the outset that we will find neither national purpose nor personal satisfaction in a mere continuation of economic progress, in an endless amassing of worldly goods. We cannot measure national spirit by the Dow-Jones average, nor national achievement by the gross national product.

The gross national product does not allow for the health of our families, the quality of their education or the joy of their play. It does not include the beauty of our poetry or the strength of our marriages, the intelligence of our public debate or the integrity of our public officials. It allows neither for the justice of our courts, nor the justness of our dealings with each other. It can tell us everything about America—except why we are proud to be Americans.

Scene transition: **RFK**'s *Senate office.*

Peter Edelman   Bob, this cinches it. You've got to run.

RFK   Not necessarily, Peter.

Peter Edelman   Gene McCarthy has damn near defeated a sitting President in a primary. The war is immoral. Martin Luther King has denounced it, Johnson's isolated because of it—

John Seigenthaler   Regardless of that, Bob, you can't jump into the race now. You'll look like a ruthless opportunist.

Burke Marshall   How about endorsing McCarthy? He can't win the nomination, the party'll split, and they'll turn to you.

Peter Edelman That's not good enough, Burke. This guy's a hero. Bob, Black people all over this country have pictures of you and your brother hanging on their walls—in their living rooms, in churches, in *shacks*, for Christ's sake. They're all counting on you.

John Seigenthaler Oh, my God, I can't believe this. If you run, it'll all come out—all the shit J. Edgar Hoover's been piling up, the wiretaps you authorized on Dr. King—

Peter Edelman This is bigger than that! Look, Bob, some liberal's gonna win with you or without you—and it's a shame, 'cause you could be the next President. And if you *don't* run, how many more people are gonna die in Vietnam? Hell, how many more people are gonna die in Detroit?

RFK Fellows, please—stop. I agree with all of you . . . I mean it: I'm tempted but . . . I'm not sure.

Peter Edelman What's holding you back?

RFK What John just said—all the shit—and I might not win, and . . .

Burke Marshall Are you afraid of what might happen?

RFK (*pause*) I need more time . . . Look, the Kerner Commission's report on the race riots comes out next week.

Let's see what the President says, what the reactions are . . . We don't lose anything by waiting a week.

Scene transition: Press conference, Washington.

SFX: Press conference sounds.

Commission Spokesman This is our Commission's basic conclusion: Our nation is moving toward two societies, one black, one white—separate and unequal. White racism is essentially responsible . . .

SFX: Out.

Scene transition: **RFK**'s *Senate office.*

Peter Edelman The President hasn't said shit, Bob. Now he's not only officially losing the war overseas, he's officially losing the peace at home.

RFK (*wryly*) I guess things aren't going very well for him, at that.

Burke Marshall He's beside the point, Bob. It's those two issues you should run on: war and social justice. In fact you're already doing it. I can hear it in your speeches. You're starting to sound a helluva lot like—well, you know.

RFK *and* **Martin Luther King** *are highlighted in two separate spaces.*

RFK (*over P.A.*) The fact is that the draft has been unfair, and has discriminated against those who are poor . . .

Martin Luther King (*over P.A.*) There were twice as many Negroes as whites in combat in Vietnam at the beginning of last year . . .

RFK (*over P.A.*)   Negroes, 11 percent of the population, suffer 22 percent of all combat deaths in the jungles of Vietnam.

Martin Luther King (*over P.A.*)   I see these two struggles as one struggle.

Scene transition: A Senate committee room.

RFK (*over P.A.*)   Ladies and gentlemen, thank you all for coming. I am announcing today my candidacy for the Presidency of the United States.

I do not run merely to oppose any man, but to propose new policies—policies to end the bloodshed in Vietnam and in our cities; policies to close the gaps that now exist between black and white, between rich and poor, between young and old—in this country and the rest of the world. I run because I am convinced that this country is on a perilous course and because I have such strong feelings about what must be done.

Scene transition: **RFK***'s Senate office.*

John Seigenthaler   Peter, did you bring the pitcher and ice?

Peter Edelman   What?

John Seigenthaler   We got a pile o' lemons here, and we gotta get goin' on the lemonade.

Peter Edelman   John, it's not that bad. Okay, we're a little behind in organizing—

John Seigenthaler   And in scheduling, and in fundraising, and in strategy, and—

Peter Edelman   But we've got people behind us.

John Seigenthaler   Sure do: the poor, the young, the disenfranchised—we're in great shape.

Peter Edelman   *And* the big-city bosses, the political machines. This is new, John. We're takin' it to the streets *and* the smoke-filled rooms. We're takin' it everywhere.

Scene transition: **RFK** *and* **Martin Luther King** *are highlighted in two separate spaces, in a medley of public speeches.*

RFK (*over P.A.*)   And so I say to you here at Kansas State, I am willing to bear my share of the responsibility for Vietnam. But past error is no excuse for its own perpetuation.

America is divided—the poor are invisible. I say we can do better. And I pledge to you, if you will give me your help, if you will give me your hand, I will work for you, and we will have a new America.

SFX: Wild applause and cheering.

Martin Luther King (*over P.A.*)   What we seek is the elimination of racism as an electoral issue.

Those who are poor—white and black—will develop an alliance that displaces racism as a political issue.

Act Two   171

SFX: Applause. Fade under:

RFK (*over P.A.*)   It is not just our supporters, not just those who vote for us, but all Americans, whom we must lead in the difficult years ahead. And this is why I have come at the outset of my campaign, not to New York or Chicago or Boston, but here to Alabama.

SFX: Cheers and applause. Fade under:

Martin Luther King   The government is emotionally committed to the war. It is emotionally hostile to the needs of the poor. I cannot support President Johnson for reelection.

SFX: Cheers and applause.

Scene transition: The Oval Office. A televised address.

LBJ   I have concluded that I should not permit the Presidency to become involved in the partisan divisions that are developing in this political year . . .

Accordingly, I shall not seek, and I will not accept, the nomination of my party for another term as your President.

Scene transition: A hotel room on the campaign trail in Indiana.

RFK   Reverend, how is it going there in Memphis?

Martin Luther King (*phone filter*)   Well, they say there's a big storm brewing.

RFK   You're speaking metaphorically?

Martin Luther King   No, I'm talking about the weather.

RFK   Well, I'm sure you'll, uh, weather it.

Martin Luther King   I'm supposed to be in Washington on Friday for the press conference to open our Poor People's Campaign.

RFK   Have you got the horses for this?

Martin Luther King (*chuckling*)   Actually, we're going to have mules. We're going to have mule trains, and trucks, and thousands of poor people.

RFK   Yes. Cesar Chavez told me about your getting Mexican farmworkers, and Indians, and Appalachians. I think it's wonderful.

Martin Luther King   Well, your campaign gives strength to our campaign. I appreciate that you know what it's really about.

RFK   Well, I know what's at stake, it's—as you've said, it's the soul of America. All of us. I hope you can help.

Martin Luther King   Senator, I'll do what I can. You know that we've never endorsed a candidate, but I'll do what I can.

RFK   I appreciate that.

Martin Luther King My faith is not flagging, Senator, but I'm worried about something. They're laughing at nonviolence now. You know I deeply believe in the power of nonviolence to solve the poverty problem. But they're laughing at it now.

RFK They're wrong, Reverend. And their riots haven't achieved anything. Violence never does. You keep on—and I'll keep on. We'll make America really see poor people—and do something about it.

Scene transition: Rally, Mason Temple, Memphis, TN.

SFX: Crowd noise up, then fade under:

Martin Luther King (*over P.A.*) If I were standing at the beginning of time, and the Almighty said to me, "Martin Luther King, which age would you like to live in?" strangely enough, I would turn to the Almighty, and say, "If you allow me to live just a few years in the second half of the twentieth century, I will be happy." Now that's a strange statement to make, because the world is all messed up. The nation is sick. Trouble is in the land. Confusion all around.

But I know, somehow, that only when it is dark enough can you see the stars. And I see God working in this period—something is happening in our world.

Men, for years now, have been talking about war and peace. But now, no longer can they just talk about it. It is no longer a choice between violence and nonviolence in this world; it's nonviolence or nonexistence. That is where we are today. Now, I'm just happy that God has allowed me to live in this period, to see what is unfolding.

And I'm happy that he's allowed me to be in Memphis.

Scene transition: Muncie, IN, airport tarmac.

SFX: Crowd noise cross-fade, from one crowd to another, and to small airplane motors in the background.

RFK (*over P.A.*) I'm very happy to be in Muncie, I'm grateful to you all for seeing me to the airport, and now it's back to Indianapolis and let's win in Indiana!

SFX: Small crowd cheers. fade under:

Woman Campaign Aide Senator . . . Senator, I need to talk to you.

RFK What . . . what is it?

Woman Campaign Aide . . . Have you heard about Dr. King?

RFK (*fatalistic*) No. What happened . . . Has he been shot?

Woman Campaign Aide (*taken aback*) I thought you—

RFK Tell me, how is he?

Woman Campaign Aide He's in critical condition, sir.

SFX: Plane taking off.

Scene transition: Interior, **RFK** *small campaign airplane.*

SFX: Airplane interior.

Frank Mankiewicz   Bob, are you okay?

RFK   I don't . . . I . . . I have to speak at this rally tonight, Frank. What do you think I should say?

Frank Mankiewicz   Not much . . . Something short . . . It should be like a prayer.

RFK   A prayer . . . A prayer for the country—yes. Can you work on that? . . . God, let's hope he's all right.

Scene transition: Indianapolis, airport tarmac.

SFX: Plane landing. Plane door opening.

Peter Edelman (*sad*)   Hi, Bob.

RFK   Peter, is he alive?

Peter Edelman   He's dead, Bob.

RFK (*after a pause*)   Oh, my God! . . . All this violence—when is it going to stop?

Music: Beethoven's third symphony, second movement. Fade but continue playing under:

Peter Edelman (*whispering*)   Is he thinking about . . .

Frank Mankiewicz (*whispering*)   Yes. Exactly.

RFK   What's my schedule?

Frank Mankiewicz   You okay?

RFK   Yes. Where am I speaking?

Peter Edelman   There's a rally at 17th and Broadway. The crowd's already gathered . . . It's the ghetto, Bob. There's gonna be trouble. You should send somebody in your place.

RFK   I'm going to 17th and Broadway. Frank, you go on the press bus. Keep working on those points we discussed. Have something ready for me when I get there.

Frank Mankiewicz   Will do.

Music: Fade out under:

SFX: Footsteps on airplane stairs.

Chief Churchill   Excuse me. Senator?

RFK   Yes?

Chief Churchill   I'm Chief Churchill of the Indianapolis Police. We've come to escort you to your hotel.

RFK   Well, that's very thoughtful of you, Chief, but you can escort me to 17th and Broadway first.

Chief Churchill You're not actually thinking of going down there—

RFK No, I've finished thinking. I'm going.

Chief Churchill Senator, it's the heart of the ghetto. There's going to be trouble there. You know there is. And some loony bastard might try to retaliate by shooting you. Mayor Lugar is asking you not to appear—

RFK You can tell Mayor Lugar to go to hell. I could take my wife and family and sleep safely in the street at 17th and Broadway . . . If you can't do that, that's your problem.

Chief Churchill Well, if you go, you're going without a police escort. We'll get you as far as downtown, but I'm not sending my men in there.

RFK Thanks for your support, Mr. Churchill. Peter, let's go.

Scene transition: Rally, 17th and Broadway, Indianapolis.

SFX: Sirens. Cars. Sirens fade out. Cars stop. Car doors opening and slamming. Crowd noise.

Where's Frank?

Peter Edelman The press bus didn't make it. I guess they got lost when the cops turned off.

RFK Well, I made a couple of notes . . . Earl, how's the crowd?

Earl Graves They want to hear from you. You can go right ahead.

RFK Do they know about Dr. King?

Earl Graves To a certain extent. We've left that up to you, we . . . didn't know how you wanted to handle it.

RFK (*over P.A.*) Ladies and gentlemen, I'm only going to talk to you just for a minute or so this evening.

Because I have some very sad news for all of you, and I think sad news for all of our fellow citizens, and people who love peace all over the world, and that is that Martin Luther King was shot and was killed tonight in Memphis, Tennessee.

SFX: Crowd gasps, cries.

Martin Luther King dedicated his life to love and to justice between fellow human beings. For those of you who are black and are tempted to be filled with hatred and mistrust at the injustice of such an act, and against all white people, I would only say that I can also feel in my own heart the same kind of feeling. I had a member of my family killed, but he was killed by a white man. What we need is not division; what we need is not hatred; what we need is not violence and lawlessness, but is love and wisdom, and compassion, and a feeling of justice toward those who suffer, whether they be white or whether they be black.

So I ask you tonight to return home, to say a prayer for the family of Martin Luther King, but more importantly to say a prayer for our own country, which all of us love—a prayer for understanding and that compassion of which I spoke. Let us dedicate ourselves to what the Greeks wrote so many years ago: to tame the savageness of man and make gentle the life of this world.

SFX: Applause. Fade under:

Frank Mankiewicz   Jesus, Bob. I think that's the best speech you ever gave.

RFK   No, the best speech I ever gave is the one we're going to write tonight. There are a few more things I need to say . . . Things that need to be said.

Frank Mankiewicz   Like what?

RFK   Like where this country's really headed, and where we should go instead.

Frank Mankiewicz   Bob, that doesn't exactly sound like the way to win a primary.

RFK   Not before, maybe. But I think things are different now.

Frank Mankiewicz   I hope you're right.

RFK   So do I.

RFK *crosses downstage center, appropriately highlighted. Other lights pick out characters as they speak on each side of him.*

RFK (*forcefully*)   This is a time of shame and sorrow. This mindless menace of violence in America again stains our land and every one of our lives. It is not the concern of any one race.

Louis Martin   Jesus, Bob! Who would've thought a message like that could win the Indiana primary?

RFK   The victims of the violence are black and white, rich and poor, young and old, famous and unknown. They are, most important of all, human beings whom other human beings loved and needed.

Peter Edelman   I can feel it in the crowds. People are listening to you, Bob, 'cause they know you're telling the truth!

RFK   Yet we seemingly tolerate a rising level of violence that ignores our common humanity. We calmly accept newspaper reports of civilian slaughter in far-off lands. We glorify killing on movie and television screens. We make it easy for men of all shades of sanity to acquire weapons and ammunition.

John Seigenthaler   Whupped McCarthy in Nebraska! The networks called it before the polls closed! If what you're saying gets folks in Nebraska and Indiana and South Dakota, they'll eat you up in California. This campaign has caught fire!

RFK   Only a cleaning of our whole society can remove this sickness from our soul.

Woman Campaign Aide   We love you Bobby! Keep on tellin' it like it is!

RFK   For there is another kind of violence, slower but just as deadly, destructive as the shot or the bomb in the night. This is the violence of institutions; indifference and inaction and slow decay. This is the violence that afflicts the poor, that poisons relations between men because their skin has different colors.

Earl Graves Winning California pretty much gives you the nomination. Hell, you're gonna be the next President! Let's get down to the ballroom. Bob. Gotta make sure your victory speech makes the late news back East.

Music: For the third time, Beethoven's funeral march marks an assassination—third symphony, second movement. Fade up slowly under:

RFK When you teach a man to hate and fear his brother, when you teach that he is a lesser man because of his color or his beliefs or the policies he pursues, then you also learn to confront others not as fellow citizens but as enemies.

Pause, as music plays, swells, then fade under:

Frank Mankiewicz I've been in politics all my life—never saw anything like it—before or since—right up to today. He was honest and he was hopeful—and the people followed him.

RFK Yet we know what we must do. We must admit the vanity of our false distinctions among men and learn to find our own advancement in the search for the advancement of all.

Daddy King This was more than just politics or a good campaign. This was a man who had truly seen the light, and he was spreading that light around.

RFK Our lives on this planet are too short and the work to be done too great to let this spirit flourish any longer in our land. Of course we cannot vanish it with a program, nor with a resolution.

Dr. Wheeler If he had lived, and if he had won, everything might have been different. We can't know for sure, but the way he was pointing—the dream, the hope—even if he'd fallen short, we'd be further along.

RFK But we can perhaps remember—even if only for a time—that those who live with us are our brothers, that they share with us the same short movement of life, that they seek—as we do—nothing but the chance to live out their lives in purpose and happiness.

Dr. Coles He called on us to be our best selves, and America answered. If it happened then, it can happen again—and again—and again.

RFK Surely we can learn, at least, to look at those around us as fellow men and surely we can begin to work a little harder to bind up the wounds among us and to become in our hearts brothers and countrymen once again.

Music: Cross-fade to "America the Beautiful," Ray Charles.

*Lights fade on the other actors, as **RFK** remains in the spotlight.*

Spotlight fades out.

Curtain.

Appendix

The following short descriptions list the names and approximate ages of historical personages and other characters in the play. (Where appropriate, their names as given in the script appear in parentheses.) For characters who appear throughout the play, a range of ages is given.

John F. Kennedy (JFK)—early forties—Congressman from Massachusetts 1947–53; Senator from Massachusetts 1953–60; second youngest President of the United States 1960–63; assassinated in November 1963.

Robert F. Kennedy (RFK) late thirties–early forties—John F. Kennedy's younger brother and campaign manager during JFK's 1960 presidential campaign; United States Attorney General 1961–64; United States Senator New York 1965–68; assassinated in June 1968.

Eleanor Roosevelt—late seventies—former First Lady; former delegate to the United Nations; newspaper columnist; early civil rights advocate; died 1962.

Harry Belafonte—mid-thirties—singer, actor, board member of Southern Christian Leadership Conference (SCLC); a vocal critic of the administrations of George W. Bush and Donald Trump, he remains an activist in his nineties.

Harris Wofford—mid-thirties—civil rights advisor to the 1960 Kennedy presidential campaign; Special Assistant to the President for Civil Rights, 1961–62; Associate Director of the Peace Corps, 1962–65; U.S. Senator from Pennsylvania, 1991–95; introduced presidential candidate Barack Obama when he gave his famous "A more perfect Union" speech on race, 2008; died 2019.

Martin Luther King, Jr.—early thirties–late thirties—minister, activist; President, Southern Christian Leadership Conference; Nobel Peace Prize Laureate, 1964; assassinated in April 1968.

Coretta Scott King—mid-thirties—wife of Martin Luther King, Jr.; singer; early civil rights activist; maintained her own activism and her husband's legacy, founding the King Center in Atlanta and supporting women's and gay rights; died 2006.

King aide—late twenties—male or female.

Byron "Whizzer" White (Byron White)—mid-forties—Deputy U.S. Attorney General 1961–62; appointed to U.S. Supreme Court 1962, retired from the Court 1993; died 2002.

Louis Martin—late forties–early fifties—journalist; newspaper owner; JFK campaign staff 1960; advisor to the Kennedys through his post with the Democratic National Committee, and later to President Lyndon Johnson; died 1997.

S. Ernest Vandiver (Governor Vandiver) [VAN-de-vur]—mid-forties—Democratic Governor of Georgia 1959–63, segregationist but early Kennedy supporter; died 2005.

Sargent Shriver [SHRY-ver]—mid-forties—JFK campaign aide; First Director, Peace Corps, 1961–64; married to Kennedy sister Eunice; candidate for Vice President (on the McGovern ticket) 1972; father of Maria Shriver, father-in-law of Arnold Schwarzenegger; died of Alzheimer's disease, 2011.

John Seigenthaler [SEE-gen-thal-er]—mid-thirties–early forties—journalist; administrative assistant to Attorney General RFK; RFK campaign aide and confidant; founding Editorial Director of *USA Today* 1982–91; founder of the First Amendment Center at Vanderbilt University, 1991; died 2014.

Martin Luther King, Sr. (Daddy King)—early sixties—Baptist minister and early civil rights leader; Pastor of the Ebenezer Baptist Church in Atlanta 1948–75; key supporter of the candidacy of President Jimmy Carter; died 1984.

Douglas Edwards—mid-forties—first CBS Television evening news anchor 1948–62, succeeded by Walter Cronkite; CBS radio correspondent and anchor 1942–88; died 1990.

Kenneth Keating (Senator Keating)—early sixties—Republican Senator from New York 1959–65, defeated by Robert F. Kennedy; U.S. Ambassador to India 1969–72; U.S. Ambassador to Israel 1973 until his death in 1975.

James O. Eastland (Senator Eastland)—mid-fifties—Democratic Senator from Mississippi 1943–79, a powerful Senate leader who supported the Kennedys but was resistant to change; succeeded by Sen. Thad Cochrane; died 1986.

Burke Marshall—early forties—Assistant Attorney General, Civil Rights Division 1961–64; Vice President and General Counsel, IBM Corporation 1965–69; Deputy Dean and Professor, Yale Law School 1970–86; died 2003.

Secretary—early thirties—female.

Berl Bernhard [Burl Burn-Hard]—early thirties—lawyer; government official: Executive Staff Director, U.S. Commission on Civil Rights 1958–63; chairman of the Aspen Institute 1991–95.

Dean of the University of Georgia Law School—mid-forties—male.

Radio announcer—late thirties—male.

Clancy Lake—mid-thirties—News Director, WAPI Radio and Television, Birmingham, AL.

Cop—early thirties—male.

John M. Patterson (Governor Patterson)—early forties—Democratic Governor of Alabama 1959–63, segregationist but early Kennedy supporter; Judge of the State Court of Criminal Appeals, 1984 until retiring in 1997; supported Barak Obama's presidential campaign in 2008.

George E. Cruit (Mr. Cruit) [Crew-it]—early thirties—Greyhound Bus Company supervisor, Birmingham, AL.

Southern Talk Show Host—early forties—male.

Rioter—female.

Diane Nash—mid-twenties—black activist; leader of the Nashville sit-ins, a founder of the Student Nonviolent Coordinating Committee (SNCC); a leader of the Freedom Rides; major participant in SCLC, splitting from it in 1965 due in large part to its male dominance; currently an educator and activist in Chicago.

Wyatt Walker—mid-thirties—black pastor and activist; Chief of Staff for Martin Luther King, Jr.; board member of SCLC; one of the founders and executive director of the Congress of Racial Equality (CORE); continued his activism as senior pastor of the Canaan Baptist Church in Harlem from 1967 until his retirement in 2004; died 2018.

Charles Sherrod [sher-ROD]—mid-twenties—black activist; one of the founders of SNCC; director of the Southwest Georgia Project for Community Education 1961–87; served as a chaplain at the Georgia State Prison in Homerville, Georgia.

Earl Long—mid-sixties—Democratic Governor of Louisiana 1939–1940, 1948–1952, and 1956–60; colorful and eccentric, he was portrayed by Paul Newman in the 1989 film *Blaze*; died in September 1960.

J. Edgar Hoover—mid-late sixties—Director, FBI 1924–72; died 1972.

Ross Barnett (Governor Barnett)—mid-sixties—Democratic Governor of Mississippi 1960–64; died 1987.

Nicholas deB. Katzenbach (Katzenbach)—early forties—Assistant U.S. Attorney General 1961–62; Deputy U.S. Attorney General 1962–64; died 2012.

TV commentator—mid-fifties—male.

Newscaster—late thirties—male.

Jerome Smith—early twenties—activist; participant in the Freedom Rides.

George Wallace [Archival Audio] (Wallace)—early forties—Governor of Alabama 1962–66, 1970–78, 1982–86; shot and paralyzed in an assassination attempt, 1972; died 1998.

TV announcer—early forties—male.

Myrlie Evers—early thirties—activist; author; wife of Medgar Evers; Chair of the NAACP 1995–98.

James Farmer—early forties—civil rights activist and leader; Director, CORE 1961–66; portrayed by Denzel Whitaker in the 2007 film *The Great Debaters*; died 1999.

House Committee Chairman—late forties—male.

Senate Committee Chairman—late fifties—male.

Erich Leinsdorf [Archival Audio] (Leinsdorf)—Austrian-born American conductor; Music Director of the Boston Symphony Orchestra, 1962–69; died 1993.

Lyndon Baines Johnson (LBJ)—mid-fifties–late fifties—U.S. Senator from Texas 1949–61, and presidential candidate; Vice President of the U.S. 1961–63; President 1963–69; died 1973.

Campaign Manager [see Seigenthaler, above].

Charles Evers—mid-forties—activist and political figure; brother of Medgar Evers; leader of the Mississippi branch of the NAACP after his brother's death; first African-American mayor of a racially mixed southern city (Fayette, MS).

Edward M. Kennedy (Teddy Kennedy)—early thirties—Democratic Senator from Massachusetts 1963–2009; died 2009.

Nelson Rockefeller—late fifties—Republican Governor of New York 1959–73; Vice President of the United States 1974–77; died 1979.

Dwight D. Eisenhower—late seventies—President of the United States 1953–61; U.S. Army 1915–53; died 1969.

Peter Edelman—late twenties—lawyer; legislative assistant to Sen. Robert Kennedy 1964–68; currently Law Professor at Georgetown University.

George Murphy (Senator Murphy)—mid-sixties—motion picture star; U.S. senator from California 1965–71; died 1992.

Graciela G. Olivarez (Mrs. Olivarez)—late thirties—Mexican-American farmworker and activist; died 1987.

Leroy F. Galyen (Sheriff Galyen)—early fifties—Sheriff of Kern County, CA 1955–67; died 1969.

Dolores Huerta—late thirties—activist and organizer; co-founder of the United Farm Workers of America; originator of the phrase "Si, se puede"; President, the Dolores Huerta Foundation.

Cesar Chavez—late thirties—activist and civil rights leader; co-founder of the United Farm Workers union; died 1993.

Dr. Robert Coles (Dr. Coles)—early thirties—child psychiatrist, author of the Pulitzer Prize-winning series of books, *The Children of Crisis*; Professor Emeritus, Harvard University.

Dr. Raymond Wheeler (Dr. Wheeler)—late forties—North Carolina physician; expert on nutrition and health problems of poor people in the South; died 1982.

Earl Graves—early thirties—publisher; founder of *Black Enterprise* Magazine; administrative assistant to Sen. Robert Kennedy.

Setting

Federal Building at Jackson and Dearborn

Time

1969

About the Play

The Times of London described it as "an amalgam of Arthur Miller's 'The Crucible' and an anarchic Woody Allen comedy." Set against the tumultuous events of 1969 and

1970, this was one of the most unusual courtroom spectacles in American history. The trial was of the so-called "Chicago Seven"—seven radicals accused of conspiring to incite a riot at the 1968 Democratic National Convention in Chicago.

Peter Goodchild has drawn on actual court transcripts for his dramatization, which is juxtaposed with the recollections of many of the key participants, plus the comments of outside observers. These include David Dellenger, Thomas Foran, Gene Fritz, Allen Ginsburg, Tom Hayden, William Kunstler, Bobby Seale, John Schultz, and Studs Terkel.

The following may sound like a surreal broadcast from another planet . . . but, unfortunately, we've become all too familiar with such spectacles. With each passing year, the potential for legal proceedings to turn into a kind of "theatre of the absurd" seems greater than ever . . .

Original Production

The Chicago Conspiracy Trial by Peter Goodchild was originally commissioned and produced by L.A. Theatre Works, a co-production of the BBC and WFMT, Chicago. It was recorded at the WFMT studios in Chicago in May 1993, directed by Martin Jenkins and John Theocharis. The cast was as follows:

Richard Schultz	Tom Amandes
Mayor Daley/Marshal	George Czarnecki
Woman #1	Christine Dunford
Allen Ginsberg	Richard Fire
Judge Hoffman	Kevin Gudahl
Tom Hayden	Gary Houston
Thomas Foran	Tony Mockus
David Dellinger	George Murdock
William Kuntsler	Mike Nussbaum
Woman #2	Peggy Roeder
Abbie Hoffman	David Schwimmer
Leonard Weinglass	Jeff Still
Deputy Mayor Stahl/Hunt	Ron West
Bobby Seale	Ed Wheeler
Pierson/Frapolly	Andrew White

Characters

Judge Julius Hoffman
Jury Members
Richard Schultz
Tom Hayden
William H. Kunstler
Leonard Weinglass
Bobby Seale
Thomas Foran
Marshals
Narrator
Kristi A. King
Ruth Peterson
Clerk
Robert Pierson
William Frapolly
J.M. Hunt
Allen Ginsberg
Linda Morse
Abbie Hoffman
Mayor Daley
Rennie Davis
Spectators
James Riordan
Anita Hoffman
Dellinger's Daughter
Foreman (of the Jury)
Newsreader

Scene One

The stage is dark.

Fade up Judy Collins singing "Blowin' in the Wind."

Cross-fade to the sound of chanting.

Voices (*chanting rhythmically to a climax*)   The whole world is watching, the whole world is watching, the whole world is watching, the whole world is watching!

Reveal **Narrator** *to the side of the set.*

Narrator   The whole world was indeed watching at the time of the Chicago Conspiracy Trial, one of the most extraordinary cases in American legal history. This documentary drama is reconstructed from the trial transcripts as well as the views of those who took part—lawyers, jurors, witnesses, journalists, defendants.

Reveal **Dellinger** *in the dock.*

Dellinger   We knew that something serious was going to happen because 1968 had been a catastrophic year already.

Narrator   David Dellinger, radical pacifist, leader of the demonstrations, and defendant in the trial.

Dellinger   There had been bloodshed in the streets of many cities and many campuses. State leaders such as Bobby Kennedy and Martin Luther King had been killed. And now Mayor Daley's administration in Chicago had refused to give permits for demonstrations and broadcasts at the Democratic National Convention which, under the First Amendment, we were legally allowed to hold in Chicago. So we were basically saying that democracy had to be re-born in the streets of Chicago because it had been killed in the White House and in the Senate.

Bring up the original images and sounds of the demonstrations on set screen with newsreader over.

Newsreader   The demonstrators were angered when the police attempted to arrest a young man who tried to rip down an American flag. (*Sounds of explosions.*) The police fired tear gas canisters and the demonstrators threw them back at the police. The battle, Chicago's first real battle of the day, was about to be joined. Many demonstrators, anticipating more tear gas, covered their faces with handkerchiefs. (*The sound of chanting grows.*) When chanting "Kill the Police" began, they began bombarding the police with bottles, cans, boards, fire fighters, and anything they could find. Demonstration leaders, hoping to save energy or that night, used bullhorns to try to restore order.

Bullhorn (*on the soundtrack*)   They are provoking us but we don't want to confront them now. Move back please. Move back please. Move back!

Newsreader Responding to leaders, some of the protestors joined arms attempting to bring the milling crowd under control.

Reveal **Foran** *at the prosecution desk.*

Foran Remember, they were students at the front of the demonstration.

Narrator Thomas Foran, leading Chicago lawyer and attorney for the prosecution

Foran The organizers of the protest really reached out for young kids who were caught up in the hippy movement, and the 1960s assault on authority, and the drug culture, sexual revolution, and all of that.

They were joining together to attack a police force that was made up of a whole bunch of died-the-wool middle class, and when they designed their protest they knew exactly what it would result in. They had worked it all out.

Dellinger It's now thought that we came here only to protest the Vietnam War, but not so.

The mobilization had organized a series of workshops in different centers where women's issues, prison issues, Native American issues, education, all those things were being looked at. And we were going to draw up an alternative platform to that of the Democratic Party. There had been these threats from Mayor Daley against us, but Martin Luther King was assassinated and black riots took place and so the police were more restrained to start with. But then Major Daley bawled them out and said, "Next time, shoot to maim someone who commits a misdemeanor and anyone who commits a felony, shoot to kill."

Reveal **Hayden** *in the dock.*

Hayden The night before the convention, a seventeen-year-old American was shot to death in mysterious circumstances in Lincoln Park.

Narrator Tom Hayden, student leader in the demonstrations and defendant.

Hayden The police then made clear their general intention was to drive the people out of the streets altogether and not even allow them to stay over in the parks. So the line that was drawn was that the streets themselves as well as establishment institutions would be closed to public protest. That was the friction point.

Reveal images and sounds of the angry mob, explosion, chanting.

When the police came, angry words were exchanged, certainly nothing more than bottles. But anyway the police would have attacked with teargas and jeeps mounted with huge concertina wire, and essentially they went beserk. Anybody who was in the way was gassed and clubbed.

Foran Looking back now, all Daley had to do was, for example, the night of the riot in Lincoln Park, was not to have a curfew, let them stay in the park. If anything, just feed them coffee and doughnuts, adding a note of humor to this of course.

Reveal **Schultz** *at the prosecution desk.*

Schultz   There were many speeches given by people in various parts of the U.S.

Narrator   Richard Schultz, assistant attorney for the prosecution.

Schultz   They were telling crowds to come to Chicago and to be prepared to fight the police, force the government to bring out the armed forces. It was a direct, physical, angry attack on the basic method of the selection of the President of the United States.

Narrator   The trial began September 24, 1969. It took some time to decide what the charges should be. But in March 1969 it was agreed that eight defendants should be charged with conspiracy and with crossing state lines and with making speeches with intent to, quote, "incite, organize, promote, encourage anti-war riots."

Reveal **Kunstler.**

Kunstler   The intention of the Justice Department was purely political and symbolic, and their choices had little to do with what the indivduals had done.

Narrator   William Kunstler, Civil Rights activist, radical lawyer, and attorney for the defence.

Kunstler   They chose a Black Panther, they chose a head of the national movement against the Vietnam War, and they chose a couple of people who were associated with militant student movements. Finally, they chose a couple of people associated with the so-called counter-culture-the Yippies. And that was the conspiracy.

Narrator   For the next five months the Chicago Conspiracy Trial commanded the attention of a deeply divided nation. John Schultz, journalist and local historian.

The whole set is revealed showing preparations for the arrival of the judge.

The screen shows exterior views of the federal building.

John Schultz   The federal building in Chicago was a steel and glass skyscraper in the downtown area. On the twenty-third floor was the courtroom of Judge Julius Hoffman.

He walks through the court.

As a member of the press, I came through the door at the side of the courtroom and I would first find myself looking down into the face of a light-coloured black man-slim, a marshal, a former Harlem Globetrotter. I look up into the courtroom that is walnut paneling, and the first thing I would feel is the nightmarish involvement of everyone present. And that's not a little caused by the emotional involvement of the judge, Julius Jennings Hoffman, who was at the head of the courtroom on the bench under the seal of the United States.

On my right were the eight defendants and at the defense table, their two lawyers, William Kunstler and his assistant, Leonard Weinglass.

To our left would be the prosecution table and here the head prosecutor Thomas Foran and his assistant, Richard Schultz, sat along with two FBI agents who were helping them.

The jurors were ten women and two men, two black women among the women. Virtually all of them were from Cook County suburb. The spectators' and the journalists' benches were usually full. And amongst them were a lot of people in favor of the defense, long-haired young people.

What we would be seeing is a stage, a theater, in which a bizarre and political drama concerning a division over the Vietnam War is about to be played out.

Scene Two

Bang on gavel.

Judge Hoffman Good morning, members of the jury.

Jury Good morning, Your Honor.

Judge Hoffman You are to lead for the government, Mr. Schultz, and will now outline that case.

Richard Schultz Thank you, Your Honor. Ladies and gentlemen of the jury, the government will prove in this case that the eight defendants planned to bring people into Chicago to create a riot—create a situation in this city where these people would come to Chicago, would riot, and the defendants, in perpetrating this offence, crossed state lines, at least six of them with the intent to conspire together to make this riot during the Democratic National Convention of August 1968. We will prove, ladies and gentlemen of the jury, that the defendant David Dellinger, who sits there, the defendant Rennard Davies, who sits next to him—(*Mixed reaction, largely amused, as* **Tom Hayden** *stands and makes the Panther salute.*)—and Thomas Hayden, who is standing, that these three . . .

Judge Hoffman Who is the last defendant you named?

Richard Schultz Mr. Hayden, Your Honor.

Reaction.

Judge Hoffman Let it be noted that he raised his fist in salute in the direction of the jury.

Hayden That is my customary greeting, Your Honor.

Judge Hoffman It may be your customary greeting, but we do not allow shaking of fists in this courtroom.

Hayden I implied no disrespect for the jury, it is my . . .

Judge Hoffman Regardless of what it implies, sir, there will be no fist shaking and I caution you not to repeat it. That applies to all of the defendants. You may proceed, Mr. Schultz.

The court reacts to this exchange.

Richard Schultz   Thank you, Your Honor. In promoting and encouraging this riot, the three men I have just mentioned used an organization, which they called the National Mobilization Committee, to end the war in Vietnam. They were joined by five other defendants to create the riots in Chicago at the time of the Democratic National Convention and two of these defendants, Abbie Hoffman who sits . . .

Abbie Hoffman *blows a kiss at the jury. Another largely amused reaction from the crowd.*

Richard Schultz   . . . who is just standing for you, ladies and gentlemen.

Judge Hoffman   The jury is directed to disregard the kiss thrown by the defendant Hoffman, and the defendant is directed not to do that sort of thing again.

Richard Schultz   And with them, a man named Jerry Rubin who is standing here— these two men called themselves leaders of the Yippies. Two more of these individuals are Lee Weener . . .

Weiner   Weiner!

Richard Schultz   . . . Lee Weiner, who just stood, who calls himself a Professor at Northwestern University, and John L. Froines, who is an Assistant Professor of Chemistry at the University of Oregon. And Weener and Froines joined . . .

Weiner   Weiner!

Richard Schultz   . . . joined with David Dellinger and Hayden. And the last person who joined is a man named Bobby Seale . . .

Reaction to **Seale** *waving to the court.*

Richard Schultz   . . . who is now waving to the court. And the government will prove that each of these eight men assumed specific roles and conspired together to encourage people to riot during the Convention. We will prove that the plans to incite the riot were in three basic steps. The first was to use the unpopularity of the Vietnam War . . . to urge people to come to Chicago during the Convention for the purposes of protest. The second step was to incite these people . . . against the police department, the city officials, the National Guard, the military, and against the Convention itself, so that these people would physically resist and defy the orders of the police and the military. Third, we will prove that the defendants made unreasonable demands upon the city of Chicago for certain permits, to allow thousands to sleep in city parks, and during these negotiations the defendant Rubin told Mr. Stahl, the Administrative Assistant to the Mayor of Chicago, "We came to fight in this city and tear up the town and the Convention." And, we will prove that the defendant Bobby Seale flew into Chicago to give a speech to a crowd in which he incited to attack, and he said, I quote, "If a pig comes up to us unjustly, we should bring out our pieces and start barbecuing that pork, and if they get in our way, we should kill some of those pigs and put them on the morgue slab." (*Low reaction.*) The defendant Dellinger was the principal architect of the riots which occurred on that Wednesday, August 28th. He led a so-called peaceful march taking police away from areas where guerilla action had been planned. And as the march assembled, the defendant Hayden said to the crowd, "Make sure that if blood is to flow, let it flow all over the city." The crowd then broke up. Thousands of screaming demonstrators blocked the streets and refused to clear them. They ignored police orders and the riot broke out at about eight o'clock on Wednesday night. In sum, then, ladies and gentlemen of the jury, we will prove that the eight defendants charged here conspired together to use interstate commerce to incite and further a riot in Chicago. Thank you.

Judge Hoffman   Is it the desire of any lawyer of a defendant to make an opening statement?

Kunstler   I would remind Your Honor, it is 12:30—time for the lunch break.

Judge Hoffman (*angrily*)   I watch the clock, Mr. er—er—

Kunstler   Kunstler, sir.

Judge Hoffman   And I do the driving, Mr. er—er—. Proceed

Kunstler   Ladies and gentlemen of the jury, my name is William H. Kunstler, and I am one of the attorneys for the defense in this case, along with my colleague Mr. Leonard Weinglass. We hope to prove before you that this prosecution which you are hearing is the result of two motives on the part of the government . . .

Richard Schultz (*always the terrier*)   Objection as to any motives of the prosecution.

Judge Hoffman   Sustained. You may speak to the guilt or innocence of your client, not to the motive of the government.

Kunstler   Your Honor, I have always thought that . . .

Judge Hoffman   I sustain the objection, regardless of what you have always thought, Kunstler.

Kunstler   The evidence we produce will show that the defendants came to Chicago in the summer of 1968 to protest in the finest American tradition. They were conscious of their rights as citizens to so demonstrate and protest, and it was their purpose to do exactly that. At the same time, the evidence will show that there were forces in this city and in the national government who were absolutely determined to prevent this type of protest and we hope to show by our evidence that what actually happened was not a riot caused by demonstrators but a riot engineered by the police of this city. (*Reaction.*) These demonstrators, as the evidence will show, came to demonstrate meaningfully against the war in Vietnam and join those who throughout history have faced the violation of their rights this time by the billy clubs wielded indiscriminately against the demonstrators, newsmen, women, children, men young and old, here in the streets of Chicago. Dissent did die here during the Convention. What happens in this case may determine whether it is moribund.

Schultz   Objection, Your Honor.

Judge Hoffman   Sustained. I direct the jury to disregard that last statement. Is there any other defense lawyer . . .?

There is a reaction as **Seale** *moves to the lectern.*

Judge Hoffman   Just a minute, sir, who is your lawyer?

Seale   Charles R. Garry.

Foran   Your Honor, may we have the jury excused?

Judge Hoffman   Ladies and gentlemen, I am sorry, I will have to excuse you. Mr. Marshal.

Jury starts to leave.

Marshal   Yes, Your Honor.

Judge Hoffman   Show the jury out.

Sounds of jury leaving.

Judge Hoffman   Now, Mr. Kunstler, do you represent Mr. Seale?

Kunstler   No, Your Honor, as far as Mr. Seale has indicated to me, that because of the absence of his lawyer, Charles R. Garry, who is in the hospital for a life-saving operation . . .

Judge Hoffman   Have you filed for his appearance?

Kunstler   Filed whose appearance?

Judge Hoffman   The appearance for Mr. Seale.

Kunstler   I have filed an appearance for Mr. Seale.

Judge Hoffman   All right, I will permit you to make another opening statement on behalf of Mr. Seale if you like.

Kunstler   Your Honor, I cannot compromise Mr. Seale's position. I am not his lawyer.

Judge Hoffman   I don't ask you to compromise it, sir, but I will not permit him to address the jury with a very competent lawyer seated here.

Kunstler   If I were to make an opening statement, I would compromise his position that he has not his full counsel here.

Judge Hoffman   Bring in the jury, Mr. Marshal.

Jury returns.

Seale   If my constitutional rights are denied, I can only see you as a blatant racist.

Jury freezes.

Judge Hoffman   Just a minute! Watch what you say, sir! Mr. Seale, you are not to make an opening statement. I so order you. You are not permitted to in the circumstances of this case.

Seale   I insist on Charles R. Garry as my chief counsel. I have fired all the others and you have refused to postpone this trial until my counsel is fit to attend.

Judge Hoffman   I do not recognize the function of chief counsel or trial teams in my court. This is not a baseball game.

Lighting down on the main set. **Weinglass** *moves to the side of the set followed by* **Kunstler**. *At the same time a female jury member moves downstage on the opposite side.*

John Schultz   Julius Jennings Hoffman may have been a short slight man but what he lacked in stature he made up with his wonderfully expressive voice.

He read the indictment with such flair that William here stood and objected to his reading it in the manner of Orson Welles. Hoffman beamed and said "I have never been so complimented as to be compared as to one of America's greatest actors."

Juror   Mr Magoo was what we jurors called him. A very brilliant man. You think he's sleeping and yet he hears every single word that is going on. Nothing he missed, nothing. A very unfair man, he never gave the defense a chance. Always for the prosecution.

Kunstler   And yet he was not the real villain. He was programmed to react to these defendants- to be afraid of them, to be told by the FBI agents to be prepared to slap them down on every instant when he thought they needed it. He went into that courtroom believing he was going to be victimized by these men unless he did something quickly to establish full control.

Dellinger   He totally and arbitrarily believed in what he considered were American values, which stood against everything we believed and stood for, and so there was a complete plain-out of generation gaps and communication gap, and a credibility gap.

Foran   When we were choosing the jury, I could have killed Judge Hoffman when he said, "I don't know whether any of you people have formed previous ideas of the guilt or innocence of these defenders." And 95 percent of these people raised their hands, and they were all my people on the side of the prosecution, but because they had already formed an opinion I was not allowed to use them. The ones who were pro the defendants were not so scrupulous as to tell the truth about what their prejudices were and I thought where am I going from here? The jury choice was no easy thing for the prosecution.

Speakers return to the main set.

Narrator   Sufficiently difficult, in fact, for the defense to begin to suspect that the prosecution was sabotaging the jury. On Monday, September 29, the prosecution and defense spent the morning in private session with the judge. Threatening letters had been ostensibly delivered to some of the jurors. The defense had already sensed that certain jurors were favorable to their cause—one young woman in a miniskirt had been noticed carrying a book by the black writer Jesse Baldwin. Kunstler was anxious not to lose her support, but the prosecution had noticed her too

Scene Three

Judge Hoffman   You are Miss, is it Kristi A. King?

King That's right.

Judge Hoffman Now, Miss King, the government is investigating certain letters alleged to have been received by certain jurors, including yourself. Will you look at government's Exhibit A and let me know if you have seen it at any time, Mr. Marshal.

King No, sir, I haven't.

Judge Hoffman And did any member of your family bring it to your attention or not?

King No, sir.

Judge Hoffman All right, read it, Miss King. Read it, please.

King It says, "You are being watched. The Black Panthers." It's addressed to the King family. (*She is obviously shocked.*)

Judge Hoffman This letter was received by your family who informed the FBI. Now, having seen it, Miss King, do you think you can continue to be a fair and impartial juror in this case? Do you still think you can do that?

King No, sir.

Judge Hoffman What did you say?

King No, sir.

Judge Hoffman You do not think so?

King No.

Kunstler Your Honor, I must make an objection for the record. This juror had never seen this letter before Your Honor showed it to her.

Judge Hoffman Earlier, I asked you for suggestions as to how to proceed.

Weinglass But as a matter of law, the asking of a single question of a juror is not sufficient.

Judge Hoffman That refers to prospective jurors, not someone already a member of the jury.

Weinglass But we are addressing the same issue, getting a fair panel. I will not mention the words fair trial, I know that disturbs the court.

Judge Hoffman A juror's statement under oath is sufficient.

Weinglass Your Honor . . .

Judge Hoffman Miss King, you are excused, Alternate juror Kay Richards will be substituted. So now let the juror Ruth Peterson take the witness box. You are Ruth L. Peterson?

Peterson Yes, I am.

Judge Hoffman Have you seen that document before?

Peterson Yes, it came in the mail two days ago. Then I gave it to you this morning.

Judge Hoffman And having seen it, do you still feel you can fulfill your role as a fair and impartial juror?

Peterson Yes.

Judge Hoffman (*surprised*) You do?

Peterson Yes, I think it is my duty to.

Judge Hoffman Have you discussed this letter with your fellow jurors?

Peterson Only one, Mrs. Mildred Burns—but I did not discuss its contents.

Kunstler The defense calls for the replacement of this juror.

Richard Schultz Her actions in discussing the letter with Mrs. Burns have been insignificant, Your Honor.

Judge Hoffman All right, this juror will be permitted to remain.

Kunstler Your Honor, the defendants believe those two letters were in fact sent by some agent of the government in order to prejudice these two jurors further in this trial.

Judge Hoffman I will let you try to prove that right now. That is a very grave charge against an officer of the government.

Kunstler Well, we obviously can't prove it, Your Honor.

Judge Hoffman Then don't say it!

Kunstler Once Miss Kristi King was off the jury, the judge then refused to let us have a hearing on who actually wrote that Black Panther letter. It was crazy that the Black Panthers would send a letter because their hero, Bobby Seale, agreed Kristi was great and we all wanted her. But the government obviously wanted to get rid of her, being a young person the same age as the defendants and a danger to them. Instead it had Kay Richards who was really a secret agent working for the prosecution.

Narrator Following the Black Panther scam, the judge ordered the jury to be sequestered, almost completely isolated from their everyday lives, for the entire five months of the trial. This was to have a profound effect.

Juror We couldn't listen to the radio, watch the news on TV, or read the papers. At night marshals sat outside our doors. They could have let us read some of the newspapers. There was no need for this. At night we could go to the movies, that's all there was, and all there was to see was James Bond stuff.

The first two months of the trial we were never allowed to go home, we could only have visits at weekends, and that was only three hours in the presence of a marshal. It was like a police state and that is how we lived for six months. After the trial it was just as scary. Neighbors wouldn't have anything to do with us, and we had death threats.

Narrator The heart of the government case was to be presented through the testimony of three undercover agents, but their first witness was David Stahl, Mayor Daley's Deputy.

Scene Four

Stahl *approaches the witness stand.*

Foran Mr. Stahl, as Mayor Daley's Deputy and administrative officer, you were responsible for the issuing of permits giving authority for public gatherings in this city.

Stahl I was.

Foran Were you present at a meeting on August 7, 1968 with the defendants Abbie Hoffman and Jerry Rubin, together with several of their supporters and a photographer from *Life* Magazine?

Stahl I was. Mr. Rubin started in by saying they were going to begin their Festival of Light by holding defense classes in case of police action. He said that Chicago had a reputation for being a hostile system. Abbie Hoffman then said that he was prepared to tear up the town and the Convention, and that he was prepared to die in Lincoln Park. He said their festival would include body-painting, nude-ins at the beaches, public fornication, discussion of the draft, and draft evasion.

Foran Now, to the meeting on August 26, 1968. Who was present there?

Stahl Only one of the defendants, Mr. Dillinger . . .

Kunstler It's Dellinger, Your Honor.

Judge Hoffman Derringer?

Foran Dellinger.

Stahl The defendant told me he had recently returned from Paris where he had been to study street riots by students. He said a permit to allow sleeping in the park was essential to minimizing destruction. There was much anger at the arrest of Tom Hayden and that anger was going to seek expression. He ended by asking for a meeting with the Mayor.

Foran That's all, Your Honor.

Judge Hoffman Mr. Weintraub.

Weinglass Weinglass, Your Honor. Mr. Stahl, you are appointed and subject to removal by the Mayor.

Stahl That is correct.

Weinglass On August 21, a week before the march, was Mayor Daley not reported as saying that an ounce of prevention was worth a pound of cure? Do you recall that statement?

Stahl Not exactly, but he would have believed it, I know.

Weinglass Then don't you think an ounce of prevention could have been to say, yes, let the people sleep in the park and issue the necessary permit?

Stahl No, I don't think so, Mr. Feinglass. You have got to be responsible in government. You can't afford the liberal luxury of saying, "Be more and more permissive, let anything go on." With major political figures our responsibility, we didn't want another Robert Kennedy assassination, another girl supporter of Senator McCarthy killed in the middle of the night. We didn't want that to happen so it didn't happen.

Clerk (*off mike, approaching the judge*) Your Honor, there is an emergency motion here. It is to disqualify the judge, Your Honor.

Judge Hoffman I have read it carefully.

Kunstler I understand sir, but . . .

Judge Hoffman I have read every line of it, Mr. Kunstler.

Kunstler But I think it is important to indicate generally to the court what is in it. It refers to an incident before Mr. Weinglass's opening address, Your Honor. When, according to a newspaper reporter, you were heard to say in the elevator, "Now we are going to hear this wild man, Weinglass." If that statement is correct, Your Honor, then we think that statement indicates a prejudice on your part against one of the trial counsel which cannot but affect the defendants in this case.

Judge Hoffman Madam Clerk, the motion to disqualify the Honorable Julius J. Hoffman as judge in this case, will be denied because the papers filed do not state the grounds for the relief sought. Continue Mr. Weinglass.

The courtroom reacts, but **Weinglass** *continues.*

Weinglass At your meeting of August 7, you say Mr. Hoffman told you he was prepared to tear up the town and that he was willing to die in Lincoln Park. Mr. Hoffman was not alone at that meeting was he?

Stahl That is correct.

Weinglass Do you recall telling the FBI in October 1968, when they interviewed you about this meeting, that you could not recall which individual made which statement on August 7?

Stahl Yes.

Weinglass So can you explain to us how you didn't know who made what statement in October, just about three months after August yet now you can recall, very explicitly, one year later what was said?

Stahl Well, I have had a great deal of time to reflect, to look back at my notes, and now to the best of my recollection, I can identify statements with particular individuals.

Weinglass Look back over your notes, then, and tell the jury where in those notes you say who did what.

Kunstler The judge paid particular attention to Leonard, by never pronouncing his name correctly, always calling him Weinburg, and Weinross, things like that. To such a degree, that Abbie Hoffman made a sign "Weinglass" and every time the judge would mispronounce his name he would hold it up in the way that they do in TV studios to make the audience applaud, to make the judge pronounce his name properly.

Scene Five

Kunstler *returns to his desk, while* **Pierson** *makes his way to the witness stand.*

Narrator The first of the prosecution's undercover witnesses to be called was Robert Pierson.

Schultz You are Robert Pierson and you work for the Chicago Police Department.

Pierson Yes.

Schultz Did you in any way alter your physical appearance to conduct your assignment as undercover investigator?

Pierson Yes, sir, I did. I allowed my hair to grow long, I didn't shave for four to six weeks, I purchased the attire of a motorcycle gangmember and I rented a motorcycle, in order to join a group of bikers known as The Head-Hunters.

Schultz Calling your attention to Monday August 26, were you in Lincoln Park?

Pierson Yes, I went to the park with two of the Head-Hunters, Gorilla and Banana. There I was introduced to the defendant Jerry Rubin.

Schultz Can you identify the defendant?

Pierson The defendant is in the yellow and red shirt and black armband. I found myself offering to act as one of his bodyguards. In the park, there were people tacking newspaper articles to the trees, with the headline, "The Battle of Chicago." On the 27th, Rubin said to me, "We have got to create little Chicagos everywhere, we've got to have riots in every city." One of the pictures showed a policeman with a club, Rubin looked at me and said, "Look at that fat pig. We should isolate one or two of them and kill them."

Schultz And what did you say?

Pierson I agreed with him. And then we went over to join some of their marshals and Rubin said, "We've got to do more to keep the crowd active so that we hold the park tonight," and "we want them in the park for the Bobby Seale speech tonight."

Seale   I object on the ground that my lawyer, Charles R. Garry, is not here, Your Honor, and I want my lawyer here to speak when he mentions my name and testifies against me.

Judge Hoffman   Ask him to sit down, Mr. Marshal, please.

Marshal   Sit down, Mr. Seale.

Judge Hoffman   His lawyer is Mr. Kunstler who has filed his written appearance.

Richard Schultz   Your Honor, this little episode, for the benefit of the jury, is intended simply to misconstrue the fact that this man originally had four lawyers to start with—in fact it went to five . . .

Kunstler   Your Honor, I object to calling it a little episode for the benefit of the jury. That is obviously an attempt to prejudice and inflame the jury. I think he should be admonished for it.

Judge Hoffman   You say prejudice and inflame the jury. One of your clients spoke first. I will direct the . . .

Kunstler   He made an honest effort to speak. He attempted . . .

Judge Hoffman   I will direct the jury to disregard the incident, but I shall deal appropriately with it in due course.

Kunstler   I make an objection to Your Honor's last remark.

Judge Hoffman   I overrule your objection, sir.

Richard Schultz   And so, what happened next, Mr. Pierson?

Pierson   Well, they were talking about a meeting Abbie Hoffman had had earlier in the day with a black gang called the Blackstone Rangers. The Rangers had agreed to come and help hold the park and fight the pigs, but Rubin doubted they would come. He asked me what I thought and I said I agreed with him.

Schultz   Mr. Pierson, do you recall anything of any speeches made by Bobby Seale?

Pierson   Yes, sir, he said that the time for singing "We Shall Overcome" is past, that now is the time to act, to go buy a .45 and a carbine and kill the pigs, that we've got to create guerrilla warfare everywhere.

Schultz   No further questions, Your Honor.

Judge Hoffman   Your witness, Mr. Weinglass.

Weinglass   Now, Mr. Pierson, at some time during your period in Lincoln Park, you were yourself struck by a police club?

Pierson   Yes, sir, I was.

Weinglass   How many times did that occur?

Pierson   Two or three times.

Weinglass   At that time, were you throwing rocks?

Pierson   No, I was not.

Weinglass   Did you ever throw rocks at the police during any of those days in the park?

Pierson   Yes, I did.

Weinglass   You volunteered for this undercover assignment, didn't you?

Pierson   Yes, sir, I did.

Weinglass   You testified that at a given point, Jerry Rubin told you that Abbie Hoffman had arranged for the Blackstone Rangers to come to fight in the park.

Pierson   Yes

Weinglass   If I can read your evidence to the FBI two months after the Convention, you said you were—and I quote—"never able to observe anything that would lead you to believe that any Negro group in fact joined forces with the Yippies to help hold the park." Close quotes.

Richard Schultz   Objection. That statement in no way contradicts testimony on what the witness was told by Jerry Rubin.

Judge Hoffman   I strike the question and direct the jury to disregard it.

Weinglass   Mr. Pierson, you also testified that erry Rubin said that—and I quote—"we should isolate one or two of the pigs and kill them." Is that correct?

Pierson   That is correct, sir.

Weinglass   By the Wednesday had the phrase "kill the pig" become as meaningless as "kill the umpire" at a baseball game?

Richard Schultz   I object, if the court please, this is not a baseball game.

Judge Hoffman   I sustain the objection

Weinglass   Now, Mr. Pierson, do you recall Bobby Seale in his speech late in the afternoon of the 27 August specifically saying, "Kill the pigs"?

Pierson   I recall his making reference to killing the pigs, yes.

Weinglass   Do you recall that reference being made in this context in Mr. Seale's speech, and I quote, "This is not even a Convention. It is a giant pig-pen. The city itself is flushed with pigs everywhere. Black people seem to be lost in a world of white, decadent, racist America. What I'm saying is we've a right to defend ourselves as human beings, and if some pig comes up to us unjustly, and treats us unjustly, then we have to bring our pieces out and start barbecuing some of that pork." Wasn't that the context?

Pierson   You said those words, "barbecuing some pork." That means killing the pigs, and that is how I reported it.

Weinglass   So you understand "barbecuing the pork" to mean "kill the pigs"?

Pierson Most assuredly.

Weinglass You can't say now that Bobby Seale ever said "kill the pigs"?

Richard Schultz If the court please, the witness has testified that was his recollection, his interpretation. Now . . .

Weinglass His interpretation.

Richard Schultz Now, Mr. Weinglass is . . .

Weinglass Not his recollection. I think Mr. Schultz points out a very interesting distinction.

Richard Schultz Now, Mr. Weinglass is saying, "Well did he use the words 'kill the pigs'"? The witness has said "no" and now he is asking him again.

Weinglass The witness . . .

Richard Schultz I object, if the court please, we have been through it.

Judge Hoffman I sustain the objection.

Weinglass Did Bobby Seale ever call for the assassination of Mayor Daley in his speech?

Pierson Well, we have to go down two more sentences in this report of what Bobby Seale said, "It is now our turn to kill and maim."

Weinglass Does he talk about killing and maiming political leaders?

Pierson Well, my recollection is that he was calling for both.

Weinglass And Bobby Seale used the words "to kill and maim"?

Pierson His speech had the words "barbecuing pork", which in my interpretation is killing the pigs.

Weinglass Now, Wednesday the 28th, you joined Jerry Rubin in Grant Park where there was a flag-lowering incident.

Pierson There were objects thrown at the police

Weinglass Wasn't the crowd reacting to the manner and the method used by the police in arresting the individual who had tried to lower the flag?

Schultz Objection.

Judge Hoffman I sustain the objection.

Weinglass Now, did you see the demonstrators' own marshals form a human line between the crowd and the police?

Pierson Yes, sir, I did.

Weinglass You saw the police come into the crowd?

Pierson Yes, sir.

Weinglass Can you tell the jury in what manner the police came into the crowd?

Pierson In a wedge-type formation.

Weinglass Did you see anyone get hit in the head with a club?

Pierson I saw clubs swing at people's heads.

Weinglass They were swinging their clubs over their heads and down on the demonstrators.

Pierson Yes, sir.

Weinglass Isn't it a fact, Officer Pierson, that the police charged into the crowd after the marshals had formed their human line, and the demonstrators had receded and quiet was restored?

Pierson No, sir, I don't recall it happening that way.

Weinglass Isn't it a fact, Officer Pierson, that your mission failed?

Schultz Objection, if the court please.

Judge Hoffman I sustain the objection.

Weinglass No matter what you did during those days, with Jerry Rubin and the others, you failed to encourage him or the others to throw even a pebble? Isn't that correct?

Pierson No, sir, that is not correct. I never tried to encourage him or the others to do anything of the sort.

Weinglass I have completed my cross-examination.

Foran *steps forward for an aside to the audience.*

Foran There was activity by a substantial number of the police who did not act professionally. But I don't think they instigated it. They were provoked by these defendants. For someone to walk up to a policeman and call them a pig and spit on them—it hardly surprises me that a policeman will sock them one.

Foran *returns to his desk.*

Scene Six

Kunstler Your Honor, we have made a motion for the suspension of the final schedule for tomorrow, based on the fact that tomorrow has been declared to be a day called Vietnam Moratorium. Its purpose, Your Honor, is to protest the continuation of the war in Vietnam and to urge American withdrawal. And, in passing, Your Honor ought to know that there are at least eighteen United States Senators and forty-seven Congressmen in direct support of this Moratorium. On the legal side of it, it is not unusual for courts to close in situations of this sort. Just recently, when President Eisenhower died, there was a . . .

Judge Hoffman Well, I have received no further order from the Executive or from the President, so I feel I am therefore without the authority to allow this motion.

Foran Your Honor, the government feels that there is some evidence, already presented, that these men have cynically used two tragic issues of American society, the war and the tragic flaw of American character, racism, to generate for themselves the right to tear down the legal and formal structure of the government of the United States. That these men with such cynicism should ask . . .

Kunstler Your Honor, this is no answer to a motion. A political speech is being given here.

Judge Hoffman I think yours was just a touch political, Mr. Kunstler.

Kunstler If Your Honor please, this is just a personal attack on these defendants who are making what is, I think, a rather fervent request before Your Honor. And if the courts can close for the death of one man, then they ought to close for the death of thousands whose lives have been corrupted and lost in this utter horror that goes on in your name and my name . . .

Judge Hoffman Not in my name.

Kunstler It is in your name too.

Judge Hoffman You just include yourself. Don't join me with you. Goodness, don't you and I . . .

Kunstler You are a citizen in the way I am a citizen.

Judge Hoffman Only because you are a member of the bar of this court am I obligated to hear you respectfully, as I have done.

Kunstler But we are citizens of the United States and it is done in Judge Hoffman's name and . . .

Judge Hoffman That will be all, sir. I shall hear you no further. The defendant's motion for adjournment will be denied.

Dellinger *moves down to the defense table, followed by other defendants, carrying the two flags.* **Dellinger** *moves to one side and addresses the audience.*

Dellinger At this time in the trial, the truth of My Lai and the massacre by U.S. troops there was just coming out. Over a million Americans in the largest protest in our country were gathering all over the country and in Washington, D.C. This is the kind of protest we have hoped for in Chicago the year previously but was blocked by the Chicago authorities.

So, before the court began, we tried to arrange a symbolic peace gesture in the court, by laying the American and the Vietnamese flags next to each other and then begin to read the names of the war dead. First an American then a Vietnamese name, then an American.

Scene Seven

Press conference at lunchtime: the defense, joined by **Dellinger** *and other defendants, begin intoning the names and laying out the flags. Son Lee—July 15, 1965; John Brown—December 2, 1968; Thai Trin—March 14, 1966; Travis Crocket—December 23, 1968.*

Marshal   Take that thing off the table.

Abbie Hoffman   We have a right to have it if we want to.

Marshal   Take those things away!

There is continuing disturbance in court.

Dellinger   Mr. Hoffman, we are observing the moratorium.

Judge Hoffman   I am Judge Hoffman, sir.

Dellinger   I believe in equality, sir, so I prefer to call people Mr. or by their first name.

Judge Hoffman   Sit down.

Kunstler   I wanted to explain that we were reading the names of the war dead from both sides.

Marshal   Sit down. Over here, sit down.

Kunstler   Your Honor, just one preliminary application. The defendants, who were not permitted by Your Honor to be absent today for the moratorium, have brought in an American flag and a North Vietnamese flag, which they placed upon the counsel table. The marshal has just removed both of them.

Judge Hoffman   We have an American flag in the corner. Haven't you seen it during the three and a half weeks you have been here?

Kunstler   Your Honor, I am applying for permission to have both flags on moratorium day.

Judge Hoffman   That permission is denied. That is a table for the defendants and their lawyers and it is not to be decorated.

Abbie Hoffman   We don't consider this table a part of the court and we want to furnish it in our own way.

Judge Hoffman   I will ask you to sit down. Bring in the jury, Mr. Marshal.

There is reaction in the court as the jury starts coming in.

Dellinger   We would like to propose . . .

Foran   If the court please . . .

Dellinger   A moment of silence.

Foran Your Honor, this man . . .

Judge Hoffman Mr. Marshal, take out the jury.

There is hilarity and jeering at this.

Dellinger (*to jury*) We only wanted a moment of silence.

Foran Your Honor, I object to this man speaking out in court.

Kunstler Your Honor, I just want to object to Mr. Foran yelling in the presence of the jury. You have admonished us often enough.

Foran Your Honor, that is outrageous. This man is a mouthpiece, look at him, wearing a black armband like his clients.

Kunstler Your Honor, I think the temper and tone of voice and the expression of Mr. Foran's face speaks more than any picture could tell.

Foran Of my contempt for you, Mr. Kunstler.

Kunstler To call me a mouthpiece, and for Your Honor not to open his mouth and say that this is not to be done in your court, I think violates the sanctity of this court. I am wearing an armband in memoriam for the dead, Your Honor, which is no disgrace to this country. I want him admonished, Your Honor. I request that you do that. The word "mouthpiece" is a contemptuous term.

Judge Hoffman Let the record show I do not admonish the United States attorney because he was properly representing his client, the United States of America.

Kunstler To call another attorney a mouthpiece and a disgrace for wearing . . .

Judge Hoffman To place the flag of an enemy country . . .

Kunstler No, Your Honor, there is no declared war.

Hayden Are you at war with Vietnam?

Judge Hoffman Any country that . . . Bring in the jury. I don't want . . .

Kunstler Are you turning down my request after this disgraceful episode? You are not going to say anything?

Judge Hoffman I not only turn it down, I ignore it.

Kunstler That speaks louder than words too, Your Honor.

Judge Hoffman Let that appear on record, the last words of Mr. Kunstler, and Miss Reporter, be very careful to have them on record.

Narrator The trial had now entered another phase, to become a political confrontation between the government and the defendants, and not just, as Hoffman called it, "Another criminal trial."

Throughout, Bobby Seale had remained aloof—frequently reading—but on the afternoon of October 20, he handed a paper to the clerk.

Scene Eight

Clerk   Your Honor, there is a motion here from defendant Bobby Seale to defend himself.

Judge Hoffman (*almost in a tone of consideration*)   I will hear you, Mr. Seale.

Seale   I have the constitutional right to defend myself. I ask for relief of bail, so I can interview witnesses and pursue factual research. I am not playing no game, with my life being stuck on the line!

Richard Schultz   This is a ploy. It's just a simple obvious ploy. Of course it's true that an individual has a right, if he wants, to defend himself, but he can't under the circumstances in this case fire four lawyers, and then say, "I want this one or I won't go ahead," and what's more, saying that in the middle of the trial. And they know perfectly well, as he is not a lawyer, there would be errors within two minutes and we would have a mistrial and there would be nothing we could do about it. It's a game they're playing with the court.

Seale   Your Honor, I did not make my request in the middle of the trial, but as soon as I knew the situation. Mr. Garry told me on the Thursday night, September 25, that he had to enter hospital or risk his life. The next morning, I asked to defend myself. This idea of a ploy and all, this is not true.

Judge Hoffman   As I see it, the defendant Seale is defended by competent counsel who has filed his appearance on Mr. Seal's behalf. So the motion by defendant Bobby Seale to appear "pro se" will be denied, as will his release on bail. Will you bring in the jury, Mr. Marshal?

Sounds of the jury coming in.

Seale   I would like to say, judge, that you denied my motion to defend myself and you know this jury is prejudiced against me.

Judge Hoffman   I will ask you to sit down.

Seale   You know that the jury can't go home to their loved ones and their homes, because of the phony Panther scare, and you know they have been made prejudiced against me.

Judge Hoffman   Ladies and gentlemen of the jury, you are excused.

The jury, perplexed, start to leave. The court is abuzz with anticipation.

Seale   I should be allowed to defend myself. I should be allowed to speak so I can defend myself.

Marshal   Be quiet.

Seale   Don't tell me to shut up. I got a right to speak. I want to represent myself. The Jury is prejudiced against me all right and you know it because of those so called jive threatening letters. How can they give me a fair trial?

Judge Hoffman   I will not argue with you. Mr. Marshal, direct that man to be quiet.

Seale I still want to defend myself and I know I have a right. (*Turning to the prosecution.*) I just want to let him know, That racist. That fascist...

Richard Schultz If the Court please, this man has repeatedly called me a racist.

Seale Yes you are. You are, Dick Schultz.

Rchultz And called Mr. Foran a racist.

Judge Hoffman Mr. Seale, I must admonish you that such outbursts are considered by the court to be contemptuous and will be dealt with appropriately in the future.

Kunstler Your Honor, the defendant was trying to defend himself.

Judge Hoffman The defendant was not defending himself.

Richard Schultz If the court please, this show has pointed up the reasons why Mr. Seale should not defend himself.

Judge Hoffman I admonish you, Mr. Seale, and you will be dealt with appropriately in the future. The court will recess till two o'clock.

The lights dim on the courtroom. **Foran** *moves to the side, while the screen shows images of the court house and the events outside it. He is followed by* **Richard Schultz.**

Foran The courthouse every morning was surrounded by several protests, some grossly vulgar in nature- Black Panthers who supported Bobby Seale, a regular military platoon that used to march up and down on the plaza in front of the federal building carrying guns. They would be chanting, yelling and screaming. I'd never seen anything like it. Or heard of anything like it. A pretty wild scene every day.

Schultz I had a huge fight with NBC to get all of the outcuts that they wouldn't show. But I got them and I showed the jury all the attacks on the police. We also had a naval intelligence officer on vacation who heard about the demonstrations on Grant Park, and he went, sat right in the middle of the crowd, holding the microphone up and he got everything. He had them cold. He had the wildest speech out of John Hayden, Jerry Rubin, Dave Dellinger. He had them all cold.

Scene Nine

Fade up on a rowdy crowd. The Panthers and underground press fill the public gallery.

Marshal (*shouting above the noise*) Will the court please stand.

Laughter from the crowd.

Judge Hoffman I order the court to rise. This instant.

The crowd is subdued somewhat; all but one Panther stands.

Judge Hoffman Remove that man in the public gallery who is still sitting.

The crowd reacts angrily.

Seale You're a pig for taking him out.

The crowd reacts with "oink oinks". Some shout, "Right on!"

Marshal This honorable court will now resume its session.

The noise continues.

Kunstler Your Honor, if I could make one application.

*At **Kunstler**'s interjection, the crowd quietens.*

Kunstler The other seven defendants have purchased a birthday cake for Chairman Bobby Seale, whose birthday is today, but the marshals would not let them bring the cake into court. Since the only way the defendants can get the cake to Seale is to give it to him in the courtroom, they request permission to present him with the cake before the jury comes in.

Judge Hoffman Mr. Kunstler, I won't even let anyone bring me a birthday cake. I don't have food in my chambers. I don't have beverages. This is a courthouse and we conduct trials here. I'm sorry.

Kunstler The cake is not to eat here, Your Honor.

Judge Hoffman Your application will be denied. Will you bring in the jury please, Mr. Marshal?

Marshal Yes, Your Honor.

Richard Schultz If the court please, can we wait until the other defendants appear—without their cake.

There are sounds of a commotion outside the court.

Judge Hoffman Oh, the defendants are not here? Then bring them in.

More commotion outside.

Abbie Hoffman (*off mike*) Hey, that's cake-napping!

The defendants come into court rowdily. Their supporters in the gallery cheer and clap.

Davis They've arrested a cake, but they can't arrest a revolution.

Cheers and "Right ons" from the crowd.

Judge Hoffman (*furious*) One more outburst like that, just one more, and all the spectators will be cleared!

Seale Don't say nothing, no more, brothers. Just sit in the court and observe the proceedings, okay? All right!

Judge Hoffman And, Mr. Seale, I will issue the orders around here.

Seale They don't take orders from racist judges, but I can convey orders to them and they will follow them.

Judge Hoffman (*still furious*)   If you continue with that sort of thing, you may be expected to be punished for it.

Seale (*muttered*)   We have protested our rights for four hundred years and we have been shot and killed and murdered and brutalized and oppressed for . . .

Judge Hoffman   There is another instance. That outburst may appear on record.

Seale   Good morning, ladies and gentlemen of the jury. As I said before, I hope you don't blame me for anything.

Judge Hoffman   Mr. Marshal, will you tell that man to sit down?

Seale   What about my constitutional rights?

Judge Hoffman   Your constitutional rights . . .

Seale (*shouting*)   You are denying them. You have been denying them. Every other word you say is denied, denied, denied, and you begin to oink in the faces of the masses of the people in this country. That is what you begin to represent, the corruptness of this rotten government for four hundred years.

Marshal (*quietly*)   Mr. Seale, will you sit down.

Seale   Why don't you knock me in the mouth? Try that.

Marshal   Sit down.

Judge Hoffman   Members of the jury, I regret that I am going to have to excuse you.

The jury moves out. **Seale** *addresses them as they go.*

Seale   I hope you all don't blame me for those false lying notes and letters that said the Black Panthers threatened the jury. It's a lie and you know it's a lie and the government did it to taint the jury against me. You got that? This racist government with its Superman notions and comic-book politics. We're hip to the fact that Superman saved no black people. I still demand the right to defend myself. You are not fooled after you . . . (**Marshal** *tries to get him to sit, but is ignored.*) have walked over people's constitutional rights? You have done everything you could with those jive lying witnesses up there presented by these pig agents of the government to lie and condone some rotten fascist crap by racist cops and pigs that beat people's heads. I demand my constitutional rights. Demand—demand—demand.

The **Marshal** *finally forces* **Seale** *back into his seat.*

Judge Hoffman   Will you bring the jury back now please and call your next witness.

Scene Ten

Narrator   The third of the government's four main witnesses from the Chicago Red Squad, the Chicago plain clothes agents, was William Frapolly, a student at North Eastern Illinois College. It was a measure of his commitment to police work that he had allowed himself to be expelled from college rather than blow his cover. He also had infiltrated the mob and had been present at one of the meetings with the city.

Foran   And where were you the afternoon following the riots, Mr. Frapolly?

Frapolly   I was in Grant Park with the accused, John Froines, and Lee Weiner. He was talking about the butyric acid he had used in hotels and restaurants the night before. It had cleared out the restaurants, he said. Butyric acid smells like vomit. And then we began talking about creating a diversion at Grant Park underground garage and Froines said he was going to firebomb it. He was either going to do that or use the butyric acid again.

Foran   Do you recall anything else being said at that meeting?

Frapolly   No, my recollection is pretty well exhausted.

Foran   That's all, Your Honor.

Kunstler   Mr. Frapolly. How many meetings have you had with Mr. Foran and Mr. Schultz, the government's attorneys before today?

Frapolly   About three.

Kunstler   Now, did Mr. Foran comment at one of these meetings that your previous testimony before grand jury didn't implicate the defendants enough and you ought to elaborate more?

Frapolly   No, he didn't.

Kunstler   Is it not true that the defendants said absolutely none of the things you have attributed to them about the troops and the police?

Frapolly   They said all those things.

Kunstler   But did you tell the grand jury they said those things?

Foran   Objection.

Judge Hoffman   I sustain the objection. That is not the way to do it.

Kunstler   Then, Your Honor, I guess the Appeals Court will have to tell me how to do it.

Judge Hoffman   Oh, I don't threaten very easily, sir.

Kunstler   I am not threatening, sir. I just think this is classic impeachment lying here.

Judge Hoffman   Your client has a right to appeal, sir. I shall continue to do my best here. Continue.

Kunstler   Mr. Frapolly, did you tell the grand jury that a David Baker, who is not a defendant here, made those remarks about the security forces?

Foran   Objection.

Judge Hoffman   I sustain the objection.

Kunstler Did Mr. Baker discuss the federal troops?

Frapolly Yes.

Kunstler And did he not say similar things to the ones you are now attributing to the defendant, Rennie Davis?

Foran Objection.

Judge Hoffman I sustain the objection. The fact that a witness omits to say something to a grand jury which he says at a trial is not relevant, Mr. Kunstler.

Kunstler But this man has readily admitted reading someone else's report to the Grand Jury and now may be embellishing it for this court.

Judge Hoffman Well, what he did there is of no importance here.

Kunstler I have no further questions.

Seale I would like to cross-examine the witness.

Judge Hoffman You have a lawyer here. Request refused.

Seale You have violated Section 1892 of the United States Criminal Code. You are violating it because it states a black man cannot be discriminated against in his legal defense.

Judge Hoffman That man is your lawyer.

Seale That man is not my lawyer! Hey, Mr. William Frapolly, did you make some statements to the F.B.I. that I was supposed to have made some racist statements about black people taking on white people. Did you? Do you know another lying police witness, Robert Pierson? You seem very interested now. You turn your head to look this way.

Judge Hoffman I am warning you, sir, that the law . . .

Seale Instead of warning me why . . .

Judge Hoffman I am warning you that the court has the right to gag you. I don't want to do that, but under the law, you may be gagged and chained to your chair.

The audience, already excited, is shocked by this.

Seale Gagged! I am being railroaded already.

Judge Hoffman The court has that right, and I . . .

Seale The court has no right whatsoever.

Judge Hoffman The court will be in recess until tomorrow morning at ten o'clock.

Marshal Everyone will please rise.

Seale I am not rising. I am not rising until he recognizes my constitutional rights. He is not recognizing . . .

Judge Hoffman *had begun to move, but he stops.*

Judge Hoffman (*furious*) Mr. Marshal.

Seale I am not rising.

Judge Hoffman Mr. Marshal, see that he rises.

Marshal Mr. Seale.

Judge Hoffman And the other one too. Get all of the defendants to rise.

Marshal Mr. Hayden, will you please rise.

Judge Hoffman Let the record show that Mr. Hayden has not risen.

Marshal Mr. Kunstler, will you tell your clients to rise?

Weinglass If the court please, it is my understanding that there is no constitutional or legal obligation on the part of the defendants to rise provided that . . .

Judge Hoffman You are advising your clients not to rise?

Weinglass I have no obligation. He is doing nothing disruptive.

Judge Hoffman We will determine that later.

Kunstler My clients are protesting what you have done to Bobby Seale's right to defend himself.

Weinglass They are sitting silently.

Judge Hoffman Mr. Kunstler, will you advise your clients to rise?

Kunstler Your Honor, if you direct me to, I will advise them.

Judge Hoffman Then I direct you to.

Kunstler Then I will pass on the direction. They are free and independent and they have a right to do what they please.

There is a pause waiting for a reaction.

Judge Hoffman Let the record show that none of the defendants has risen.

As **Judge Hoffman** *leaves the courtroom, fade to black.*

Scene Eleven

Fade up on a group of young Panthers and a number of armed marshals spread around the court. During the narration, **Seale** *comes in. He reacts to the armed marshals as if this was not what he was expecting. He sits on the corner of the defense table, and addresses the Panthers.*

Narrator October 29, 1969. In the morning, Bobby Seale came into the courtroom before the judge appeared. He had been requested by the marshals, many of whom were black, to appeal to young Panthers in the courtroom not to create a disturbance.

The audience buzzes with anticipation.

Seale   Brothers and sisters in the audience, I want to say a few things to you. See those pictures there on the wall: Washington, Jefferson, Franklin. They were all slave holders, every one, and this court is their court. They have denied me my right to defend myself, refused my constitutional rights as a black man. But brothers and sisters, whatever happens today just stay cool. You got the right to observe, but I don't want you cats out there to get upset and emotional and start doing anything that's out of the ordinary. But if anybody attacks you, you know what to do. We defend ourselves but keep cool. Right on brothers. Okay, all right?

Audience reaction.

Marshal (*enters*)   Court will be upstanding.

Judge Hoffman *enters.*

Judge Hoffman (*very tense*)   Mr. Marshal, bring in the jury.

Abbie Hoffman   Mr. Judge, there is a small army of marshals in here now and they all got guns.

Weinglass   Your Honor, the jury cannot fail to be moved by this armed display. It's not right, it's not good, and it's not called for.

Richard Schultz   If the court please, before Your Honor came into this courtroom, Bobby Seale stood up and addressed this group . . .

Seale (*overlapping*)   That's right, brother. That's right.

Richard Schultz (*continuing*)   . . . and he told these people in the audience, if the court please, and I want this on the record, that if he's attacked, they know what to do. He was talking to these people about an attack by them.

Seale   You're a lying, dirty liar! I told them to defend themselves. You're a rotten racist, pig, fascist, liar. I said they had a right to defend themselves if they are attacked and I hope that the record carries that tricky Dick Schultz is a liar, and we have a right to defend ourselves, and if you attack me, I will defend myself.

Through this speech the crowd is growing increasingly restive, punctuating **Seale***'s words with "Right ons," etc..*

Richard Schultz   If the court please, this is what he said, just as he related it. In terms of a physical attack by the people in this . . . . . .

Seale   A physical attack by those damned marshals, that's what I said.

Judge Hoffman   Let the . . .

Seale (*shouting*)   And if they attack people, they have a right to defend themselves, you lying pig!

Marshals *restrain* **Seale***, pushing him into his chair.*

Judge Hoffman Let the record show that the tone of Mr. Seale's voice was one of shrieking and pounding on the table and shouting. That will be dealt with appropriately at some time in the future.

Kunstler Your Honor, the record should show that Mr. Schultz was also shouting.

Judge Hoffman Yes, he raised his voice, but what he said was the truth. I can't blame him. We are going into recess now, young man. If you keep this up . . .

Seale Look, old man, if you keep up denying me my constitutional rights, you are being exposed to the public and the world that you do not care about people's constitutional rights to defend themselves.

Judge Hoffman I will tell you what I indicated yesterday might happen to you.

Seale Happen to me? What can happen to me more than what Benjamin Franklin and George Washington did to black people in slavery? What can happen to me more than that?

Judge Hoffman I might add that as it's said all the defendants support you in your actions, I might consider they are bad risks for bail.

Heavy reaction to this.

Seale I still demand my constitutional rights and to cross-examine.

Judge Hoffman Make him sit down, Mr. Marshal.

*Three **Marshals** struggle with **Seale**. **Dellinger** joins in.*

Seale (*struggling*) I want my constitutional rights. How come you won't recognize it?

Richard Schultz May the record show that the defendant Dellinger is physically attempting to interfere with the Marshals as they try to seat the defendant Seale.

Judge Hoffman Mr. Kunstler, if you can't control your client . . .

Kunstler I am not his lawyer.

Judge Hoffman You told me you were his lawyer.

Kunstler Your Honor.

Judge Hoffman I have the transcript here.

Kunstler Your Honor, we have gone over that.

Judge Hoffman I will tell you this, Mr. Kunstler, over the noon hour I will reflect on whether the defendants are good risks for bail, and I shall give serious consideration to the termination of their bail.

Seale You're trying to make jive bargaining operations and that's different from the right I have. Take your hands off me!

*The **Marshals** lunge at **Seale**, pushing him down.*

Richard Schultz May the record show the Defendant Dellinger is interfering again.

Judge Hoffman I saw it myself, Mr. Schultz. It will be dealt with later. Mr. Seale, I didn't think I would ever live to sit in a courtroom where George Washington was assailed by a defendant in a criminal case and a judge criticized for having his portraits on the wall. Mr. Marshal, we shall recess.

The set goes to black. After a short pause a light finds **Seale** *at the side of the stage.*

Seale They set me down in the chair, there was no leg cuffs, no hand cuffs, and they put me in a chair that in no way kept me there. They put six inch of tape around the corner of my mouth and onto my cheeks and they picked me up in that chair and brought me into the courtroom in this chair and sat me down. And the judge comes in and asks whether Mr. Seale over there will indicate whether he would be quiet and sit in the corner—and bang bang bang. I was sitting there and so he asked me a question, But the tape is not holding, and so I said "Clang, clang, clang"—that was my first response and then the tape wasn't holding so I blew it up into my face.

The next day, I came into court and I said again, you're barring my testimony and so—(*Two figures come in with a different chair and strap* **Seale** *to it as he is talking.*) they put me on this big mahogany chair, no hand cuffs but a big thick two-inch wire strap around my legs, round the legs of the chair with locks and keys and pulled tight.

Bring up lights slowly on the court. Noises can be heard from the courtroom which gets louder.

They wrapped my mouth with bandage all the way up my head and around my neck. "If you choke me," I said to the Marshal, "I will kill you, you son of a bitch." He thought about this and he decided to loosen it. But still they brought me into the courtroom.

Marshals *pick him up in the big chair and carry him into the court.*

Seale As we went in they were cutting my air, my blood circulation. While I was doing this Jerry Rubin is cussing the judge—it's a personal argument, and with this going on, one of the marshals comes up, a real Goliath—knocks my head back, hits me in the balls.

Defendants and others try to free **Seale** *from the chair.*

Weinglass If Your Honor please, the buckles on the leather strap holding Mr. Seale's hand are digging into his hand and he appears to be trying to free his hand from that pressure. Could he be assisted?

Judge Hoffman If the Marshal concludes he needs assistance. Mr. Marshal.

Marshals *around* **Seale** *set to adjusting his straps.* **Seale** *squeals in protest.*

Kunstler Your Honor, what are they doing, they are tightening them! This is a disgrace.

There is a real struggle as **Seale** *is tipped over in his chair.*

Rubin That guy put his elbow in Bobby's mouth and it wasn't necessary.

Kunstler This is no longer a court of order, Your Honor. It is a medieval torture chamber. They are assaulting other defendants as well.

The chair plus **Marshals** *are in amongst the press reporters.* **Seale** *manages to get his gag off in the melee.*

Seale Don't hit me in the balls!

Kunstler Your Honor, this is an unholy disgrace, and I, as an American lawyer, feel a disgrace.

Foran Created by Mr. Kunstler.

Kunstler Created by nothing but what you have done to that man.

Seale (*his gag having slipped*) You fascist dogs! You rotten low-life son of a bitch! Fuck you!

Judge Hoffman The Marshals will replace that gag.

Dellinger Someone go to protect him.

Foran May the record show that Mr. Dellinger is interfering yet again.

Rubin May the record show that Foran is a Nazi.

Pandemonium has broken out, with **Hayden**, **Davis**, *and* **Dellinger** *trying to calm the spectators.*

Kunstler Your Honor, we are going to ask for a judicial review of this entire treatment of Bobby Seale.

Judge Hoffman Don't point at me in that manner, Mr. Kunstler. You should be ashamed of your conduct.

Kunstler What, when a client is treated like this.

Judge Hoffman Take that down.

Narrator Seale was then removed to outside the courtroom. Next day, with Seale still chained and gagged, Kunstler attempted to break the impasse.

Kunstler I am moving now on behalf of the other seven defendants that this be stopped. Let this man defend himself. You could stop this instantly, stop any disturbances in the courtroom if you let him defend himself.

Judge Hoffman If that is a motion, I deny the motion.

Kunstler Your Honor, before the jury comes in, the defense would like to move to adjourn until Monday so that we can have an opportunity to send the lawyers to California to consult with Mr. Garry. We feel that it is impossible for white men to sit in this room while a black man is in chains.

Judge Hoffman I wish you wouldn't talk about the distinction between white and black men in this courtroom. I have lived a long time and you are the first person who has ever suggested that I have discriminated against a black man. Come into my chambers and I will show you on the wall what one of the great newspapers of this city said editorially about me in connection with a school desegregation case.

Kunstler Your Honor, this is not the time for self-praise on either side of the lectern.

Judge Hoffman It isn't self-praise, sir. It is defense. I won't let a lawyer stand before the bar and charge me with being a bigot.

Kunstler For God's sake, Your Honor, we are seeking a solution of a human problem here, not whether you feel good or bad or I feel good or bad.

Judge Hoffman Please don't raise your voice to me. I don't like that. Mr. Schultz, Mr. Foran, are you willing for an adjournment?

Foran The government would have no objection to a recess until ten o'clock on Monday morning.

Judge Hoffman As you have no objection then I will go along, but with reluctance. I believe we should have assurances that there will be no speeches vilifying the court or you. I don't want to be lying in bed peacefully looking at television to suddenly see one of the defendants characterizing me as a blackmailer. I don't want that to happen. So you are accepting certain risks and responsibilities, Mr. Foran. Mr. Marshal, the court is recessed until Monday morning at ten o'clock.

Dim the lights.

Narrator No solution to the impasse was found. Seale's continuing to demand his legal right to represent himself. Hoffman now decided to sentence Seale for contempt and to separate his trial from that of the other seven defendants. He read from a long document, listing all of Seale's outbursts. He found him guilty of sixteen separate acts of contempt, adding up to a total sentence of four years. Before imposing sentence, Hoffman invited Seale to speak.

Lights up.

Scene Twelve

Judge Hoffman Mr. Seale, you have the right to speak now. I will hear you.

Seale How come I couldn't speak before?

Judge Hoffman This is a special occasion.

Seale Wait a minute. How are you going to try to—you are going to attempt to punish me for attempting to speak for myself before? Now I don't understand it. What kind of court is this? Is this a court? It must be a fascist operation.

Judge Hoffman I don't want to be questioned further. The law gives you the right to speak out now in respect to possible punishment for contempt of court, sir.

Seale Well, the first thing. I'm not in no contempt of court. I know that I make requests hoping that once in one way along this trial you will recognize my rights as a human being, a black man living under the scope and influence of a racist decadent America where the government of the United States does not recognize the black people's constitutional rights . . .

Judge Hoffman Are you addressing me, sir?

Seale I'm talking. You can see I'm talking.

Judge Hoffman That's right, but if you address me you'll have to stand.

Seale Stand? Stand now? It's going to a higher court, possibly the highest court in America.

Judge Hoffman I find that the acts, statements, and conduct of the defendant Bobby Seale constitute a willful attack upon the administration of justice, an attempt to sabotage the functioning of the federal judiciary system. And the defendant Seale will be committed to the custody of the Attorney General of the United States for imprisonment for a term of four years. (*Court reaction.*) There will be an order for a mistrial.

Seale Hey, wait a minute. I got a right—what's this cat trying to pull now? I'm leaving the—I can't stay?

Judge Hoffman Bobby G. Seale is severed from this case and will be tried at a later date. The court will recess until tomorrow at ten o'clock.

Seale I'm put in jail for four years—for nothing? I demand an immediate trial now. You can't call it a mistrial. I want my coat.

The spectators have begun to chant, "Free Bobby! Free Bobby!"

The lights dim except for the defense and prosecution tables; the chanting dies away.

Weinglass When Bobby Seale was bound and gagged, I was not in favor of going back into that courtroom. But some of the defendants were ambivalent, and one of them, Tom Hayden, was persistent. He argued that they were "on trial for their identity" and that not only would they be unable to make their defense properly but we couldn't go around the country explaining all the things the trial was about. So we kept going.

Kunstler As far as the atmosphere was in court, it was deadly from beginning to end, except when the defense took over and began their case. The defendants tried to make it light and airy—political. They brought in books, reading matter. Abbie Hoffman did cartwheels into the well of the court over the railings . . .

Foran Yeah, they did all sorts of things in court, like wearing judges' robes and trampling on them and so forth. It was rubbish. They used posters of Jerry Rubin copulating with his girlfriend, both of them in the nude. They brought in the American flag, used it as a tablecloth and sprinkled it with marijuana. The language, the language was "you mother fucker you."

Kunstler   We had these intelligent and humorous defendants who were fighting for all the young people in America, in spite of a venomous judge and two prosecutors who did everything evil you could imagine to convict, and a sort of impassive jury. That contrast created an impression throughout America. We were on the news nationally every single day of the trial, so the general public were getting an eyeful and an earful.

Scene Thirteen

Weinglass   We decided we were going to put the government on trial and we were going to do that with the kind of witnesses we brought in to testify. So few of the prosecution witnesses were ordinary members of the public, but we found them. The first was J. N. Hunt, a solid businessman who happened by chance to be in the park when the police raid occurred.

During the last speech, **Hunt** *has moved to the witness stand. Lighting up on the court.*

Hunt   The police marched directly into the crowd, in step, broke ranks, and then chopped their way a hundred yards into a tightly packed crowd, beating people all the way.

Weinglass   What happened then, Mr Hunt?

Hunt   Some of them started turning around and walking back, hitting a few people on the way. The attack was simply a punitive assault on the crowd. There was no provocation.

Foran   I object to this.

Hoffman   The last statement of the witness may be struck out.

Weinglass   No further questions.

Hoffman   Cross-examination.

Foran   Mr Hunt, did you hear the defendant Dellinger say from the stage over that loudspeaker, "We are coming alive and we're fighting back"?

Hunt   I heard many statements to that effect, it was very difficult . . .

Foran   Can you answer yes or no. Did you hear it?

Hunt   Your Honour, I am unable to answer the question.

Foran (*frustrated*)   I have no further questions.

Hunt *leaves the stand and is replaced by* **Morse**.

Weinglass (*to audience*)   Not only did we have witnesses to the police brutality and who created the riot, but also on why the people were there. We thought they would be able to talk about what was happening among the youth, which society must pay attention to, and while they wouldn't completely agree with it, they would have to interact with it and not treat them as outcasts.

Morse moves to the stand.

Weinglass   One of our witnesses was a young woman, Linda Morse, a Quaker and a former pacifist.

Kunstler   Now, Miss Morse, you came to Chicago around Convention time?

Morse   Yes, I did.

Kunstler   Calling your attention to Friday, August 23, do you know what you did on that particular day?

Morse   I went to the Mobilization Centre and met Dave Dellinger. He asked me to come with him to see Mayor Daley to discuss the crisis in the city of Chicago, with no march permits and no permit to sleep in Lincoln Park. We went to City Hall.

Kunstler   What happened at City Hall?

Morse   We went into a waiting room outside of the Mayor's offices and sat around for quite a long time asking to see Mayor Daley, and finally a city official came out and said that Mr. Daley would not see us and that the matter was closed.

Kunstler   No further questions.

Richard Schultz   Miss Morse, you practice shooting an M1 rifle, don't you?

Morse   Yes, I do.

Richard Schultz   You also practice karate?

Morse   Yes, I do.

Richard Schultz   That is for revolution, isn't it?

Morse   After Chicago I changed, from being a pacifist to the realization that we had to defend ourselves. A nonviolent revolution was impossible. I desperately wish it was possible.

Richard Schultz   And the way you are going to change this country is by violent revolution, isn't that right, Miss Morse?

Morse   The way we are going to change this country is by political revolution, sir, but we have to defend ourselves.

Richard Schultz   Miss Morse, isn't it a fact that in your opinion there is no alternative to revolution.

Morse

Richard Schultz   And are you prepared to kill and die for this?

Morse   Yes. (*Pause.*) In self-defense.

Richard Schultz   And is this part of the reason you are learning to fire an M1 Rifle?

Morse I still don't know if I could kill anyone. I haven't reached that point yet. I believed that we could create a different kind of society, a society of love which would change the attitudes of the police and the government by loving them. Now I know that the police-state that existed inside the Convention also existed outside the Convention and that nonviolent methods would not work to change that. We had to defend ourselves or be wiped out.

Dim the set lights and fade up Judy Collins' version of "Blowin' in the Wind." As the music fades, **Kunstler** *is picked out at the defense table.*

Kunstler We had such singing stars as Judy Collins, but the judge wouldn't let them sing but he did let them recite what they would have sung. I remember Judy started to sing "Where Have All the Flowers Gone?" and a martial clapped his hand across her mouth, on the stand. The judge said "Shut that woman up," and so she recited that great anti-war poem by Pete Seeger. And then she was cited. And so it was quite normal to have these people. We had Norman Mailer, we had Allen Ginsberg, all these people took the stand"

Ginsberg *enters on the edge of the stage.*

Dellinger Maybe a mixed case was Allen Ginsberg. He was such a majestic figure and so forth but he was also a homosexual which was one of our issues.

Scene Fourteen

Ginsberg I was one of the people who had projected the Festival of Life and the Yippies.

Narrator Allen Ginsberg.

Ginsberg My function here was to be a sort of spiritual counselor, a spiritual activist let's say. Since I'd been in India, I'd been involved in some chanting, basically of a pacifist nature, and had been involved in a number of anti-war demonstrations.

The set comes to life. **Ginsberg** *moves to the witness stand.*

Weinglass Mr. Ginsberg, do you recall what you said at your meeting with Mr. Abbie Hoffman in February 1968?

Ginsberg Yippie!—among other things. And he said that politics had become theater and magic, that the manipulation of imagery through mass media was confusing and hypnotizing the people in the U.S. and was making them accept a war which they really did not believe in: that people were involved in a lifestyle which was intolerable to them, which involved brutality and police violence as well as a larger violence in Vietnam. And that we ourselves might be able to get together in Chicago to present different ideas of what we could do to make society more sacred and less commercial, less materialistic.

Weinglass Now, do you recall a meeting in March in New York in which you described the objectives of the Festival of Light?

Ginsberg Yes, my statement was that the earth at present was endangered, that it was a planetary crisis that had not been recognized by any governments. But since the younger people did know, we were going to invite them there and the central motive would be the desire for the preservation of the planet as manifested by the great mantra to the preserver god, Vishnu. I then chanted the mantra Hare Krishna for ten minutes to the television cameras and it goes, "Hare Krishna, hare Krishna, Krishna, Krishna, hare, hare, hare rama, rama rama."

Judge and prosecution counsel laugh.

Weinglass Now, in chanting that did you have musical accompaniment? Your Honor, I object to the laughter of the court on this.

Judge Hoffman I don't, I don't understand it because it was—the language of our courts is English.

Kunstler But you don't laugh at other languages.

Judge Hoffman I didn't laugh. I didn't laugh at all. I wish I could tell you how I feel. Laugh—I didn't even smile. All I could tell you was I didn't understand it because the language the witness . . .

Ginsberg Sanskrit, sir.

Judge Hoffman Well, that's one I don't know. And I don't laugh at the witnesses, I protect them. The only language is English here unless you have an interpreter. You could use an interpreter if you wish.

Weinglass *gives* **Ginsberg** *a little squeeze box.*

Weinglass That won't be necessary, Your Honor. Mr. Ginsberg, can you identify this object?

Ginsberg *begins playing.*

Foran Your Honor, this is outrageous.

Judge Hoffman You asked him to examine it and instead he played it. I sustain the objection.

Ginsberg It adds spirituality to the case, sir.

Judge Hoffman Will you remain quiet, sir.

Ginsberg I am sorry.

Weinglass Now, at approximately 10:30 p.m., August 24, where were you?

Ginsberg I was in Lincoln Park. There were several thousand people gathered waiting, late at night. There were bonfires burning in trashcans. Then there was a sudden burst of lights in the center of the park and a group of policemen moved in fast where the bonfires were and kicked over the bonfires. There was a great deal of consternation and movement and shouting and I turned surprised because it was early. The police had given 11 p.m. as the time.

Weinglass What did you do next?

Ginsberg I started the chant, "Ommmmmmmmmm, ommmmmmmmmmm."

This goes on for several seconds.

Foran All right, we have had a demonstration.

Judge Hoffman All right.

Ginsberg And when we began chanting, there was one central sound, vocalized by all the people, and a slow quieting of the physical behavior of all the people, slowly moving out of the park, away from the police, calmly.

Weinglass Now, can you relate to us the incidents of the 28th of August?

Ginsberg I was in Grant Park and Dave Dellinger asked me to join the front line of the marchers with Jean Genet, and with Terry Southern who had written *Dr. Strangelove*. And we marched until we came to a halt in front of a large guard of armed human beings in uniform with machine guns, jeeps, police. And I heard Dave Dellinger saying, "This is a peaceful march. All those who are not peaceful, please go away and . . ."

Weinglass Did you go over with him?

Ginsberg Yes, and I also brought a little armful of flowers that had been given us.

Weinglass And what did you do with the flowers?

Ginsberg Mr. Dellinger and the police officials were talking together and whenever they seemed to be agitated, I took the flowers and put them in between their faces, shook them around a little.

Weinglass Then what did you do?

Ginsberg I think Mr. Dellinger announced soon after that the march was over, and the government had simply forced us to abandon our citizens' rights.

Weinglass I have no further questions.

Foran Your Honor, I need to get some materials to properly cross-examine this witness, and I wonder if I could request an early recess?

Judge Hoffman All right, we will go till two o'clock.

Kunstler Your Honor, we asked for five minutes two days ago and were refused.

Judge Hoffman You will have to cease this disrespectful tone.

Kunstler That is not disrespect, that is an angry tone, Your Honor.

Judge Hoffman Yes, it is, yes, it is. I will grant the motion of the government.

Kunstler You refused us five minutes the other day.

Judge Hoffman You are shouting at the court.

Kunstler Oh, Your Honor . . .

Judge Hoffman I never shouted at you during this trial.

Kunstler Your Honor, your voice has been raised.

Judge Hoffman You have been disrespectful.

Kunstler It is not disrespect, Your Honor.

Judge Hoffman And sometimes worse than that.

Ginsberg Ommmmmmmmmmm.

Judge Hoffman Will you step off the witness stand!

Kunstler He was trying to calm us both down, Your Honor.

Judge Hoffman Oh no, I needed no calming down. That will be all.

Narrator In cross-examining Ginsberg, Foran asked the poet to read some of his verse, the intention being to show that he was a homosexual as well as an advocate of free love in public places.

Foran You've been named as a sort of religious leader of Yippies. Would you recite your poem "The Night-Apple" for us?

Ginsberg *reads out "The Night-Apple."*

Foran Could you explain to the jury, having said that, what the religious significance of the poem is?

Ginsberg I could, if you would take a wet dream as a religious experience. It is a description of a wet dream, sir.

Narrator Foran then went on to infer homosexual tendencies between Ginsberg and others of the defendants. Ginsberg pleaded that universal sexual communion as expressed in his poetry was the only basis for true democracy. He then read his long poem "Howl." By the end, most of the defendants were in tears.

Ginsberg *reads a section from "Howl."*

Foran Goddamned fag!

Lighting dimmed to leave **Ginsberg** *still lit on the stand.*

Ginsberg *leaves the stand and* **Hoffman** *takes his place.* **Dellinger** *moves to the side.*

Scene Fifteen

Narrator Only two of the defendants took the witness stand. The first was Abbie Hoffman.

Dellinger If I was to choose the most colorful of us eight defendants, it would have been Abbie Hoffman. What Abbie did was to supply a certain kind of irreverent humor to the whole week, the whole period, the whole trial. He was the only one to establish any rapport with the judge, who thought him—funny too.

Weinglass Will you identify yourself for the record?

Abbie Hoffman My name is Abbie—an orphan of America.

Weinglass Abbie, where . . .

Richard Schultz Objection. He isn't Abbie. He's a thirty-three-year-old man who should be called Mr. Hoffman.

Weinglass Where do you reside?

Abbie Hoffman I live in Woodstock Nation.

Weinglass Will you tell the court and jury where that is?

Abbie In my mind and in the minds of my brothers and sisters. It does not consist of property or material, but rather of ideas and certain values . . .

Richard Schultz (*interrupting*) That doesn't say where Woodstock Nation is, whatever it is.

Abbie Hoffman This is going to be a very exciting cross-examination.

Judge Hoffman We want an address. Now you said Woodstock. In what state is Woodstock?

Abbie Hoffman It is a state of mind, in the mind of myself and my brothers and sisters. (*Pause.*) It is a conspiracy.

Weinglass Mr. Hoffman, can you tell us your occupation?

Abbie Hoffman I am a cultural revolutionary.

Weinglass What do you mean by that phrase?

Abbie Hoffman Well, it is a person who tries to shape and participate in the values and customs of a new people.

Weinglass And is that what you were intending in Chicago?

Abbie Hoffman Yes, a free festival which would bring a new program, a new kind of lifestyle to Chicago. We went to the Parks Department with a permit application. It said the festival would be entirely free, that a hundred entertainers had already agreed to participate, and that those attending will need to sleep in the park. We also asked for portable sanitation and for cooperation in setting up kitchens as there would be food sharing.

Weinglass Did you receive a reply to this application?

Abbie Hoffman Not to my knowledge.

Weinglass Then where, if anywhere, did you go?

Abbie Hoffman We went to see Deputy Mayor Stahl. And we presented him with a copy of the permit application, rolled up in a Playmate of the Month that said, "To Dick, with love. The Yippies." And we gave him a kiss and put a Yippie button on him and he was very embarrassed. But he said that we had followed the right procedure, things like that.

Weinglass Did you speak to Deputy Mayor Stahl again?

Abbie Hoffman Yeah, it was the morning of Monday the 26th. The police had just broken up the music festival. It was two in the morning and I phoned him at home. I told him that driving the people out of the park was the dumbest military tactic since the Trojans let in the Trojan horse. I again pleaded with him to let people stay in the park the following night. "There will be more people coming," I said "And they should be allowed to sleep." I told him that his boss Daley, was totally out of his mind. That I had read in the paper the day before that they had two thousand troops surrounding the reservoirs in order to protect them against the Yippie plot to dump LSD in the drinking water. I said there wasn't a kid in the country, never mind a Yippie, who thought such a thing could even be done. He said this was a very difficult situation.

Weinglass What happened then?

Abbie Hoffman I walked to the Free Theatre. There were perhaps two or three hundred young people in small groups in the courtyard huddled around camp—fires with blankets over them. Many people had bandages over their heads with blood showing through. I had seen the birth of a new society in Lincoln Park, a revolutionary youth culture dedicated to love. I had seen that society brutally attacked by the police who had gone crazy. The Yippies were being treated the way black people have been treated for hundreds of years. I said that the Democratic Party was a facade of democracy, but underneath was a brutal system bent on destroying any way of life that challenged the way of life of those in power.

Weinglass What happened when you left there?

Abbie Hoffman I came back to the park, where I met with a group of ministers.

Weinglass Do you recall what was said?

Richard Schultz I object as to what the ministers said to Mr. Hoffman.

Abbie Hoffman I sustain the objection.

Weinglass Did you meet and talk with anyone else that afternoon?

Abbie Hoffman I met a man who said he was from a group called the Blackstone Rangers.

Weinglass I notice Mr. Schultz does not object when the words Blackstone Rangers are mentioned. Apparently we can have conversations with them, but not with ministers.

Judge Hoffman I'm not here to be quizzed, sir.

Richard Schultz Mr. Weinglass, it's because the defendant arranged with the Blackstone Rangers, which is a black gang, to come and fight in the park, with weapons. That's why and we will establish that.

Judge Hoffman Continue with your examination, Mr. Weinglass—please!

Weinglass What happened the following morning?

Abbie Hoffman The police came to a restaurant where I was having breakfast, and arrested me. They said they arrested me because I had the word "fuck" on my forehead. They said it was "obscene."

Weinglass How did that word come to be there?

Abbie Hoffman Well, I was tired of seeing my picture in the paper and I know if you got that word somewhere visible, they aren't going to print your picture in the paper, and it also summed up my attitude about what was going on in Chicago. But I like that four-letter word. I thought it was kind of holy actually.

Weinglass Abbie Hoffman, did you enter into an agreement with David Dellinger, John Froines, Tom Hayden, Jerry Rubin, Lee Weiner, or Rennie Davis to come to the city of Chicago for the purpose of encouraging and promoting violence during the Convention week?

Abbie Hoffman An agreement?

Weinglass Yes.

Abbie Hoffman We couldn't agree on lunch.

Weinglass I have no further questions.

Richard Schultz Mr. Hoffman, the Yippie myth was created to get people to come to Chicago, isn't that right, Mr. Hoffman?

Abbie Hoffman That's right, Mr. Schultz.

Richard Schultz Now, in this festival where you thought you were going to have over 500,000 young people, you were going to have a liberated area where people could do what they wanted and be free from city control, city and state laws?

Abbie Hoffman Not all of the laws. If somebody pulled a gun and started shooting people, I assume he would be arrested and taken away.

Richard Schultz And you told Deputy Mayor Stahl you were going to have nude-ins in your liberated zone didn't you? Public fornications?

Abbie Hoffman A nude-in? No, I don't believe I would use that phrase. I don't think it very poetic, frankly.

Kunstler Are we ever going to reach the end of this prurient interest in sex, Your Honor?

Richard Schultz I wish to demonstrate that the city authorities were right to deny applications to such irresponsible applicants. In your book *Revolution for the Hell of It*, you state, and I quote, "A liberated area is only the beginning of an expansion into other areas." We would have had drug-crazed kids with guns in Lincoln Park that night and I quote, "We'll burn Chicago to the ground." Isn't that right?

Abbie Hoffman No.

Richard Schultz And was there L, to your knowledge, in both the honey and the brownies they were eating in the park?

Abbie Hoffman It is colorless, odorless, tasteless. I would have to be a chemist to know that for a fact.

Richard Schultz Weren't you trying to create a situation so that it would appear that the Convention had to be held under military conditions. Isn't that a fact, Mr. Hoffman?

Abbie Hoffman You can do that with a yo-yo in this country. That's easy. You can see just from the troops in this courtroom.

Richard Schultz And you wanted it to happen, did you not?

Abbie Hoffman We did not come to—we did not come to fight the troops, no. Never. No.

Richard Schultz You were ready to die over your right to be in Lincoln Park, isn't that right?

Abbie Hoffman I explained that to Mr. Stahl. Yes.

Richard Schultz You felt that defending the liberated land in Lincoln Park meant more to you than your feelings on the war in Vietnam, isn't that right?

Abbie Hoffman I'm not sure when I came to Chicago that those were my feelings, but afterwards I felt that the issue became one of assembly and free speech.

Richard Schultz Mr. Hoffman, while you were negotiating with city officials, you were secretly attending meetings and planning for spontaneous acts of violence during the Convention. Isn't that right?

Abbie Hoffman How do you plan spontaneous acts of violence? I would have no idea how to do that.

Reaction.

Richard Schultz Mr. Hoffman, did you not deliberately tell your police tails that you had a fight with the defendant Jerry Rubin?

Abbie Hoffman Yes, deliberately.

Richard Schultz In order to destroy any charge of conspiracy, isn't that right?

Abbie Hoffman Yes. God I was sneaky. It didn't work, obviously.

Reaction.

Richard Schultz Did you say you were going to wreck society?

Abbie Hoffman I said that the institutions in America were crumbling, and all we had to do was sit here, smile and laugh, and the whole thing would come tumbling down because it was basically corrupt and brutal.

Richard Schultz So the answer is yes. That is all, Your Honor.

Weinglass Mr. Hoffman, have you had any change in your personal philosophy since Chicago?

Abbie Hoffman I began to see what had been called democracy in this country in a new light: underneath it was really a police state. I began to see it in a way that black people and Puerto Rican people and Indians and I suppose all the minority groups in this country—in fact the way the Vietnamese were seeing it: that it was a police state based on brutality, and there was a facade that protected it, that gave a semblance of some kind of debate, of some kind of democratic-type decision-making, but underneath it was the police state and that that could only be protected by sheer police power.

Lights dimmed.

Scene Sixteen

Narrator On January 6, 1970, the atmosphere in the courtroom was electric. The prosecution had decided not to call Mayor Daley as a witness so the defence had subpoenaed him to appear as one of theirs. However, as their witness, they could not subject him to the cut and thrust of cross-questioning. So they were setting out to provoke him enough have him declared a hostile witness and then they could question him.

Lights up.

Kunstler What is your connection with Mr. Foran, Mr. Daley?

Daley I think he is one of the greatest attorneys in the United States.

Kunstler I see. (*Pause.*) Now, following the riots in Chicago after the assassination of Martin Luther King, Jr., did you not, in April 1968, order your police department, publicly, to shoot and kill and to shoot and maim black people in this city?

Foran Your Honor, I object, that is a leading question.

Kunstler Your Honor, I have to ask a leading question.

Judge Hoffman No, you don't have to. I won't permit you.

Kunstler Where were you on April 15, Mayor Daley?

Daley I was at my home on Lowe Avenue.

Kunstler And did you leave your home at any time to go to a press conference?

Foran I object to that?

Judge Hoffman I sustain it.

Kunstler Then at this moment, Your Honor, I move to have the Mayor declared a hostile witness.

Judge Hoffman Why? The Mayor has been a most friendly witness. I deny the motion.

Kunstler Your Honor, I have made no argument . . .

Judge Hoffman Please, go ahead. Your motion is denied.

Kunstler Calling your attention, Mayor Daley, to the week of August 28, 1968, did you say to Senator Ribicoft . . .

Foran Oh, Your Honor, I object.

Kunstler And I quote—"Fuck you, you Jew son of a bitch, you lousy motherfucker, go home." Close quote.

Foran Listen to that, Your Honor.

Judge Hoffman Sir, this is your witness and you may not ask . . .

Kunstler I have the source, Your Honor.

Judge Hoffman I order you now, Mr. Kunstler, not to ask leading questions.

Kunstler Mayor Daley, in your fifteen years as Mayor, have you knowledge of anyone sleeping in Lincoln Park overnight?

Foran Your Honor, I object. It is leading.

Judge Hoffman Objection sustained.

Kunstler Mayor Daley, do you believe people have the right to demonstrate against the war in Vietnam?

Foran Objection.

Judge Hoffman Objection sustained.

Kunstler Your Honor, in view of the way in which the questioning has gone, I want to read into the record an offer of proof of what we had hoped to prove if we had been given permission to treat him as a hostile witness. This will go to a higher court.

Judge Hoffman I will excuse the jury. Mr. Marshal, show the jury out.

Marshal Yes, Your Honor.

Jury moves out.

Kunstler Your Honor, the defendants would have offered proof that there was a conspiracy overt or tacit between Mayor Daley and the Democratic administration to prevent any significant demonstrations against war, poverty, imperialism, or racism at the Convention. That in furtherance of his conspiracy, Mayor Daley procured this indictment to shift the deserved blame for the disorders . . .

Spectator Right on!

Kunstler . . . surrounding the Democratic Convention from the real conspirators to other individuals symbolizing dissent from government policy and to punish those individuals as a deterrent.

This speech is greeted by more "right ons" and sporadic applause.

Foran Objection.

Judge Hoffman Sustained, Any questions, Mr. Foran?

Foran In your conversation with anyone, did you ever tell anyone to deny them their permits?

Daley No.

Judge Hoffman Thank you, Mayor Daley, you are excused. Court will be recessed.

The courtroom starts the recession.

Abbie Why didn't you cross-examine Daley, Mr. Schultz?

Richard Schultz I was so intimidated by him, I couldn't ask a question.

Laughter. The lights dim.

Scene Seventeen

Narrator The trial became a battle far wider than the two political factions; it became a battle between two fundamentally different philosophies battling for the soul of a nation. It reflected a struggle of almost religious dimensions, with both sides fighting in fancy dress. The other main defense witness was the second defendant to take the stand. Rennie Davis. A seasoned campaigner for liberal causes, older than the rest, a pacifist who had served time for his beliefs, his stance was that of the reasonable man. He had recently returned from Vietnam.

Rennie Davis When one of these bombs exploded, about 640 of these round steel balls I was holding here were spewed in the sky. When they landed, they burst back to produce about 300 steel pellets and they will kill 90 percent of every living thing over an area of a thousand yards long and . . .

Foran Your Honor, the government objects. The Vietnam War has nothing whatever to do with this indictment, which concerns whether people have the right to travel in interstate commerce to incite a riot.

Judge Hoffman I sustain the objection.

Weinglass Your Honor, before you . . .

Judge Hoffman I am not trying the Vietnam War here.

Weinglass But that is the heart of our defense, Your Honor. They did not come here for riot purposes. They came here as citizens to demonstrate their concern over a social issue.

Judge Hoffman I order you to continue to examine this witness.

Kunstler (*stands in protest*) Your Honor, why can't Mr. Weinglass complete the argument? Mr. Foran has . . .

Judge Hoffman I ask you to sit down, sir.

Kunstler But, Your Honor . . .

Judge Hoffman I direct the Marshal to have this man sit down.

Dellinger Force and violence.

Judge Hoffman That man's name is Dellinger.

Marshal Will you be quiet, Mr. Dellinger.

Dellinger (*also stands*) After such hypocrisy, I don't particularly feel like being quiet. I've said before, the judge is the chief prosecutor, and he's proved the point.

Marshal Be quiet, sir.

Dellinger You gagged Bobby Seale because you couldn't afford to listen to the truth.

The spectators warming to this new outburst begin applauding.

Marshal Sit down please and be quiet.

Dellinger Oh, very well.

Dellinger *sits and the audience settles again.*

Weinglass Mr. Davis, did you say anything in the course of your speech in March 1968 about the forthcoming election?

Davis Someone in the audience asked about whether or not there should be civil disobedience at the Convention.

Weinglass Do you recall your answer?

Davis I said that our objective was to reach the largest numbers of people who, on the whole, had never participated in a peace march, perhaps never picketed, never been in a demonstration, and to achieve that it was essential that this demonstration be legal and nonviolent.

Weinglass No further questions.

Weinglass *and* **Foran** *exchange places.*

Foran Mr. Davis, isn't it a fact that you wanted violence in order to impose an international humiliation on the people who rule this country?

Davis I did not want violence, Mr. Foran. I wanted the world to know that there were thousands of young people saying "no" to Johnson's war.

Foran Your Honor . . .

Judge Hoffman The jury will disregard the words after, "I did not want violence."

Foran And you believe, don't you, that there can't be any peace in the United States until every soldier is brought out of Vietnam, and the government is discredited?

Davis The government has discredited itself, Mr. Foran.

Foran You decided to fight the battle of Chicago by incitement to riot, didn't you?

Davis No, no, sir. No, I am trying to find a way that this generation can make this country something better than what it has been.

Foran Your Honor, he is not responding to the question.

Judge Hoffman Strike the last part of the answer.

Foran No further questions.

*As **Davis** leaves the stand, he is hugged and congratulated by the other defendants.*

Judge Hoffman I have never presided at a trial where so much physical affection has been demonstrated. With defendants hugging and embracing each other.

Spectators Right on!

Judge Hoffman Perhaps this is part of the love-in. I don't know. But it's not the proper place for it.

Kunstler Well, Your Honour, love is love.

Scene Eighteen

Narrator The defense's main objective witness was to have been Ramsey Clark, the Attorney General at the time of the Convention. Clark had been appalled by what he had seen of the police action in Chicago and had said so. However, on a technicality, Judge Hoffman ruled that his evidence was inadmissible. But then another prestigious witness suddenly became available.

Lights up.

Kunstler Your Honor, we have now Dr. Ralph Abernathy to be a witness for the defense in this case. When we made enquiries some time ago, he was out of the country, but he has just returned and indicated that he would be willing to appear. He is arriving at the moment at Chicago airport.

Judge Hoffman I certainly am not going to wait for him. Who will speak for the government?

Richard Schultz Your Honor, we believe Dr. Abernathy's evidence will be hearsay and will not be admissible.

Kunstler Your Honor, I think what has just been said is about the most outrageous statement I have ever heard from a bench, and I am going to say my piece right now, and you can hold me in contempt right now as you wish. You violated every principle of fair play when you excluded ex-Attorney General Ramsey Clark from that stand as a defense witness. *The New York Times,* among others, has called it the ultimate outrage in American justice.

Spectators Right on! (*They applaud.*)

Scene Eighteen

Kunstler   I am outraged to be in this court before you. I discovered on Saturday that Ralph Abernathy can be here. I am trembling because I am so outraged. I haven't been able to get this out before, and I am saying it now, and then I want you to put me in jail if you want to. You can do anything you want with me. Ralph Abernathy has relevant testimony. I know that doesn't mean much in this court when the Attorney General of the United States walked out of here with his lips so tight he could hardly breathe—and his wife told me he had never felt such anger at the United States government as when you prevented him from testifying.

Spectators   Right on!

Kunstler   I am going to turn back to my seat with the realization that everything I have learned throughout my life has come to naught, that there is no meaning in this court, that there is no law in this court . . .

Spectators   Right on! (*They are increasingly angered and excited.*)

Kunstler   . . . and these men are going to jail by the virtue of a legal lynching . . .

Spectators   Right on!

Kunstler   . . . and that Your Honor is actually responsible for that.

The courtroom speaks out with applause and cheers.

Judge Hoffman   Those applauders . . .

More reactions.

Judge Hoffman   . . . out with the applauders.

Richard Schultz   Your Honor, may we proceed with the trial?

Kunstler   We ask only for the court to wait a few minutes, and we will produce Dr. Abernathy for the court.

Richard Schultz   Your Honor, we are ready to go ahead now.

Judge Hoffman   Let the record show the defendants will not proceed, have, in effect, rested their case. Bring in the jury, Mr. Marshal. And Mr. Kunstler, you will not mention Dr. Abernathy in front of the jury.

Kunstler   We have a right to state our objection to resting before the jury.

Judge Hoffman   Don't do it.

Kunstler   I am going to have to put my liberty in your hands on that score.

Richard Schultz   Mr. Kunstler is simply inviting it.

Kunstler   Of course I am, because what Your Honor is doing is a disgrace in this court.

Dim the lights.

234   The Chicago Conspiracy Trial

Scene Nineteen

Narrator As they ended their case, the defendants were furious at the negative way the judge had handled their witnesses. They were demoralized, and apprehensive at the prospect of imprisonment. Now they faced the prosecution's rebuttal of their evidence and they feared that the government had left their most damaging witnesses for this. A number of them were police officers present during the riots. One of them, James Riordan, was a Deputy Chief of the Chicago Police.

Bring up lights. **Riordan** *is moving to the witness box. Court is now quiet.*

Riordan On the day of the Presidential nomination, at 5:45 p.m., there were about fifteen hundred people on the sidewalk of Columbus Drive. This was a group of people that wanted to march.

Richard Schultz Did you see the defendant Dellinger?

Riordan I did. He was confronting me at the head of the march.

Richard Schultz What, if any, announcements were made?

Riordan Thirty or forty yards from the front of the march, an unknown man announced with a loud speaker that, as the march had been stopped, to break up in small groups to penetrate into the establishments where the police could not get at them, and then disrupt normal activity.

Richard Schultz What, if anything, did you observe the people do?

Riordan The march disintegrated.

Richard Schultz Did Dellinger say anything when this announcement was completed?

Riordan I don't recall anything, but I did notice he left with the head of the march.

Dellinger Oh, bullshit!

Judge Hoffman Did you get that, Miss Reporter?

Dellinger That is an absolute lie!

Judge Hoffman Did you get that, Miss Reporter?

Dellinger Let's argue about what I stand for, but let's not make things up like that.

Judge Hoffman I have never heard in more than half a century of the bar a man using profanity in the courtroom.

Abbie Hoffman I've never been in an obscene court either.

Dellinger You're a snake, Dick Schultz. We have to try and put you in jail for ten years for telling lies about us.

Marshal Be quiet, Mr. Dellinger.

Dellinger When it's all over, the judge will go home to Florida, but if he has his way, we'll go to jail. We're fighting not just for us, but all who are being oppressed.

Davis   Damn right. Assert ourselves.

The noise is growing, as is spectator agitation.

Spectators   Right on!

Judge Hoffman   Take that man into custody. Mr. Marshal, take that man into custody.

Spectators keep reacting and chanting.

Richard Schultz (*surprised*)   Into custody?

Judge Hoffman   Into custody.

Davis (*crossing to* **Richard Schultz**)   Go ahead, Dick Schultz, put everybody into jail.

Dellinger   Dick Schultz is a Nazi, if ever I saw one.

Richard Schultz   Your Honor, will you please tell Mr. Davis to walk away from me?

Dellinger   Put everyone in jail.

Judge Hoffman   Mr. Davis, will you take your chair?

Abbie Hoffman   Nazi jailer!

Judge Hoffman   Time and time again, as the record reveals, the defendant David Dellinger has disrupted the session of this court. Today he used vile and obscene language. I propose to end the use of such language if possible, and such conduct, by terminating the bail of the defendant.

Reaction.

Kunstler   Your Honor, is there not going to be any argument about this?

Judge Hoffman   No.

Kunstler   I would like to say my piece. He is my client and I think this is utterly . . .

There is mounting disorder.

Davis   This court is bullshit!

Judge Hoffman   There he is saying the same word again.

Davis   No, this time I said it.

Richard Schultz   It was Davis, the defendant Davis, who just uttered the last . . .

Rubin   Everything in this court is bullshit!

Davis   I associate myself with Dave Dellinger, completely, 100 percent. This is the most obscene court I have ever seen.

Rubin   You're not going to separate us. Take us too. Take us all. Show us what a big man you are. Take us all.

Abbie Rubin, *Rubin's wife is reacting to this.*

Schultz Your Honor, I ask that you do not do them the favor they ask.

Judge Hoffman You didn't think I would?

Amidst the uproar, **Abbie Rubin** *is hustled by* **Marshals.**

Davis Mr. Rubin's wife, they are now taking . . .

Rubin Keep your hands off her. You see them taking away my wife?

Davis Why don't you gag the Press too, and the attorneys, gag them.

Kunstler Your Honor, there was no need for your action.

Judge Hoffman The court will be in recess, Mr. Marshal.

Kunstler Your Honor, is there no decency left here?

Judge Hoffman You can't stand there and insult the United States District Court.

Kunstler I am not insulting you. I am asking for argument. Everything you characterize as an insult . . .

Judge Hoffman Yes you are. The case is recessed.

Marshal Everyone please rise.

Judge Hoffman Clear the courtroom.

Davis You can jail a revolutionary, but you can't jail the revolution.

Abbie Hoffman You are a disgrace to the Jews. You are a Jew behaving disrespectfully in front of Gentiles. You would have served Hitler better.

Marshal That was Mr. Hoffman, Your Honor.

Judge Hoffman I saw him and I heard him.

Rubin You're a fascist, Hoffman.

Judge Hoffman Clear the courtroom, Mr. Marshal.

Abbie Hoffman You got to cut our tongues out, Julie, to order us.

Davis Get as many people as you can. Just like the Convention all over.

Marshal Clear the court!

Judge Hoffman Clear the court!

Anita Hoffman You little prick!

Rubin You are a fascist!

Marshal Let's clear the court, get out of the courtroom. Let's go. Clear the court please! Will the defendants leave the counsel table?

Fade on this last speech which rises above the hubbub.

Scene Twenty

The defendants congregate and pass out academic gowns to one another and parade back to the dock.

Narrator   With Dellinger jailed for his part in the day's outburst, the defendants decided on as heavy a disruption of the court as possible. They reasoned that if they were all jailed together, that would help Dellinger. Thus their appearance at the start of the session dressed in black academic robes.

Judge Hoffman   We have come to the point in this trial when the lawyers make their final arguments to the jury. Mr. Schultz will open for the government.

Richard Schultz   Ladies and gentlemen of the jury, the defendants claim they came to Chicago for peaceful protests. They said they wanted the grassroots people of America to have a counter-convention while the Democratic Convention, which didn't represent the people, took place. A very peaceful and legitimate claim. And why would anyone want to incite a riot? Why would anybody want to incite a situation where policemen are beating demonstrators, where demonstrators are beating policemen? Well, in answering this question, we can look at the defendants' own statements. Davis said, and I quote: "There will be war in the streets until there is peace in Vietnam." Davis and Hayden sought to impose this by creating a riot, and then blaming it on an illegitimate government fighting for its survival, destroying people in the streets. They wanted it to look as though it was some kind of people's uprising. Dellinger referred to the people in Chicago as freedom fighters. Hoffman stated that he wanted to smash this system by any means at his disposal. Vietnam, as Hayden said, would come home, barbed wire, bayonets would be used by the government here, fighting for its survival. Now, a good part of the government's case, especially the part dealing with the planning activities, was presented by four witnesses, who had penetrated the conspiracy. Those witnesses related the defendants' plans for fighting, for storming the hotels, for having weapons for use against the police. Of course the defendants deny all of these plans, revealed at meetings and in conversations. It is your duty to determine who is telling the truth.

Richard Schultz *sits down,* **Weinglass** *takes over.*

Weinglass   Ladies and gentlemen of the jury. The government's case is that seven men, long active in the peace movement, men who from all indications worked hard to change and better the future, suddenly decided to embark on a totally insane and completely inexplicable course. Analyze, if you will, who the prosecution witnesses were. They produced only four, four private citizens. For the rest, they brought city officials, policemen, undercover agents, youth officers, paid informers. In all of this time, couldn't they find one good human, decent person to come in here to support the theory of conspiracy that the prosecution has given you? Who is trying to project the truth in this courtroom?

My clients wouldn't change a single garment to curry favor. They wouldn't put on a tie, wouldn't wear a suit, they wouldn't get a haircut. They want you to judge them as they are. There is no make-believe here. This is the way we are. These men follow in the footsteps of Abraham Lincoln, who was vilified and derided for speaking out against the immorality and illegality of the war in Mexico—they follow Jesus Christ and Clarence Darrow—This court evokes memories of the Salem Witch Trials . . .

Richard Schultz Oh, objection, Your Honor!

Laughter.

Judge Hoffman Sustained.

Weinglass Ladies and gentlemen of the jury, I think while you deliberate, history will hold its breath.

Weinglass *sits,* **Kunstler** *takes over.*

Kunstler Ladies and gentlemen of the jury. This is the last voice you will hear from the defense. We are followed by the government and the government has the last word. I want you to know, first, that these defendants had a constitutional right to dissent and to agitate. No one would deny that, not Mr. Foran, not I, not anyone else. The reason for these rules, that people have the right to travel freely and have the right to agitate against social and political conditions, is that most of the reform in the United States and the world has come from such people.

Foran I object to this type of argument.

Kunstler Just fifty years ago, in a criminal court building here in Chicago, that fine lawyer, Clarence Darrow, said "When a great idea necessary for mankind is born, where does it come from? Not from the police force, or the prosecuting lawyers. It comes from the despised, from jails and prisons. It comes from men who have claimed to be rebels and think their thoughts, and their faith has been the faith of rebels." We are living in troubled times. These are rough problems, terrible problems, they are so enormous that they stagger the imagination. But they don't vanish by sending men to jail. They never did and they never will. You can kill Che Guevara; you can jail a Bobby Seale. You can assassinate Robert Kennedy or Martin Luther King but the problems remain. There are no solutions. Suddenly all importance has shifted to you the members of the jury and it is your responsibility to speak boldly and unafraid, and to live and die free.

Kunstler *sits. It is now* **Foran***'s turn.*

Foran May it please the court, counsel, ladies and gentlemen of the jury. The defense has argued that because four men who gave evidence are undercover agents, they cannot be honest men. That statement is a libel on every FBI agent, every single policeman who goes out alone and unprotected into some dangerous area of society to find out information, helpful to his government. Now these men are sophisticated and well educated, and they are as evil as they can be. There are millions of kids out there who naturally resent authority. There is another thing about a kid, as we all remember, that you have an attraction to evil. Evil is exciting and evil is attractive. Kids in the sixties are disillusioned. They feel that John Kennedy went, Bobby Kennedy went, Martin Luther King went, and the kids do feel that the lights have gone out in

Camelot. These guys take advantage of them—evilly—and use them for their purposes. What has happened to us? The bad people are the policemen, the FBI agents. You are only a good guy if you like the homosexual poetry of Allen Ginsberg? What they want is to stand on the rubble of a destroyed system of government. The First Amendment is not now and never was intended to protect those who violate the law. True freedom and substantial justice don't come from violent altercation and incendiary dissent. The First Amendment permits advocacy, not incitement. You can't say "Fight the Police." To incite is not protected by law. These men have named St Matthew and Jesus, they have named Lincoln and Martin Luther King. Can you imagine supporting these men?

Dellinger's Daughter (*interrupting*)   Yes, I can. I can imagine it because it's true.

Judge Hoffman   Remove these people.

Dellinger   That's my daughter.

Dellinger's Daughter   I don't have to listen to any more of these disgusting lies.

Dellinger   They're hitting my daughter. Don't hit my daughter that way.

Judge Hoffman (*reassuringly*)   The Marshals will retain order.

Dellinger   But they don't have to hit my daughter, who knows I was close to Dr. King.

Foran   Isn't it interesting that these believers in free speech do not believe that the United States attorney has the same right. The lights that Camelot kids believe in need not go out. The parade will never be over if people remember what Jefferson said; "Obedience to the law is the major part of patriotism." These seven men have been proven guilty beyond a doubt. Do your duty.

Narrator   The next day, Judge Hoffman gave his instructions to the jurors, who then left for their deliberations. He then turned to sentencing the defendants for contempt, each being asked if he had anything to say before sentencing. This is Dellinger.

Dellinger   I want to point out first the aggression against Vietnam and the racism in this country are two issues that this country refuses to take seriously.

Judge Hoffman   You are not speaking strictly to what I gave you the privilege of speaking to. I don't want you to talk politics.

Dellinger   You have tried to keep what you call politics, which means the truth, out of this courtroom, just as the prosecution has.

Judge Hoffman   I will ask you to sit down.

Dellinger   You wanted us to be like good Germans, supporting the evils of our decade, and now you want us to be good Jews, and go quietly and politely to the gas chambers, while you and this court support freedom and truth. This is a travesty of justice . . .

Judge Hoffman   Take him out.

Spectators   Tyrant, Tyrant!

Rubin Heil Hitler! Heil Hitler! Heil Hitler!

The court is now in uproar.

Kunstler My life has come to nothing. I am not anything anymore. You have destroyed me and everyone else. Put me in jail now, for God's sake, and get me out of this place.

Narrator Hoffman sat impassively through Kunstler's emotional outpouring. Then, with the jury still deliberating, he sentenced Dellinger to six months for reading the names of the dead on Moratorium Day and five months for saying "bullshit"—altogether he sentenced Dellinger to twenty-nine months and thirteen days. The sentencing continued.

Hayden Before your eyes you see a vital element of your system collapsing.

Judge Hoffman Oh don't be so pessimistic, Mr. Hayden. Our system isn't collapsing. Fellows as smart as you could do awfully well under the system.

Abbie Hoffman We don't want a place in the regiment, Julie.

Judge Hoffman What did you say? Your turn's coming up!

Abbie Hoffman I'm being patient, Julie.

Judge Hoffman He thinks that annoys me . . . addressing me by a name that I've been called since I was a boy.

Hayden The point I was trying to make is what I regretted most about punishment. I can only state one thing that affected my feelings and that is that I would like to have a child. (*He sobs.*)

Judge Hoffman That is where the federal system can do you no good.

Hayden Because the federal system can do you no good in trying to prevent the birth of a new world.

Narrator Hayden was sentenced, and, like the rest of the defendants, led out of the courtroom. Abbie Hoffman.

Abbie Hoffman The only dignity that free men have is the right to speak out. When the law is tyranny, the only order is insurrection.

Judge Hoffman Sentence. Eight months and six days.

Scene Twenty-One

Narrator The judge then listed the contempt charges against William Kunstler.

Judge Hoffman . . . for calling this court a medieval torture chamber when the defendant Seale was in altercation with the Marshals, three months. For arguing in "an angry tone" at the conclusion of the witness Ginsberg's testimony that the court should not be recessed early, as the government requested, three months. For asking

Mayor Daley eighty-three questions which were objectionable, six months. In all, I sentence the attorney William Kunstler to four years and thirteen days for the twenty-four counts of contempt. Mr. Kunstler, you have something to say?

Kunstler *stands at the defense table.*

Kunstler   Your Honor, until today I have never once in more than twenty years at the bar been disciplined by a judge, federal or state, although a large part of my practice has been in hostile southern courts.

However, I have the utmost faith that my beloved brethren at the bar, young and old alike, will not allow themselves to be frightened out of defending the poor, the persecuted, the radicals and the militants, the black people, the pacifists, and the political pariahs of this, our common land. I may not be the greatest lawyer in the world, Your Honor, but I think that I am this moment, along with my colleague Leonard Weinglass, the most privileged. We are being punished for what we believe in.

The spectators begin to cheer and applaud.

Judge Hoffman   The Marshals will remove those who have applauded from the courtroom. Remove them from the courtroom! The circus has to end sometime. Please remove everybody who has applauded.

Spectators removed.

Judge Hoffman   Mr. Kunstler, a man charged with a crime has a right to defense properly made, and that does not include what has gone on in this courtroom. For you to have sat through that Bobby Seale incident and never to have made an attempt to say something like this to him, "Bobby, hush. Cool it." But you let him go on and you never made any attempt to keep him from calling a judge a fascist pig, a racist pig. I only mention the Seale episode because I didn't want anyone to think I was obtuse and didn't know what was going on. I didn't want the press to get the impression that I didn't know what was really the time of day.

Kunstler   Your Honor, I am glad you spoke, because I suddenly feel nothing but compassion for you. Everything else has dropped away.

Lights dim. A **Juror** *moves down stage to the audience.*

Narrator   In the jury room, the jurors were as divided as they had been at the beginning of the trial, eight wishing to convict on all counts and four wishing to acquit.

Juror   There were four of us, Frida, Mary, Shirley, and Jean, and we were the four that were for acquittal. The rest were all for guilt and they wouldn't listen. Even when we sat down to eat they would congregate at the other end of the table, and there was never any agreement about anything. They wanted them guilty and that was all there was to it. Our foreman, Edward Kratzke, sent out a hung jury message to the judge and his response was "keep deliberating" and for us to remember that he could keep us there as long as he wanted. In the end the four of us gave in, that was what happened. We weren't getting anywhere, so we just gave in.

Scene Twenty-Two

Richard Schultz Your Honor, before the jury is brought in, can I ask that, considering what has gone on in this courtroom before, it is cleared of all spectators except the press.

There is a reaction from the spectators.

Judge Hoffman You think a rule of exclusion here should apply to the wives of the defendants?

Richard Schultz Yes, Your Honor, they have probably been in contempt more than any of the others.

Kunstler Your Honor, we want to voice the strongest possible objection and that at long last Your Honor will deny a motion made by the prosecution.

Judge Hoffman No, I will decide to enter this order.

Vigorous reaction from the spectators.

Anita Hoffman (*shouting*) The ten of you will be avenged. They will dance on your grave, Julie, and the grave of the pig empire!

Chaos breaks out.

Spectator They are demonstrating all over the country for you. Right on!

Richard Schultz For the record there is screaming in the court and the hallway.

Dellinger That's my thirteen-year-old they're beating her up.

Abbie Hoffman Why don't you bring your wife in, Dick, to watch it?

Dellinger You ought to be a proud man.

Judge Hoffman Marshal, bring in the jury.

The courtroom quietens down as the families are excluded and the jury is brought in.

Judge Hoffman I am informed by the Marshal, ladies and gentlemen, that you have reached a verdict, or some verdicts.

Foreman Yes, Your Honor.

Judge Hoffman If you will hand the verdicts to the Marshal, I will direct them to be read out.

Clerk We the jury find the defendant David T. Dellinger guilty as charged in count two of the indictment and not guilty as charged in count one. We find the defendant Rennard D. Davis guilty as charged in count one of the indictment, and not guilty as charged in count one.

*The **Clerk** continues to read the repeat charges in the background as the **Narrator** takes over.*

Narrator There were compromises. All were acquitted of conspiracy. Froines and Weiner were found innocent of teaching and demonstrating the use of incendiaries. No concrete evidence of this was presented throughout the entire Trial. The other five, however, were found guilty of the new law of crossing state lines with the intention to incite a riot. They were each sentenced to five years in jail, plus a fine of $5000.00, together with the costs for the prosecution. Each defendant made a statement before sentence was imposed.

Dellinger Throughout this trial, Judge, you have behaved as a man who has had too much power over too many people for too many years. I do admire your spunk, but then I keep comparing you to King George the Third of England, trying to hold back the tide of history.

Davis In judging my actions, my jury will be in the streets tomorrow. I am going to be "the boy next door" and we are going to turn the sons and daughters of the ruling class into Viet Cong.

Hayden If you had left us alone on the streets of Chicago, we would hardly have been notorious at all. But instead we were turned into the architects, the masterminds and the genius of a conspiracy to overthrow the government. We were your invention.

Abbie Hoffman You find us guilty of incitement. In 1861, Abraham Lincoln delivered his Inaugural Speech where he said that when the people are weary of their government, they will exert their revolutionary rights to overthrow the government. If he had said that in Lincoln Park in August of 1968, he would be on trial right here in this courtroom, because that is an "inciteful" speech, a speech intended to create a riot.

Rubin This copy of my book is for you, Judge. On the flyleaf I have inscribed—"To Julius, the demonstrations in 1968 were the first steps in the Revolution. What happened in this courtroom is the second step. Julius, you radicalized more young people than ever we could. You are the country's top Yippie."

Scene Twenty-Three

Narrator The decisions went to appeal and by November 1972 all the convictions had been reversed. Initially, one of the appellate court's main reasons for this was Judge Hoffman's "deprecatory and often antagonistic attitude towards the defence." Then later it emerged that throughout the trial, and with the knowledge and complicity of Judge Hoffman and the prosecutors, the FBI had bugged the offices of the Chicago defense attorneys. This was not only an indication of how seriously the government had been taking the conspiracy, but as the appeals panel put it, "the wrongdoing of FBI agents would have required reversal, in themselves."

Foran *moves from behind his desk.*

Foran You know, the thing I disapproved of so strongly was how they gave no credit at all for the fact that Judge Hoffman was just tortured for whatever error or wrongdoing he committed. Generally the law says that individually generated errors, like his, are not excusable or reversible. Well, to people who say that, I reply, you should have been there.

John Schultz, Dellinger, Kunstler, *and a* **Juror** *move to front stage.*

John Schultz   That trial was like a pivotal focal point of the protests and everything that happened in the 1960s. You are talking about the Vietnam War, about racism—I mean civil rights struggles were top of the news for a year everywhere. And at that point it was a direct threat on the structure of power, and all its interlinked aspects, from the presidency to J. Edgar Hoover, to the courts. That was what it was all about, the very state of the nation.

Dellinger   It was a special time, high on the hypertension that sometimes accompanies an inability to deal with major problems like racism and war. I only wish that we'd been smarter, more dedicated, more united to make the best use of it. I wish we could have reached out to the Judge Hoffmans, the Schultzes, the Forans and convince them of the necessity of revolution.

Kunstler   It taught people how to fight in a courtroom. It also taught the American public that the courts were being used by the government to stifle dissent. I was frightened by my own government and what they were capable of, and frightened by my fellow lawyers.

So I came out of it a people's lawyer, if you can use that term,

Juror   I was very frightened by my own government. It changed me very much. When I came back, I was a lot more liberal than I'd ever been in my life. Reading more, very interested in politics. I was for Nixon 100 percent—his first time that is.

Foran   I think it's good to remember it as a piece of theater. There were some outrageous things committed by the defence, but they were to show up the nature of authority when mindless. So perhaps it's about the evil of banality. The danger of mindlessness, the danger of mindlessness fused to banality, of banality fused to muscle, to clout.

Narrator   Beyond the political, moral, and personal assessments of the trial, there remains the question of whether the conspiracy was an invention of the government as Tom Hayden proposed or could have become an actual embryo revolution. That, as the writer Norman Mailer pointed out, the alleged conspirators had discovered that they didn't have to attack the fortress anymore. All they had to do was surround the fortress, make faces at the people inside, and let them have nervous breakdowns and destroy themselves.

Dellinger   I only wish that we'd been smarter, more dedicated, more united to make the best use of it. I wish we could have reached out to the Judge Hoffmans, the Schultzes, the Forans and convince them of the necessity of revolution.

Foran   The nation's children are still being lost to a freaking fag revolution, and we've got to reach out to them. Our kids don't understand that we don't mean anything by it when we call people "niggers." They look at us like we're dinosaurs when we speak like that.

John Schultz Over the years, most of the participants in the trial prospered. At first, when they were released, the defendants planned to form a permanent revolutionary party called The Conspiracy, but separate interests drove them apart. Tom Hayden became a politician, a Californian state senator. Abbie Hoffman continued as a strong radical voice until his death, probably from suicide in 1989. David Derringer continued with international pacifist activities, and Jerry Rubin became a businessman. The defense lawyers were threatened by their Bar Associations, but they became very successful criminal lawyers. Thomas Foran and Richard Schultz went into practice together and prospered.

The judge alone perhaps was the one who suffered. For a while he was praised and feted, but as one appeal after another went against him he was shunned by the very people who supported him. He died a very lonely man, and the very sum of his existence became this trial. At the end when his effects were auctioned, Abbie Hoffman was invited to bid for his gavel. He declined.

The gavel echoes as it is struck twice.

Fade up "Blowin' in the Wind."

A Note from the Writer

In 1992, when this play was commissioned by the BBC, with L.A. Theatre Works as co-producer, many of the past main participants in those events in Chicago in 1968 and 1969 were still alive. Many of them were also willing to collaborate with us and it was a wonderful opportunity to capture the color, the context, and the atmosphere surrounding a trial which summarizes so vividly the situation in late 1960s America. I was there at the time working for the BBC, and I remember the feeling that values and mores were changing before your eyes and that society might just fracture under the pressure irreparably.

And so I first worked up the dramatic structure from the trial transcripts. Then the two producers, Martin Jenkins and John Theocaris, used it as a framework for interviews which were then integrated into the drama.

In producing this version for publication, however, we obviously cannot use the original interview recordings which were such a feature of the first production. However, we do have the texts of what was said, and we have threaded them into the dialogue and structure of the drama, using them verbatim as asides to the audience.

Peter Goodchild

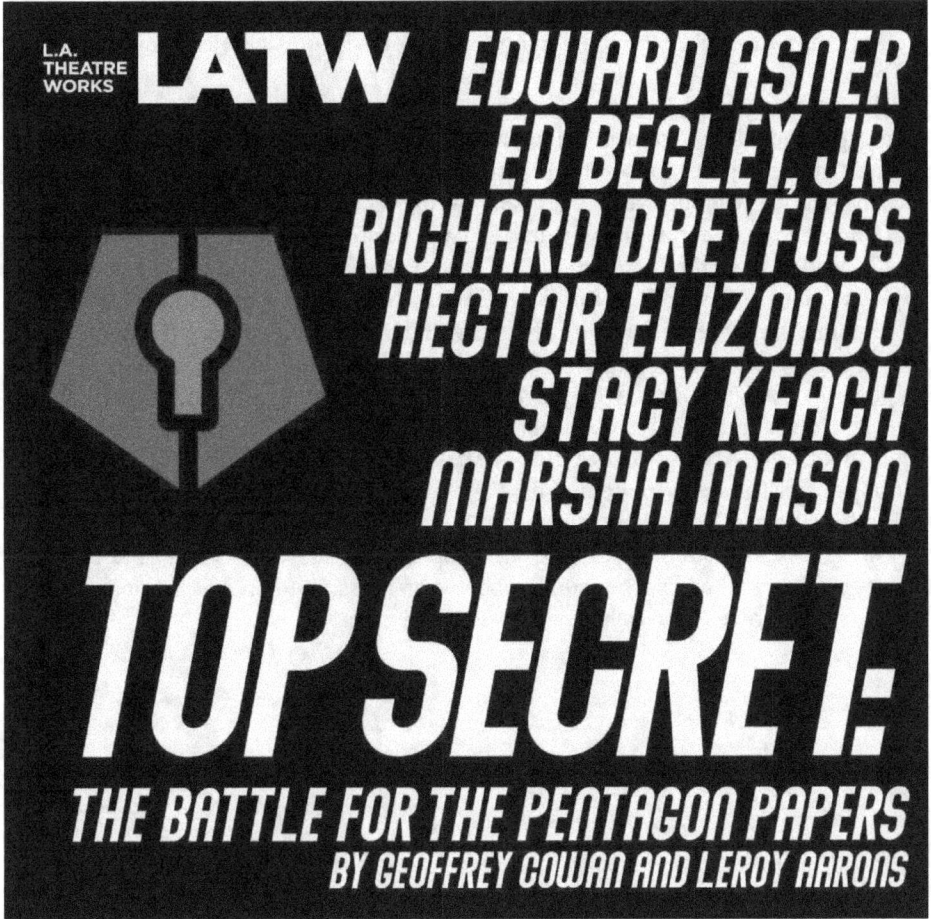

Setting

Time: Summer, 1971
Act One: Ben Bradlee's Living Room, June 17, 1971
Act Two: Federal Courtroom, June 21, 1971

About the Play

In a democratic society, should a government be allowed to protect secrets in the name of national security if those secrets are used to cover up politically damaging actions taken by that government? *Top Secret: The Battle for the Pentagon Papers* is an inside look at the *Washington Post*'s decision to publish the top secret study documenting U.S. involvement in Vietnam. The subsequent trial tested the parameters of the First Amendment, pitting the public's right to know against the government's desire for secrecy. The epic legal battle between the government and the press went to the nation's highest court—arguably the most important Supreme Court case ever on freedom of the press.

This play is based on interviews with the participants and on the actual trial transcripts, including transcripts of the in camera portions of the proceedings that were released under the Freedom of Information Act. For dramatic purposes we have taken certain liberties without, we think, changing the facts. While the play focuses on the *Washington Post*, the trial dialogue in Act Two uses material from the *New York Times* case as well as from the *Washington Post* case. Each case was heard by a trial court, an appellate court, and the U.S. Supreme Court. The lawyers and the judge, therefore, represent a composite of the many lawyers and judges who participated in those cases.

For clarity and simplicity, we have also consolidated a few *Washington Post* employees. George Wilson, who played a crucial role during the trial, actually wasn't present in Ben Bradlee's home on June 17, 1971. Yet we have placed him at Bradlee's home in Act One. Also, since it would have been unwieldy to include all of the important participants at Bradlee's home that day, a few key reporters and editors, most notably Philip Geyelin and Don Oberdorfer, have, to our regret, been omitted from the drama.

For more about our sources, and the people and issues involved in the Pentagon Papers case as well as in other conflicts between press freedom and national security, you may want to visit our website at topsecretplay.org.

Geoffrey Cowan and Leroy Aarons

Original Live Theatre Production

Top Secret: The Battle for the Pentagon Papers by Geoffrey Cowan and Leroy Aarons was originally produced by L.A. Theatre Works. It premiered and was recorded before a live audience at the Double Tree Suites, Santa Monica in March 1991. It was directed by Tom Moore. The cast was as follows:

Chal Roberts	Philip Abbot
Bailiff/Clerk	Irene Arranga
Ben Bradlee	Edward Asner
George Wilson	Ed Begley, Jr.
Eugene Patterson/Carl Coogan	Jack Coleman
Narrator	Richard Dysart
Fritz Beebe	Hector Elizondo
Soldier	Bo Foxworth
Ben Bagdikian	Robert Foxworth
Murray Marder	Robin Gammell
Robert Mardian	Gerrit Graham
Fritz Beebe	Howard Hesseman
John Mitchell	Stacy Keach
Darryl Cox	Darrell Larson
Meg Greenfield	Nan Martin
Katharine Graham	Marsha Mason
Lamont Vanderhall	Richard Riehle
Richard Nixon	Harry Shearer
Ron Ziegler	Joe Spano
Judge Martin Peel	James Whitmore
Henry Kissinger	Harris Yulin

Additional Production

There was a subsequent recording of *Top Secret: The Battle for the Pentagon Papers* before a live audience at the Skirball Cultural Center, Los Angeles in March 2008. It was directed by John Rubinstein. The cast was as follows:

Meg Greenfield	Diane Adair
George Wilson/Eugene Patterson	Bo Foxworth
Ben Bagdikian	John Getz
Murray Marder/Judge Martin Peel	James Gleason
Brian Kelly	Gregory Harrison
Ben Bradlee	John Heard
Robert Mardian/Ron Ziegler	Raphael Sbarge
Soldier/Darryl Cox/Clerk-Bailiff	Russell Soder
Katharine Graham	Susan Sullivan
Fritz Beebe/Dr. Henry Kissinger	Peter Van Norden
Dennis Doolin/President Richard Nixon	Tom Virtue
General John Mitchell/Chal Roberts/Lamont Vanderhall	Geoffrey Wade

Characters

Benjamin Bradlee
Ben Bradlee served as Executive Editor of the *The Washington Post* from 1965 to 1991. He became famous for overseeing the publication of Bob Woodward and Carl Bernstein's stories documenting the Watergate scandal. For decades, Bradlee was one of only four publicly known people who knew the true identity of Deep Throat, the other three being Woodward, Bernstein, and Deep Throat himself.

Ben Haig Bagdikian
Ben Bagdikian has made journalism his profession since 1941. As an editor at *The Washington Post*, Bagdikian was leaked portions of the Pentagon Papers by Daniel Ellsberg.

Frederick Sessions ("Fritz") Beebe
After arranging the purchase of *Newsweek* for one of his best clients, the Post Co., Beebe abandoned his law practice at Cravath, Swaine, & Moore to become the *Post*'s chairman of the board in 1961.

Dennis James Doolin
Dennis Doolin was Deputy Secretary of Defense for International Security Affairs. He was called upon by the government to testify as to the propriety of classifying the Pentagon Papers as top secret.

Katharine Meyer Graham
Publisher and Chairman of the Board of *The Washington Post*.

Meg Greenfield
Known for her wit, Meg Greenfield was a Washington insider and the editorial page editor for *The Washington Post*. She was awarded journalism's highest honor, a Pulitzer Prize for editorial writing, in 1978.

Henry Kissinger
National Security Advisor and Secretary of State under Richard Nixon.

Murray Marder
Was a staff reporter for *The Washington Post* during the Pentagon Papers episode and later became the paper's chief diplomatic correspondent.

Robert Mardian
Assistant Attorney General under Richard Nixon.

Richard Nixon
37th President of the United States.

Eugene Patterson
Eugene Patterson won the 1967 Pulitzer Prize for his civil rights editorials in *The Atlanta Constitution*. Later he served three years as Managing Editor of *The Washington Post*.

Chalmers ("Chal") Roberts
Chal Roberts was a senior Washington correspondent for *The Washington Post*.

George C. Wilson
Reporter and military correspondent for *The Washington Post*.

Ronald Ziegler
White House Press Secretary and Assistant to the President in the Nixon administration.

Producing Director Notes

Susan Loewenberg

Around 1990, I called my friend Geoff Cowan seeking information about a First Amendment issue I was researching. Geoff was teaching at UCLA at the time and was known to be an expert in the field. He answered my questions, and then told me about a docudrama he had written with his friend Leroy Aarons called *Top Secret: The Battle for the Pentagon Papers*. Leroy, a Pulitzer Prize-winning journalist, was *The Washington Post* bureau chief at the time of the "dust up" over the Papers. Though the play piqued my interest, it sat on my desk along with a pile of other scripts I liked but could not yet find a place for in our season.

When the Gulf War began in 1990, my eye happened to fall on Geoff and Roy's manuscript. Suddenly, a light bulb went off: *Top Secret* resonated perfectly with the then-current debate: national security vs. the people's right to know. The play dramatically re-enacted the very issues we were experiencing at the height of the Gulf War.

We shifted into high gear, quickly contacting our local NPR station, NPR headquarters, and LATW's cadre of top actors—Edward Asner, Marsha Mason, Hector Elizondo, and Ed Begley, Jr., among others—to see if they would participate. KCRW (our local station) agreed to record the show for broadcast nationwide and NPR agreed to national distribution; we were off and running. The idea was to "go live" in Los Angeles and delay the broadcast for one day so the East Coast and Midwest would hear it at a reasonable hour. Geoff, Roy, Ruth Seymour from KCRW, and I put our heads together to come up with a wish list of post-performance panelists. Of course, the first on our list was Ben Bradlee, the editor of the *Post* at the time of the Pentagon Papers (not to mention the center of the storm a few years later, uncovering the Watergate scandal). I called him—cold—and to my delight he answered the call. I gave him my pitch, and his first question was, "Who's playing me?" I replied, "Ed Asner," and he seemed pleased. After a pause he asked, "And who is playing Kay?" When I told him Marsha Mason, he chuckled, told me he had danced with her once at the White House, and signed off with, "I'm on board."

After that coup, the rest was easy.

Six weeks later, with the war in the Gulf still raging, we were in the ballroom of the Guest Quarters Suite Hotel (which had been transformed into a recording studio) with 500 audience members practically hanging from the rafters. Our director, Tom Moore, had worked intensely with the authors to polish the script, and we had assembled a dream cast. We had a spectacular panel with Bradlee and Carla Robbins, the head of the reporters' pool in the Gulf, calling in from the NPR studios in Washington; with us in Los Angeles were George Wilson, the actual reporter who figures prominently in the play, Robert Scheer, one of the prominent left-wing journalists who was a major critic of the government during the Vietnam War, Bob Maynard, the editor of the *Oakland Tribune*, and Peter Braestrup, a former Vietnam-era journalist and Senior Editor and Director of Communications at the Library of Congress. The play wrapped up around 1 a.m. EST, so we made sure Ben Bradlee and Carla Robbins back in D.C. had plenty of hot coffee and treats to keep them going for the post-show discussion.

Both the docudrama and the panel afterwards were grand successes, and we won the Corporation for Public Broadcasting's Gold and Silver Awards for the Best Radio Drama Production that year. In retrospect, I am glad I placed the call to Geoff that day. I am delighted to be bringing this ever-relevant work back to universities and performing arts centers worldwide as we continue to confront national security vs. the people's right to know.

A Note from Geoffrey Cowan

This play had its origins in a classroom, so it seems appropriate that it is now being performed at universities around the United States. In the mid-1970s, when teaching an undergraduate lecture course in media law, I found that the most important and dramatic way to start the class was with a discussion of the Pentagon Papers case.

The case was of signal importance since it pitted the interests of a free press against the government's need for secrecy when national security may be at risk. Moreover, the facts were riveting. In the midst of a war in which more than 50,000 American soldiers were killed, *The New York Times* gained possession of a huge trove of documents that traced the origins of the war and described the U.S. government's internal deliberations. Importantly, many of the documents showed government deception—of the press and the public.

The documents, which soon became known as the Pentagon Papers, had been commissioned by Robert McNamara in 1967, while he was the Secretary of Defense. He wanted the government to be able to gain a greater understanding of the origins and decision-making process of the war in Vietnam. Just after President Nixon took office in 1969, the Defense Department published the forty-seven-volume, 7,000-page study, which included about 4,000 pages of contemporaneous documents. It was the most limited of editions. There were only seven copies—five of which were held under lock and key within the United States government at the departments of State and Defense and at the National Archives. The sixth copy was in the possession of Secretary McNamara, who had become the President of the World Bank. The seventh volume was in Santa Monica, at a think tank called the RAND Corporation, which conducts highly sensitive studies for the Department of Defense.

Practically no one read them. But one of those who did was Daniel Ellsberg, a former Defense Department employee, a one-time fervent supporter of the war (or "hawk," in the parlance of the era), who had come to believe that the war was a tragic mistake. With the highest security clearance, he was working at RAND. He quickly became convinced that the Congress and the American people needed to understand what the papers had to say; that they could help to end the war by explaining the series of mistakes and deceptions that had led us to enter Vietnam and to remain there. He and his colleague Anthony Russo secretly copied the documents. First, Ellsberg tried to share some of the documents with Senator William Fulbright, Chairman of the Senate Foreign Relations Committee, hoping that he would hold hearings and make them public. When that failed, he gave the volumes to a reporter at *The New York Times* named Neil Sheehan who had just published a book review discussing the possibility that those who had been involved in conducting the war (perhaps including Ellsberg himself) might be guilty of war crimes.

Against the advice of their outside lawyers, who argued that the publication of top secret documents could be illegal, but following the advice of their internal lawyer, the publisher and editors of *The New York Times* set up a secret team to scour the papers and prepare a series of front-page articles that made heavy use of the documents. When the first story appeared on June 13, 1971, President Richard Nixon's initial reaction was surprisingly benign; after all, the material in the papers ended in 1968, before Nixon took office. But he quickly became concerned about the need to protect government secrets, and he instructed the Attorney General to go to court immediately to block the rest of the series. The government argued that the Pentagon Papers were filled with vital information including codes and battle plans that could put American lives at risk. The district court granted an immediate injunction, pending a formal hearing. And here is where our story and that of *The Washington Post* begins.

In the early 1980s, having told the story to students for almost a decade, I decided to write a play that would use the techniques of contemporary political dramas based on documents such as *Are You Now or Have You Ever Been* and *In the Matter of J. Robert Oppenheimer*, both of which use the transcripts of government hearings to examine the excesses of anti-communism during the Cold War. Since the *Post*'s story was so much more compressed, I decided to tell the story from the perspective of that paper rather than the perspective of *The New York Times*, though both cases were dramatic and the *Times* is, properly, more indelibly identified with the case. I was quickly joined by my friend, the late Leroy Aarons, an immensely talented former *Washington Post* reporter who had a flair for theater and knew all of the newspaper's participants. How Roy would have loved this new production.

Roy and I interviewed most of the key participants and used all of the documents that were available at that time. It should be noted, however, that some additional materials, including some highly revealing White House recordings, have become available during the past decade. Some of those documents, along with other material that may be of interest to students and others, are available on the website of the USC Annenberg Center for Communication Leadership at www.topsecretplay.org

As I write these words, issues of the press and national security are very much in the news. During the war in Iraq, *The New York Times*, *Washington Post*, and other papers have printed stories that the government says compromise our efforts in the war on terror. *The Washington Post*'s Dana Priest won a 2006 Pulitzer Prize for her reporting about the CIA's interrogations of al Qaeda suspects at secret prisons (referred to as "black sites" inside the government) in eight countries, including some in Eastern Europe. At the government's request, she withheld the names of those countries. In awarding the prize, the Pulitzer committee commended Priest "for her persistent, painstaking reports on secret 'black site' prisons and other controversial features of the government's counterterrorism campaign."

Meanwhile, James Risen and Eric Lichtblau of *The New York Times* won a Pulitzer for their stories describing the administration's decision to engage in widespread domestic surveillance without a court order—a practice that has since been changed. The *Times* reporters were cited by the Pulitzer jury "for their carefully sourced stories on secret domestic eavesdropping that stirred a national debate on the boundary line between fighting terrorism and protecting civil liberty."

Many people in and out of government regarded those and similar recent stories as great journalism that has helped to protect our constitutional liberties and America's democratic form of government. Others questioned the wisdom of publishing those stories and some went so far as to charge the papers with treason and wanting America to lose the war. (In his radio program, for example, former Secretary of Education Bill Bennett said of the *Times* reporters, "I think what they did is worthy of jail.")

In June 2007, in a widely debated decision, the CIA decided to release a trove of CIA secrets sometimes known as the "Family Jewels." The Director of National Intelligence, Michael Hayden, explained that he had ordered release of the documents because openness can help build trust for the CIA and because the more that the agency can tell the public, the less chance that misinformation among the public will "fill the vacuum."

In any case involving top secret national security documents, there are a series of decision makers: those in the government who classify the materials in the first place; the person with access to the material who decides to give it to the press; the reporters, editors, and publishers who decide whether to use the story; the leaders of government who decide whether to take the case to court; and the court itself, which has to decide whether to stop the press from printing—or to punish the press for what it has printed. The stories that gain public attention are naturally those where the material is "leaked" and where a publication decides to use the material. Those concerned with the battle over government secrets should always be mindful that the best reporters and editors have had access to scores of national secrets that they have decided not to print and that such reporters and editors maintain that they only print those stories which they are convinced have been improperly classified and where the benefits to the public far outweigh any risks to national security. But there are those who believe that new risks will be presented, and new rules may evolve, in an era dominated by the Internet and by concerns about international terrorism.

Interview Highlights

Susan Loewenberg   The central issues raised by *Top Secret: The Battle for the Pentagon Papers* are as relevant today, if not more so, than they were in 1971. In a democratic society, should a government be allowed to protect secrets in the name of national security—if those secrets are used to cover up politically damaging actions taken by that government?

To discuss this, I was joined onstage after the performances by co-author Geoffrey Cowan and a distinguished panel of experts: former Nixon White House counsel and author John Dean, journalist and author Robert Scheer, and Congresswoman Jane Harman, who served as the ranking Democrat on the Intelligence Committee and currently chairs the Homeland Security committee. Here's Geoffrey Cowan.

Geoffrey Cowan   John Dean has actually written a very interesting movie about the Pentagon Papers which covers some of the same material, but more importantly John Dean lived through this entire period inside the White House. I think, John, you were saying beforehand that this marked the turning point in the history of the Nixon administration. Maybe you could talk for a minute about seeing this from inside the White House.

John Dean   I've got to first say that the number of microphones on this stage about equal to what was in the Oval Office and somehow I always managed to sit down in front of one—thank God, later I said. The point you make, though, that I had mentioned at the break how important this particular event is portrayed in the play was to the Nixon presidency cannot be underestimated. Those of us who have talked about what happened after the fact have all come to almost a unanimous conclusion we all agree that the Pentagon Papers leak, and Nixon's handling of it, became a turning point in the Nixon White House. There had been hanky-panky before, there have been newsmen put under surveillance trying to track down who is leaking national security information, but nothing quite like what happened after the Pentagon Papers leaked. So a lot of us have always been interested in what did happen.

I remember hearing the story the Monday after Tricia's wedding. When Nixon came in the office on Sunday, he first looked to see what the coverage had been in the *New York Times*—he had the *Post* there also—but he would look first at the *Times* to see how the coverage of the wedding had been. Which was pretty good, pretty happy with that and it. Then he looked over and saw this major story, the first installment of this study of the release of the causes of the war in Vietnam, which caught his attention. His first reaction is that this is wonderful! This is going to show how duplicitous the Democrats have been and how they have dragged us into this war by deceiving the American people. And this is his initial thought in his initial frame of mind.

It's really not until Monday when Henry Kissinger comes back, as you portrayed briefly in the play, Henry turns to the President, talks about the effect this is going to have the inability of him to control the papers of his administration's highly confidential material. It'll affect first of all these negotiations with the North Vietnamese, and Paris, and the secret Paris peace talks. But more importantly, Henry is escalating it when he tells him it's going to affect your ability for you to carry out your China initiative, which then was still in development, and was the centerpiece not only of what he conceived of as his re-election campaign, but his entire presidency. He knew his decision and his China initiative would really change history, and change his place in history.

But there's one line you missed in the tapes that has always fascinated me that really got to Nixon. Henry knew exactly which buttons to push and how hard to push. And at one point after, as you report, how Henry is describing his former student and former colleague Dan Ellsberg, and what a nasty man he is making things up that have no basis in truth, but really trying to get Nixon all excited about it. And he tells Nixon after this brief colloquy, he says—if you can't deal effectively with Ellsberg, if you can't go after him and deal with his stealing of these papers, and releasing them, Mr. President, the world is going to see you as a weakling. Well, Henry pushed the manhood button and this button is one that Nixon always reacted to.

And after that, you hear Nixon thumping on the table pounding and saying I'm going to do this and that. This is where he claims at one point he learns that apparently the Brookings Institute has a copy of the Pentagon Papers, and he orders a break-in into the Brookings Institute. He says I don't care how you get them just go in there and get them.

Geoffrey Cowan Bob, you lived through this in many ways then, and you to some extent are living through it now, and I wonder if you could talk a little bit about these issues of secrecy and the public's right to know as you perceive them as they existed then, and how it strikes you in terms of today's world.

Robert Scheer I think the issue was framed by the founders. You cannot have a republic and an empire. You have to make a choice. And the reason that Washington and Jefferson warned about foreign entanglements, foreign engagements, is they knew it's incompatible with a democratic society.

So we should just recognize that. If you're going to be involved in building empires, if you're going to be involved in these foreign escapades, truth will be destroyed. And the proof of that is that despite all the great lessons of the Pentagon Papers, and everything, *The Washington Post* and *The New York Times* fell for the lies about Iraq! Boom! Gone! Where was freedom of the press after 9/11? Where were the vigilant guardians of the gate? They collapsed!

Geoffrey Cowan Jane, you're privy to some secrets, probably not all in these jobs that you've had, but certainly have an insight as to what the public is told, what's kept from the public—and I wondered if you could share some perspectives on that.

Congresswoman Jane Harman In the play, Congress played almost no role, except fortuitously, the critical piece of evidence had been published in a hearing report. But otherwise at least, you don't hear about a role that Congress played. Congress, subsequent to this chain of events, did play a role. I joined John Tunney's staff in 1972. And as Watergate unfolded, Congress was all over it, and I think played a very constructive role. I remember a role I played that I still recall was on Sunday after the Saturday Night Massacre. You'll all remember that there was a series of resignations in the Justice Department, and finally, someone agreed to fire Archibald Cox who had been doing an investigation.

There was a secret meeting in the Congress of key Democrats on the Senate Judiciary Committee, and each could bring one aide, and I was John Tunney's aide and I was the only woman.

I remember thinking about how cataclysmic this all was, and thinking that Washington would break out in gunshot. I mean if there was a risk with this could happen. The secret meeting was about how does Congress—of course Ted Kennedy was there, Birch Bayh was there, it was an interesting cast of characters—how does Congress assert its authority? And in that meeting, it was decided we must get into this, and we must make certain that this plays out in a way that saves the Republic. And it did play out in the way that saves Republic. And I don't mean to claim all the credit for Congress. But I sensed at that moment the awakening of courage in Congress.

Note

This play is based on interviews with the participants and on the actual trial transcripts, including transcripts of the *in camera* portions of the proceedings that were released under the Freedom of Information Act. For dramatic purposes we have taken certain liberties without, we think, changing the facts. The scenes in the Oval Office are adapted from various transcripts and accounts of those events. While the play focuses on the *Washington Post*, the trial dialogue in Act Two uses material from the *New York Times* case as well as from the *Washington Post* case. Each case was heard by a trial court, an appellate court, and the U.S. Supreme Court. The lawyers and the judge, therefore, represent a composite of the many lawyers and judges who participated in those cases. The final scene is a dramatic invention based on the characters and issues as we have come to understand them.

Since the judge is a composite character with a fictional name, we should stress that Judge Murray Gurfein, whom John Mitchell praises when he issues the first restraining order against the *New York Times*, ultimately issued a ringing endorsement of the importance of the First Amendment.

For clarity and simplicity, we have also consolidated a few *Washington Post* employees. George Wilson, who played a crucial role during the trial, actually wasn't present in Ben Bradlee's home on June 17, 1971. Yet we have placed him at Bradlee's home in Act One. Also, since it would have been unwieldy to include all of the important participants at Bradlee's home that day, a few key reporters and editors, most notably Philip Geyelin and Don Oberdorfer, have, to our regret, been omitted from the drama.

Those interested in learning more about our sources, and about the people and issues involved in the Pentagon Papers case as well as in other conflicts between press freedom and national security, may want to visit our website at topsecretplay.org.

Characters (in order of appearance)

Katharine Graham
Richard Nixon
John Mitchell
H. R. (Bob) Haldeman
Ron Ziegler Ben
Bradlee Eugene
Patterson Ben
Bagdikian Chal
Roberts Murry
Marder George
Wilson Brian Kelly
Meg Greenfield
Fritz Beebe
Henry Kissinger
Soldier
Robert Mardian
Reporter 1
Reporter 2
Reporter 3
Clerk-Bailiff
Judge Martin Peel
Lamont Vanderhall
Dennis Doolin
Darryl Cox

Act One

Graham Hello, I'm Katharine Graham. It is now almost forty years since the events to be depicted this evening, events which had such a profound impact on our newspaper and on the nation—as well as on my own life. It was June of 1971, and I was still getting my sea legs as publisher of *The Washington Post*, the daily which my father had bought at a bankruptcy auction in 1933, and which was published by my husband for twenty-four years, until he ended his own life.

June is a time for weddings in Washington, D.C., with glorious weather and roses in bloom. No wedding that year promised to be as newsworthy as that of President Nixon's younger daughter Tricia and Edie Cox, a Harvard-trained lawyer. Our editors had assigned a talented but somewhat sharp-penned reporter to cover the event. She had once compared Tricia to an ice-cream cone (beat) vanilla. Frankly, I'm not sure that I would have wanted her to cover my own daughter's wedding. But when the White House barred her from the affair I got drawn into the story.

Apparently, the White House did not want the episode to get out of hand, so for the first and only time during his years as President Nixon's Chief of Staff, Bob Haldeman called me directly. I'm sure I would have handled the whole thing differently later—but I was still learning what it means to be a publisher, and I tried my best to avoid a confrontation.

Thinking back on it, it's a bit embarrassing to remember my words, and my nervous laugh, as I tried to accommodate Haldeman. Well. My naïve effort as a negotiator failed, and the *Post* was banned from the wedding that Saturday.

Despite some intermittent showers, President Nixon managed to escort his daughter down the staircase, past the columns of the south portico and into the Rose Garden. It was the first outdoor wedding in White House history.

Coincidently, I was a guest at another rain-interrupted wedding that Saturday, the wedding of Jimmy Reston, the son of the great *New York Times* reporter and editor Scotty Reston. While there, I learned that the *Times* had access to a much more important story that would be on the front of the paper the next day.

Scotty told me that the *Times* would be publishing a series of articles about a secret history of the decision-making that led us into the Vietnam War. It had been commissioned by my friend Bob McNamara in 1967, while he was still Secretary of Defense. He wanted to help future scholars understand what had happened and why.

We had been scooped by the *Times* on a bombshell of a story—which drove our editor, Ben Bradlee, wild with competitive envy. Ben wanted the *Post* to be every bit as important as the *Times*—and he hated the idea of rewriting stories that had been first published elsewhere.

Their story appeared the next morning on the front page of the *Sunday Times*—right next to the one about Tricia's wedding.

Ben was mortified, even more so the following day when the *Times* published another installment of what promised to be a multi-part, blockbuster series.

As it happened, on Monday evening, I had dinner in New York with some friends, including Abe Rosenthal, the editor of *The New York Times*.

Over a glass of wine, Abe told me that the Attorney-General, John Mitchell, had just called the *Times*, and threatened to take them to court if it published again the next day.

Nonetheless, the *Times* published the third installment on Tuesday morning, and we at the *Post* continued to play catch-up.

At the time, I couldn't understand why Nixon cared so much about documents that were several years old—and some much older than that—and that seemed most likely to embarrass the Democrats. But a couple of years later, thanks to Watergate, we found out that Nixon had been secretly taping his own White House meetings. We learned what he and his top aides were thinking and saying. We could even listen in on Nixon having a late afternoon visit in the Oval Office on June 15, 1971, with Attorney-General John Mitchell and White House Chief of Staff Bob Haldeman.

The Oval Office of the White House.

Nixon Well, John, I hope you had some time off, that they didn't bother you to death with Kent State and all that. Did you do any fishing?

Mitchell We fished, and we went out in the boat with Bebe Rebozo a couple of times.

*Haldeman We didn't bother you too much?

*Mitchell No, not you fellows.

Nixon I'd like a little consommé. Want some consommé?

Mitchell I'd love some. So, it was absolutely great. The weather was wonderful.

Nixon Yeah [*static, unintelligible*] . . . wish we were as lucky. Goddamn weather over Hanoi . . . [*unintelligible*]. Damn it, if any of you know any prayers, say them, 'cause we need some clear bombing weather. The bastards have never been bombed like they are going to be bombed this time, but you've got to have weather.

Mitchell Is the weather still bad?

Nixon Huh! It isn't all that bad. The goddamn Air Force won't fly. The Air Force isn't worth . . . [*unintelligible*]. I mean, they won't fly . . .

*Haldeman It's the strangest thing. In World War II they flew those bombing runs all the time and they couldn't see a thing.

*Nixon I know.

Mitchell Are the Navy pilots as bad?

Nixon Oh, they're better, but they're all under this one command. It's all screwed up. The weather will clear up. It's bound to. When they do, they'll hit something—and there are a lot of brave guys—you've got to say. After all that POW crap, those poor guys who got shot down. They're over there starving on that damned rice. It's all right, we'll give 'em hell . . . How's your consommé?

Mitchell   Quite good, thank you.

Nixon   Too salty . . . Okay, what about the *New York Times* situation?

Mitchell   Well, as you know, we're waiting for the judge's decision in New York on our request to stop the *Times* from publishing further excerpts from the Vietnam papers. If that works, we'll start looking at criminal action. We've got to stop these goddamn leaks.

*Nixon   It's treasonable. Boy, if I were the publisher of a great newspaper, I wouldn't print this stuff. I don't give a damn about the information in the Vietnam papers; that all happened under the Democrats. Politically, it might even be a plus. But it makes my blood boil to have those goddamn newspapers printing stolen government documents.

*Haldeman   What's the use of the classification system? Why the hell do we classify anything if a newspaper feels no compunctions about printing it?

*Mitchell   It's an outrage.

*Haldeman   What motivates the intellectuals—and must help motivate the *Times*—is the knowledge that it hurts the government. Don Rumsfeld was making that point this morning. For the ordinary guy, all of this is a bunch of gobbledygook. But out of the gobbledygook comes a very clear thing, which is: You can't trust the government, you can't believe what they say and you can't rely on their judgment. And as a result, the implicit infallibility of presidents, which has been an accepted thing in America, is badly hurt by this, because it shows that people do things the president wants to do even though it's wrong. And the president can be wrong.

*Nixon   You're right! And we've got to ferret out the leakers, too. They're the lowest vermin. Let's get the guy who leaked the Pentagon material—and tell Ziegler to freeze out the *Times* completely . . . Oh, here he is now . . . Ron, we were just talking about you.

Ziegler   Mr. President, I thought you'd like to know that the judge slapped a restraining order on *The New York Times* this afternoon barring them from printing any more of the Vietnam papers, pending a hearing.

Mitchell   Good for him! I told you that judge was a good man.

Nixon   Great! Now we can move.

Mitchell   I'll start right now to get a grand jury convened to seek criminal indictments against the *Times*.

*Nixon   And, Ron, *The New York Times* is finished in the White House. Henry talked to that damn Jew Max Frankel all the time. He's bad. You know? Don't give them anything. No one but you and me even talks to any of those bastards. Do I make myself clear?

Ziegler Absolutely, Mr. President. If those guys are aching for a fight, we'll take our gloves off too.

Mitchell We're going to go after the whole crowd.

Nixon Wonderful. Wonderful.

Graham When the court stopped the *Times* from printing the next installment, Ben Bradlee was determined to track down a copy of the papers and seize the story for the *Post*. Technically, *The Washington Post* was not covered by the court's injunction. But Ben also knew that if the government found out that we planned to pick up where the *Times* left off, they would come after us with guns blazing. On Tuesday night, the *Post*'s Assistant Managing Editor, Ben Bagdikian, called Bradlee to say that he had made a contact to acquire a copy of the papers. So, early on the morning of June 17, 1971, Bradlee secretly summoned a group of his top reporters to his (lovely) townhouse in Georgetown, where they waited for Bagdikian to arrive with the contraband materials. Almost no one else on the *Post* staff knew what was happening—except for our Managing Editor, Gene Patterson, who kept calling Bradlee to make sure that we would really be able to launch our own series for the next day.

Phone rings.

Bradlee Bradlee here.

Patterson Ben?

Bradlee Gene?

Patterson I need to alert the composing room crew down here. Are we really going to be able to go with it tonight?

Bradlee You're goddamn right we will. It burns me to be beaten on a Washington story by *The New York Times*. Now that they're barred from publishing we have a golden opportunity.

Patterson Okay. Who's gonna write it?

Bradlee I've asked Roberts, Marder, and Wilson. And to come directly here. I'm not taking any chances on the Feds learning about this.

Patterson I heard a report that the *Times* got the stuff from a guy named Ellsberg. Is he our source, too?

Bradlee Damned if I know. All I know is, Bagdikian shot out of town yesterday headed somewhere in a hurry. Next thing, he calls me at some God-awful hour and says he's on his way back with the goods. I hope he didn't get hijacked. (*Doorbell rings.*) Wait, maybe that's him now. I'll call you back. (*Opens door.* **Bagdikian** *enters.*) Bagdikian, you son of a bitch. You made it. So this is it. Christ, there must be thousands of pages in that carton.

Bagdikian Four thousand, four hundred and fifteen, to be exact. And he didn't give me everything he had. (*He wipes himself with a handkerchief.*) It's damn hot. Have you got a glass of water?

Bradlee   You look like you need one. It's a scorcher out there. (*He goes into the kitchen to get the water.*)

Bagdikian (*shouting after him*)   Guess who I met on the plane? Stanley Karnow.

Bradlee (*returning with the water*)   No kidding? What happened?

Bagdikian   Well, mostly small talk at first, how glad he was to be joining the *Post* after all of his years at *Time* Magazine, stuff like that. I was in first class, me in one seat, the carton in the other, both trying to look inconspicuous. Suddenly, the son of a bitch figured it out and yells, "You got it!"

Bradlee   Christ, What did you say?

Bagdikian   I said, "Got what, Stanley?" He looked blank for a minute, then his face turned red as a beet, and he just said, "Oh," and skulked away.

Bradlee   This gets more like a spy movie every minute. (*The doorbell rings.*) Here come the guys. (*He talks while going to answer the door.*) I've asked Chal Roberts, Murry Marder, and George Wilson to work on it.

Bagdikian   You certainly have the first team.

Roberts   Damn, it's good to get my hands on the original after rewriting the goddamn *New York Times* for three days. You did good, Bagdikian.

*****Bradlee** (*to* **Wilson**)   Weren't you supposed to move to Virginia today, George? What did you tell your wife?

*****Wilson**   She wasn't too happy. But I guess that's one virtue of covering the Pentagon. There's always some urgent mission you can't talk about.

*****Bradlee**   Lots of guys would kill for the opportunity to use that excuse.

Marder (*looking over the papers*)   This is a mess. Some of it isn't even numbered. It's out of chronological order. It's going to take us days just to sort it out.

Bradlee   Days, my ass. This is our shot. I want to stick it to the *Times*. This is the biggest story of government deception in decades and if we sit on the goddamn thing the government might find out and try to stop us. I want a story for tomorrow's paper.

Marder   Tomorrow! Ben, that's totally unrealistic.

Wilson   C'mon, Murry. I heard that you once actually produced a story for the next day's paper—I think it was April 10, 1955—all three paragraphs. We know you can do it again.

Marder   Wilson, you'd be a howl if this wasn't damn serious business. The *Times* had three months to consider this stuff and to produce some great reporting. We're expected to sort it, read it, understand, and write it in seven hours? Hell, I don't mind going to jail for publishing a leaked document, but I am not going to go to jail for stupidity!

Bagdikian   Gentlemen, *The Washington Post* is a daily newspaper and this is a breaking story. I suggest we treat it as such. So, let's tackle it and do our best and take a reading in a couple of hours when you have it somewhat sorted out. Okay?

Roberts   Where to?

Bradlee   There's tables and paper set up in the den. Good luck.

Marder (*as they begin to exit*)   George, give me a hand with this box.

Wilson (*grunting sounds*)   God, this mother is heavy.

Roberts (*as voices drift off*)   How are we going to divvy this thing up? By chronology, or subject?

Wilson   How about by weight?

Bradlee   Whew! I'm going to get myself another drink before the lawyer shows up.

Bagdikian   Lawyer?

Bradlee   Yeah. Our usual guy is handling a big case in Chicago, so the law firm is sending down some heavy hitter from New York. Name is Kelly. We gotta run this past him.

Bagdikian   Makes sense. It's definitely a hot one. I don't expect him to be too thrilled.

Bradlee   Maybe. Maybe he'll love it. I dunno.

Bagdikian   I highly doubt it. The Secretary of State used to be the head of their firm. Ben, you said these papers get printed or the *Post* will be looking for a new executive editor.

Bradlee   And I meant it, goddamnit! This puts us on the map. It makes the *Post* a national paper. Don't you think it's odd that McNamara ordered the study. It could only make him look bad. He was the Secretary of Defense during the whole thing.

Bagdikian   He wanted a historic record of the whole bloody mess, to learn from our experience. What he got was a detailed account of all the manipulations and lies, the self-delusions.

Bradlee   What's that adage, be careful what you wish for. So tell me how you engineered this thing?

Bagdikian   I can't say too much, even to you. But when the story broke in the *Times* last Sunday, I began calling all over the country trying to find a copy of the papers. Two nights ago, after the *Times* was ordered to stop publishing, I struck oil. I got a call from a source. He had lots of worries, but mostly I had to promise we'd use the stuff.

Bradlee   Source, huh? Every news report in the country this morning is saying it's this guy Ellsberg.

Bagdikian   They're saying who they think the *Times*' source is. I'm not saying who mine is.

Bradlee   Okay, okay. Go ahead.

Bagdikian That's when I called you and got your assurances. Then I headed for Boston.

Bradlee Boston! I thought you went to Los Angeles.

Bagdikian No. My guy was in a motel in Boston. Talk about spy movies! I was directed from one phone booth to another and from checkpoint to checkpoint, until the drop was finally made. It's 2:30 in the morning. I get the Papers into a carton and grab a cab to a hotel. By this time I'm paranoid, convinced I'm being tailed.

Bradlee That's not paranoia. The way the government's been reacting, that's common sense. I hope nobody beside Karnow saw you.

Bagdikian I was pretty careful. This morning, after a few hours' sleep, I had a cup of coffee and began looking for some twine to tie the carton so I could carry it on the plane. Naturally there was no rope to be found anywhere in the hotel at 6 a.m. So I managed to find a piece they had used to tie a dog to a fence a few days ago. Let history record that it took a dog leash to transport the Pentagon Papers.

Bradlee's *den. The sound of typewriters.*

Graham In Bradlee's den, Roberts, Marder, and Wilson had begun to sort through the carton of documents. It was 11:35 a.m.

Roberts (*taking off his shirt*) Ahh . . . that's better.

Marder Jesus, Chal, first you took your jacket off, then your tie, and now your shirt. You planning to audition for the *Cosmo* centerfold?

Roberts Huh? Oh, it's goddamn hot in here.

Wilson Hot? That air-conditioning is so cold my fingertips are developing icicles. Chal's trying to get us enjoined for indecent exposure.

Marder (*oblivious, discovering something*) Listen to this. You remember Pleiku in early 1965? The North Vietnamese attacked the big air base there and killed a bunch of our soldiers?

Wilson Of course I remember. That's why we started bombing North Vietnam.

Marder So we were told. Our old pal Mac Bundy was in Vietnam at the time, assessing the situation for LBJ. He was so angry that he recommended a massive escalation of the war.

Roberts So, get to the point.

Marder The point is, it was all a lie. These papers show that Bundy and LBJ had already decided to bomb the North. They were just looking for an excuse, and Pleiku gave them what they needed. Bundy says—Pleikus are like streetcars. You catch them as one comes along. His outrage was just a ruse to fool the public.

Wilson That shouldn't shock you, of all people. You're the guy who invented the term "credibility gap"!

Marder   I certainly had my suspicions, but I could never prove it. And I wasn't quite sure the *Post* would print it if we could prove it. Much as I admire Bradlee and Mrs. Graham, they always seemed a bit too cozy with the administration. You did, too, Chal. You used to have those elaborate parties with all your pals from the State Department. They all looked like ambassadors—straight from central casting.

Roberts   Except you. You looked like Peter Falk in *Columbo*. Always sure that someone in the room had committed a crime. It's still hard for me to believe all of this. In those days I just couldn't imagine that the government and the President would lie to us.

*****Wilson**   Well, things are simpler now. Now we just *assume* they're lying to us.

*****Roberts** (*still at his work*)   That's a sad commentary about *something*.

Bagdikian *has entered the room*

Roberts   Bagdikian, welcome to our cell.

Bagdikian   What've you got?

Wilson   I've been going through to see what's been printed before and what's new. I remember seeing a lot of this material before in other forms—in magazines, official public documents, and so on.

Roberts   The most concise sequence—the easiest to grab hold of—goes back to the Eisenhower administration, the French period in Indochina. It's not the sexiest stuff in the world, but there're some important revelations. Ike actually tried to stall an election in Vietnam in 1954 because Dulles was warning it might go to the communists. That, combined with the surprise that the *Post* has the Papers, should make a hell of a good package.

Bagdikian   Fine. That'll be our lead story for tomorrow, but I'd like everybody to keep working as if they were writing for tonight's deadline . . . we should be aiming for finished copy no later than 5 p.m. (*Looking at his watch.*) It's nearly noon. Any questions?

Marder   Did I hear Meg Greenfield in the living room?

Bagdikian   Yeah. She's looking to do an editorial. And there's a lawyer named Kelly, flew down from New York, presumably to protect us from any legal bloopers. You guys need anything?

Wilson   How about a double scotch?

Roberts   Tell 'em to turn up the air conditioning.

Bagkikian   You got it.

*****Marder** (*after **Badkikian** closes the door*)   I told you they'd get cold feet. It's Marder's rule: never trust the lawyers.

Fade-out of typewriters. **Bradlee***'s living room.*

Graham While the reporters were in the den, intoxicated by the aroma of a great story, a top-flight attorney from New York, a man named Brian Kelly, arrived at Ben's house. As it happened, I had never met him, but he had a reputation as a great litigator. Kelly was in the living room, delivering a sermon on the law to Bradlee, Bagdikian, and my good friend Meg Greenfield, one of our finest editorial page editors.

Kelly I can understand how you guys feel—you're newspapermen . . . er . . . and women. And it's your job to print news without necessarily making any judgments as to . . .

Greenfield (*interrupting*) Oh, c'mon, Mr. Kelly, give us a little more credit than that . . .

Kelly (*interrupting back*) Wait a minute, wait a minute, let me finish my point. And please call me Brian. I'm simply trying to put it in some perspective. Back in 1931 . . . where's my citation? (*Finding it, he continues.*) Back in 1931, in a case called Near versus Minnesota, the Supreme Court said that the government has the right to prevent publication of material that could endanger human lives—like naming the sailing dates of transports, or the number and location of troops . . . now you guys got 4,000 pages of top secret war-related material, and inside of eight hours you plan to dump it on the public without a careful, responsible analysis of what's in it.

Bradlee Brian, that's ridiculous. The *Washington Post* has no intention of publishing troop movements or anything else that we regard as sensitive material.

Kelly Yeah, but how do you know? You rush into print with something that on the face of it looks innocent . . . But what if, as a result, some agent or operative in Vietnam gets executed? How would the *Post* look?

Bagdikian My soapbox may be showing, but I'm convinced that by printing the Pentagon Papers, the *Post* will *save* lives, not cost lives. And the families of tens of thousands of Americans killed in this damned war—not to mention the Vietnamese—may even want to know why it wasn't done earlier.

Kelly Well said, sir, but I'd hate to have to prove it in a court of law. It might go down better at an anti-war demonstration.

Bagdikian Wait a second, Brian, I resent the suggestion that we're staging some kind of street-corner demonstration here. The three men in that room among them have seventy years of distinguished coverage in their field. Chal Roberts, the senior Washington correspondent of this newspaper, is retiring in two weeks after thirty-eight years of government reporting. George Wilson is the most trusted Defense Department expert in the business. Murry Marder knows more about the State Department than the damn Secretary of State.

Kelly I'm not questioning anybody's credentials.

Bagdikian No, you're questioning their judgment. We're big boys, Brian, not a bunch of kids playing newspaper. We make these kinds of decisions every day.

Kelly Gentlemen. I hope we can avoid getting into personalities. We're all on the same side in this situation. My job is to lay out the legal options. The government went into court and said that continuing publication of the Pentagon Papers by the *New York Times* would do irreparable damage to the security of the United States. The court accepted that argument, at least to the extent that it ordered the *Times* to cease publishing until the facts can be determined in a formal hearing. The presumption, it seems to me, is that the court intends that the issue be aired in the courtroom, not in the press. If the *Washington Post* goes ahead and prints, isn't it in effect flouting the court's injunction?

Bradlee It's a hell of a good argument. Let's publish and find out.

Greenfield I confess I have trouble following the logic that suggests that because the government declares something off limits, all newspapers should fall in line like a bunch of Marines. That's one hell of a precedent.

Bagdikian Besides, the way our first story is lining up, the events we're writing about all took place in the fities. Nothing sensitive about that.

Kelly If it's not sensitive, why has the U.S. government chosen to keep it secret for twenty years?

Greenfield Brian, that's positively naive. Look, the government labels practically *everything* "top secret," including the menu of the Pentagon cafeteria, and then leaks things selectively when it serves its purposes. Without leaks, both the government and the press might as well close up shop. It's an intimate, symbiotic relationship.

Bradlee Brian, let me relate a personal experience. I covered Jack Kennedy in the sixties. Do you remember his big summit with Khrushchev? Well, it was a disaster, and as a result the administration labeled everything connected with the dialogue "top secret." Off limits. However, Jack was interested in getting out the fact that Khrushchev had agreed to relax some restrictions on mutual arms inspections, a victory of sorts. So, he arranged for me to get hold of the file for that part of the discussion, and, of course, I went with it. A scoop for me, a propaganda coup for him.

Kelly Ben, that's a totally different situation. That was the President exercising his right to declassify a document.

Bagdikian It doesn't matter whether it's the President or the director of federal fisheries! The point is that this tacit arrangement between the press and government in Washington has gone on for a long time. Most of it produces pablum. But once in a while, a journalist manages to ferret out something really meaningful. Sure, it might embarrass a federal official, or an entire administration. But do we have a right to suppress it, or to give the government that power?

Kelly Who's talking about suppression? I'm not arguing against publication. I'm arguing against *rushing into* publication. What is the rush?

Bradlee I'll tell you what the rush is, Brian. For three days the *Times* beat the living bejesus out of us, and I'll be goddamned if I'm going to let the story slip away now.

Kelly   In short, a scoop at any cost.

Bradlee   No. Calculate the cost as best you can. Then go for the scoop.

Bradlee's *den. The sound of typewriters.*

Roberts   Hey, listen to this. I've found an incredible passage about Diem's assassination. It seems the Kennedy administration was involved in the 1963 coup all the way up to its eyeballs.

Wilson   Hey, wait a minute. I thought JFK liked Diem.

Roberts   So he did. So did my friends at the State Department. And so did some of our most important military brass. General Harkin, our top field general at the time, fired off a protest to Washington saying, quote, "rightly or wrongly, we have backed Diem for eight long, hard years. It seems incongruous now to get him down, kick him around, and get rid of him." Harkin sent that telegram on October 30, 1963.

Wilson   Thursday. The day before the coup.

Marder   How the hell do you always remember that kind of shit?

Roberts   Listen to this. It seems that our ambassador, and probably the rest of the administration, were helping the plotters. Here's a telegram from McGeorge Bundy in the White House to Ambassador Lodge in Saigon. "Once a coup under responsible leadership has begun," Bundy says, "it is in the interest of the U.S. government that it should succeed."

*****Marder**   Ah, hah! All these years I have been telling you to be more skeptical of what you hear from your friends in government. So Jack Kennedy actually helped overthrow Diem?

*****Roberts** (*troubled*)   It seems he sure as hell didn't try to stop it.

Sound of typewriter fades. **Bradlee**'s *living room. Doorbell rings.* **Beebe** *enters.*

Bradlee   Fritz, how was your flight?

Beebe   The usual Eastern Shuttle luxury.

Bradlee   Brian, you know Fritz Beebe, of course, Chairman of the *Post* Company. (*Ad-lib introductions.*)

Beebe   Who's the kid out on the steps selling lemonade at ten cents a shot?

Bradlee   That's my nine-year-old capitalist, Marina.

Beebe   Well, if the *Post* gets shut down, the Bradlee family can always switch to the soft drink business.

Bradlee   Not at those prices. I told the kid to charge a quarter. But she's already a bleeding-heart liberal.

Bagdikian *and* **Roberts** *enter.*

Bagdikian   Ben, Chal has a start.

Bradlee Great, let's see. (*Shuffling of papers as he scans.*)

Roberts It's early stuff, but I think it's interesting. It shows that we were tampering with their politics as far back as the fifties.

Bradlee Shouldn't we start with something more current?

Bagdikian Not necessarily. This sets up the entire series. Don't worry, it'll build.

Bradlee Okay. Keep churning it out, Chal. It's after three o'clock.

Roberts (*exiting*) I'll get back to it.

Kelly Ben, there's another issue to consider. (*A pause, then:*) Espionage.

Bradlee Espionage?!

Kelly Look, even if the court lets us go ahead and print, the government might still bring criminal charges against the *Post*—under the Federal Espionage Act.

Bradlee Which says what?

Kelly It's part of the Criminal Code. (*He picks up a marked volume.*) Section 793(e) . . . Here it is. Let me read it to you:

"Whoever has unauthorized possession of . . . information relating to the national defense, which information the possessor has reason to believe could be used to injure the United States . . . and who willfully communicates that information to anyone not entitled to receive it . . . shall be fined not more than $10,000, or imprisoned not more than ten years, or both."

Bradlee No problem. One, the *Post* has no "reason to believe" it has harmful information. And, two, if we did, and it was *really* harmful, we wouldn't print it.

Kelly Ben, the truth is you don't know what you've got. And you skipped point three: unauthorized possession. The news accounts say the papers were stolen.

Bradlee It's an old newspaper tradition—we never discuss our sources.

Kelly I know that. But I'm convinced the government can make a substantial criminal case against you if something damaging slips into the newspaper. They've already waved the espionage flag at the *Times*.

Bradlee So, who goes to jail?

Kelly Maybe you, for starters.

Bradlee Well, if that's espionage, then every top official in this administration and every top reporter and editor in the country will be there with me—for divulging this kind of thing all the time. Listen, why don't you guys get some lunch? There're sandwiches in the kitchen. I need to chat with Fritz for a few minutes.

Bagdikian Good idea, I haven't had anything to eat for two days. (*He and* **Kelly** *exit into the kitchen. Sound of swinging door.*)

Greenfield (*staying behind a moment, she whispers to* **Bradlee**) Ben, you're not taking this seriously, are you?

Bradlee At the rate we're paying this guy. I'm at least going to listen to what he has to say.

Greenfield But it's insane. He has no idea how the system works.

Bradlee I know. But he's not the key. Beebe is. Let me talk to him.

Greenfield (*resigned*) Okay. (*She exits to kitchen. Sound of swinging door.*)

Bradlee How about a stiffener? (*Going to the bar.*)

Beebe Lemonade and scotch, my favorite drink.

Pause.

Bradlee Fritz, we really need this one. When Katharine made me editor six years ago, I told her this paper could go two ways—toward greatness or mediocrity, and I had no intention of presiding over the latter.

Beebe Ben, you know my blood has more ink in it than it has profit-and-loss ledgers. Just the thought of a story like this makes me light-headed. But I'm also a businessman, and when I look through the lens of Chairman of the Board of the *Post* Company, I get damned nervous.

Bradlee What about?

Beebe The survival and economic health of this company. Look what's on the table if we end up facing criminal charges. The *Post* stock went public only two days ago—we've got a million three hundred thousand shares outstanding. Our deal doesn't firm up until next week, and it includes a clause that says the entire stock issue could be cancelled by a, quote, catastrophic event. To my mind, a criminal indictment for violating espionage laws adds up to a catastrophic event.

Bradlee Fritz, there isn't going to *be* a criminal action. I've been around this town thirty years, and no President has been dumb enough to take on the press in that manner. Sure, Nixon hates our guts—he'd love to stick it to us. But he doesn't have the balls to go the criminal route.

Beebe What makes you think he hasn't got something? There's such a thing as *real* secrets, after all. We almost lost the Battle of Midway when the *Chicago Tribune* printed the fact that the U.S. had cracked the Japanese code.

Bradlee Yeah, I remember. I was in the Navy. Thank God the Japanese didn't read the *Chicago Tribune*.

Beebe But you can be damn sure that Hanoi is reading the *Washington Post*. Anyway, all Nixon needs is an indictment. Don't forget, we've also got TV and radio licenses. If we get involved in a felony case, his FCC will pull our licenses faster than you can pronounce the call letters. What we're talking about here is a $193 million corporation on the line.

Bradlee (*pensive*) That's quite a scenario, Fritz. If I didn't know you better, I'd call it a cheap shot. You knew, of course, that I'd have to hear this not only as a newspaperman, but as a member of the board of the company.

Beebe Ben, don't get paranoid. I'm dealing with you straight. It's not my style to play games. I'm here to protect Kay Graham and her newspaper.

Bradlee I know, Fritz, and I respect that. You're her best friend, her lawyer, her biggest shoulder, and, I may add, her smartest adviser.

Beebe Thanks, you're overly kind.

Bradlee Don't worry, I'm not stepping out of character. I need to know the bottom line . . . what if you had to decide this minute?

Beebe (*pause*) . . . I'd have to say I'm leaning against.

Bradlee And where thou leanest, so leanest the Lady Graham.

Sound of typewriters. **Bradlee**'s *den.*

Roberts (*talking to himself as he types*) . . . and reported directly to the President the result of the talks . . . Okay, that's page seventeen . . . (*He beings shuffling papers.*) What the hell happened to my add sixteen? Goddammit! Have you guys been—oh, here it is.

Marder (*ignoring* **Roberts**) Ha! They missed it.

Wilson Who missed what?

Marder The Papers. They haven't got the story of the Vietnamese general and his mistress.

Wilson What story is that?

Marder One of the generals had his mistress at the Paris Peace Talks all through 1968. She was listed as a secretary.

Roberts So?

Marder So, he jilted her. She got mad, and defected. The CIA debriefed her for eighty hours straight.

Wilson Yeah, what'd they get?

Marder Not much. This particular secretary could neither read nor write. (*Laughter, except for* **Roberts**.)

Roberts Jesus Christ, can you guys get serious? We're damn close to deadline and I've got at least three more pages.

Wilson Relax, Chal. In a few hours you'll be famous.

Sound of typewriter. **Bradlee**'s *living room.*

Kelly Okay. Let me be precise about what I'm proposing. What we do is postpone publication one day, notify the government we have the Papers and give it the opportunity to tell us which portions it finds objectionable. We still plan to go ahead and publish, but this way we're not spitting in the face of the government or the court.

Bagdikian   I don't get it. By announcing we have the Papers, aren't we inviting the government to come in and try to stop us from publishing entirely?

Kelly   Sure, it's a risk—but by showing an attempt to be responsible, we're in a far stronger position to assert the right to publish.

Bagdikian   I always thought the way to assert the right to publish is to publish.

Kelly   What do you think, Ben?

Bradlee (*with an exhausted sigh*)   Maybe. Meg?

Greenfield   Frankly, I'm confused.

Bradlee   Fritz?

Beebe   It's got possibilities.

Sound of typewriters. **Bradlee**'s *den.*

Roberts   Two more lines to go!

Wilson   Can you believe this? August, 1964. Our glorious leaders are secretly planning to bomb the crap out of North Vietnam while LBJ is campaigning as the peace candidate against Barry Goldwater.

Marder   Oh, yeah. I remember the speech Lyndon made at a Texas barbecue. (*He breaks into an LBJ-Texas drawl.*) Ah will not commit a good many Amurican boys to fightin' a war that ought to be fought bah the boys of Asia . . .

Roberts (*sound of paper ripped from carriage*)   Finished!

Wilson   Great!

Bagdikian *enters.*

Wilson   Bagdikian, come on in. We're done! . . . What's the matter?

Marder (*overlapping*)   "We have lost 200 men . . . we think it is better to lose 200 than 200,000 . . ."

Bagdikian   Fellas. Fellas!! The story is in trouble.

Roberts   What do you mean?

Bagdikian   I mean . . . I think we're losing it to the lawyers.

Wilson   What are you talking about?

Marder   Let's get out there.

The **Reporters** *charge into the living room.*

Roberts   What's going on?

Bradlee (*clearly uncomfortable*)   Sit down, you guys . . . There's a proposal on the floor . . . just a proposal, mind you. Our lawyer, Brian Kelly here, is concerned that we may be inviting criminal charges if we go ahead without letting the government know we've got the Papers. He suggests we wait a day to inform the Attorney General before we publish.

Wilson (*stunned*)   That's the shittiest idea I've ever heard!

Roberts   Wait a minute. Are you suggesting that after all this, we crawl on our bellies to John Mitchell and ask his permission to publish?

Kelly   No, no, you misunderstand . . .

Bradlee   Just hold it, Brian.

Roberts   I can't believe I'm hearing this.

Marder   Ben, if we do this, everyone and his mother'll know by morning that the *Washington Post* ran for cover on a monumental First Amendment issue. We'll never recover from it.

Roberts   Ben, you can go ahead and kill this story if you want, it's your right. But it's my right to resign from this newspaper and make a public statement explaining why. Come on guys. (*They exit.*)

Bagdikian (*to* **Bradlee**)   Ben, you're going to have a revolt on your hands.

Phone rings.

Greenfield (*answering phone*)   Yes, just a minute, Gene . . . Ben, it's Gene Patterson. He says we need a decision now on the first edition. He can't hold the presses much longer.

Bradlee   Tell him forget it for the first edition. Fill in with house ads we can kill later.

Greenfield   What about the late city?

Bradlee   I don't know. We'll call him as soon as we have something definite.

Greenfield   We'll call you as soon as we know, Gene.

Bradlee (*turning to others*)   It's got to go to Katharine.

Bagdikian   I agree.

Beebe   So do I. (*Looks at his watch.*) Problem is she's in the midst of a big lawn party at her home right now. A farewell bash for the circulation manager. I'll give it a try. (**Beebe** *goes to the phone near the couch, stage center, and dials. There is an expectant silence.*)

Beebe   Mrs. Graham, please. Fritz Beebe calling . . . Yes, I know. Tell her it's urgent. No, do not wait please. This is urgent. (*To the others.*) She's in the middle of her speech to Harry Gladstein. (*After a pause.*)

Graham   Hello?

Beebe   Kay? Sorry for the interruption, but I'm afraid we're at a stalemate on the matter we've been dealing with. We're on deadline and it needs a decision at the top.

Graham (*the sounds of the party can be heard in the background*)   Isn't this a news decision, Fritz? I try to stay out of those.

Beebe   I wish you could, but this is more than a news decision. The legal advice we're getting is that publishing tomorrow could expose the company to grave consequences.

Graham   Like what?

Beebe   Possible criminal indictment, charges of espionage . . .

Graham   Espionage! Who's giving us this advice?

Beebe   Brian Kelly, the lawyer from the New York office of our law firm.

Graham   Do you agree?

Beebe   I'm concerned.

Graham   Fritz, you're asking me to do something over the phone that it took the *Times* three months to do . . . All right, is the lawyer there with you?

Beebe   Yes, I'll ask him to get on the line.

Bradlee   Katharine, it's Ben. I'm on the other extension. Look, if we fail to publish, we're coming down on the government's side against the *Times*. It's going to look like the *Washington Post* is endorsing prior restraint as a legitimate weapon against the press.

Kelly   Mrs. Graham, this is Brian Kelly. What I have been arguing is that by immediately publishing secret documents the reporters have hardly had time to examine, the *Post* could inadvertently reveal sensitive and damaging material. The paper could be accused of endangering lives in wartime.

Bradlee   The government can accuse us of a lot of things. The question is, would any of it stick? This is not about national security, and it's not about espionage. It's about politics. It's about control, about embarrassment. They don't want us to expose their cover-ups and their lies. To Nixon, we're the enemy, and if they think they can get away with it, they'll use all kinds of *threats* to intimidate us.

Kelly   Mrs. Graham, this is an unprecedented situation. We can't predict what the government might resort to in this case.

Bradlee   I'm convinced it's a game of chicken.

Graham   But Ben, if Mr. Kelly and Fritz are right, it could destroy our newspaper.

Bradlee   I understand what Fritz is saying, but there's more than one way to destroy a newspaper.

Graham   All right everybody, hold on a second. Mr. Kelly, I'm not all together clear why you feel our reporters aren't able to distinguish between so-called good and bad information.

Kelly I have great respect for the *Post*'s magnificent staff, Mrs. Graham. But unlike the *New York Times*, we haven't had three months to study this material—and we're staring in the face of an injunction that was handed down by the court in New York. However, I think maybe we could cure this by holding off for a single day.

Bradlee Yeah. A day in which we let the government know we have the papers.

Graham Is that what's being proposed?

Beebe Brian is suggesting we give the government a chance to tell us what sections of the papers they consider most sensitive.

Bradlee Chal and Murry and George have gone through the stuff, and they agree there's nothing in it that threatens the security of the country. I'll stake my reputation on it.

Kelly Mrs. Graham, I'm sure Fritz Beebe can tell you better than I that there's a lot more than reputation at stake.

Bradlee (*angry, playing his hole card*) I'll tell you this: if the *Post* caves on this issue, Katherine, you're gonna lose some of your top reporters, and maybe an editor or two.

Graham Just who are you talking about?

Bradlee Chal just threatened to publicly resign if we don't print tomorrow.

Graham My God, Ben, he can't be serious.

Bradlee I'm afraid he is. Look, we all feel the *Post* has vital information about what really happened in Vietnam which our government tried to suppress. These documents show that the government has been lying to us, all along playing us for dupes. If under a threat from that government, we back off, we might as well become a shopping mall giveaway.

Graham Okay, I've got your arguments. Let me talk to Fritz alone.

Kelly *and* **Bradlee** *hang up, leaving it to* **Beebe**.

Greenfield (*aside to* **Bradlee**) Ben, what's happening?

Bradlee She's tossing it to Fritz.

Beebe Well, you're aware of the stock issue, of course, and the FCC licenses. From a purely fiscal viewpoint, I have to advise you that we could be very vulnerable. Naturally, that has to be weighed against the journalistic consequences.

Graham Well, Fritz . . . What do you think?

Beebe What do I think? . . . On balance . . . I think I wouldn't.

Bagdikian (*groaning, hand to head*) That's the ball game!

Beebe (*finally*) But ultimately it's up to you.

Graham (*long pause*) Go ahead. Go ahead. Go ahead. Let's go. Let's publish.

Beebe All right. Thanks, Kay. Goodbye. (*He slowly cradles the phone. Then, quietly, to those assembled.*) We publish.

There is an outburst of cheers and applause. The **Reporters** *rush in and join the excitement.*

Roberts (*handing* **Bradlee** *the rest of his story*) Here's the finish.

Bradlee Great. (*To* **Bagdikian**.) Hey, Bagdikian . . . let's get this down to the paper right now. We've got less than half an hour to make the late city edition.

Greenfield (*to* **Bagdikian**) I'll drive you down.

Beebe I can't say I'm sorry it turned out this way, Ben.

Bradlee Mother Graham is a gutsy broad, I gotta say that for her.

Beebe Yep, and she's got a big fight on her hands. I'll be at the Mayflower if you need me. (*He exits.*)

Kelly Ben, we're diving blindfolded into a pool of sharks. But I want you to know I'll give it our all. We know for sure the government is going to haul us into court on a civil injunction, just like the *Times*. If we can win big there, I don't think we have to worry about criminal charges. But, it's a big "if."

Bradlee's *eye catches* **Wilson**, *who is halfway out the door.*

Bradlee (*shouting*) Hey, George.

Wilson Yeah, chief.

Bradlee Mr. Kelly here says we're probably going to be socked with a court action for blowing defense secrets. That's your territory. I want you to give him a hand.

Wilson Great. When do we start?

Kelly Right now. It gives us a few hours before the *Post* hits the streets—and the Shinola hits the fan. (**George** *exits.*)

Sound of bell, newspaper presses, and then a series of broadcast news stories.

End of Act One.

Act Two

Graham Why did I do it? Why did I decide that we should publish? When Fritz and Ben called in the middle of my farewell toast to Harry, I was surrounded by dozens of our best *Post* employees. It was a beautiful June day, and the party had spilled out of the house and onto the terrace and lawn. I was trying to look natural, but I was tense and frightened.

I had always trusted Fritz Beebe to help me find my way through any crisis. When he said that ultimately the decision to publish was mine, something about that phrase or maybe it was something in his tone, gave me the confidence that I needed. I knew the risks were incalculable, but somehow I then had the courage to give the editors the go-ahead, knowing that we were provoking a possibly disastrous confrontation with a President who seemed to consider the *Post* the enemy, and, who would like nothing better than to destroy us.

Once again, Nixon's White House taping system allows us to hear what he was actually saying, this time in a conversation with Henry Kissinger.

The Oval Office.

Kissinger (*exploding*)   There can be no foreign policy in this government. No foreign policy, I tell you! We might as well just turn it all over to the Soviets and get it over with. These leaks are slowly and systematically destroying us.

Nixon You're right, Henry, damn right. What if someone blows the news about your secret meetings with China?

Kissinger They would never meet with me again. We would probably have to eliminate the entire operation.

Nixon We'll take care of the press in the courts, but it's not enough. We've got to turn this around from the PR angle, use it against the Democrats! After all, they're the ones who screwed up the damn war. What about this guy Ellsberg?

Kissinger He is a nut; he is the most dangerous man in America. He was once a student of mine, a genius, but mad. Mr. President, he must be stopped. He has access to very critical defense secrets of current validity, such as nuclear deterrent targeting.

Nixon Well, let's get on it. Why can't we find him? This guy should be locked up. And it's not only him. There's a whole gang of them out there, in cahoots with the Democrats, trying to pry loose government secrets for political reasons. We need to counterattack. What about the Diem study? Is that in the Pentagon Papers? I gave orders a year ago to get that damn study! It shows that Kennedy ordered Diem's assassination. I think Howard Hunt is working on that.

Kissinger (*trying to excuse himself*)   Very good. Now if you'll excuse me, Mr. President.

Nixon And we'll get them on several fronts. That goddamn *Washington Post*. Don't they have a couple of TV licenses? Let's see what we can do about those. And we'll get Agnew on it. Turn him loose on the *Post*. I'm going to order a full court press.

Kissinger (*somewhat impatiently*) Yes, Mr. President.

Nixon Don't worry, Henry.

Kissinger No, Mr. President.

Graham The judge who was assigned to our case ordered the government to provide him with a list of the most dangerous secrets in the Pentagon Papers. National security experts prepared several sworn statements, but the administration refused to let the *Post* or our lawyers see any of them. Brian Kelly alerted the judge, who was furious. He ordered the government to let our lawyers see the documents so that we could prepare for trial. Reluctantly, they agreed to admit Brian Kelly, accompanied by George Wilson, to a cramped conference room in the Justice Department. There they examined the affidavits at a small wooden table, while a military sentry kept watch. It was very early Monday morning, June 21. At around 1:50 a.m., Wilson left the room for a few minutes, and Kelly tried to strike up a conversation with the sergeant who was standing guard.

Kelly (*finally, trying to reduce the tension*) Young man. Sergeant. It's nearly 2:00 a.m. Can't you relax? Take a seat. At least go "at ease."

Soldier Thank you, sir, but no, sir. I'm being relieved in ten minutes, sir.

Kelly Look, I know you're sworn to protect the sanctity of these so-called secret documents with your life, but if we try to run off with them, you can just as easily shoot us from a sitting position.

Soldier Sorry, sir. Assistant Attorney General Mardian's orders, sir. He says this is a maximum-security situation, sir. Like a night watch in Nam.

Kelly You're joking. (*He waits a moment, but there is no reaction.*) No, of course you're not. Have you been over there?

Soldier Twenty-seven months, sir. Re-upped for a second tour.

Kelly Brave lad. I was in the Pacific Theater myself. In World War II. Marines. But my son—he's part of the "make love, not war" brigade.

Soldier Yes, sir.

Door opens and **George Wilson** *enters.*

Wilson Jesus. They even followed me into the men's room!

Kelly Really? Did they spot the microfilm camera taped to your balls? (*Then, suddenly recalling the humorless M.P.,* **Kelly** *quickly turns to him and adds:*) Only kidding, Sergeant. I hate to say it, George, but the more documents I look at, the more scared I get. My guess is that the government wins this thing if they can show the court that any document in this pile will endanger our national security. You're the military expert. How do we deal with this one?

He throws a document across the table to **Wilson**.

Wilson   What's in it? (*Starting to read.*)

Kelly   It's about a Canadian diplomat who's posing as a neutral member of the International Control Commission, while actually serving as our agent. I wouldn't want to be in his shoes when we blow his cover.

Wilson (*still looking at the document*)   I could swear that I've heard about this guy before. Maybe it's in someone's memoirs.

Kelly   Well, you've got less than six hours to find out—and to prove that each of these other documents is either innocuous or already public. (*He tosses a yellow notepad across the table.*) Remember, we've got to convince Judge Martin Peel that the Founding Fathers would have allowed us to print a bunch of top secret—and possibly even stolen documents.

Door opens and **Mardian** *enters.*

Wilson   Oh shit, here comes Mardian.

Mardian   What the hell do you guys think you're doing?

Wilson   Mr. Mardian. We were just—

Mardian   Not you, Wilson. Kelly, what have you got written on that yellow pad?

Kelly   Just some notes.

Mardian   You know damned well you can't take notes in here.

Kelly   What do you mean I can't take notes?

Mardian   This stuff is all top secret. You're not allowed—

Kelly   Not allowed! We've got to be able to respond to each of these documents in court today. I haven't got total recall, for Christ's sakes.

Mardian (*angrily*)   Look, Kelly, you better put your pencil away right now before we break it for you.

Kelly   You want to break a pencil! I'll break a pencil. (*Sound of pencil breaking.*) Now let me tell you this. I'm going to start walking out of here with my notes in hand. I know damned well that young soldier is going to try to take them away. I promise I'll give him one hell of a fight and when I go into court today battered and bandaged, I'm going to say I got beat up on your orders.

Mardian   Oh, to hell with it. At ease, soldier. We'll squash them in court.

Graham   Later that morning, Ben Bradlee and I went to the courthouse together. As we arrived, we were surrounded by reporters shouting questions.

As **Mrs. Graham** *walks toward the courtroom, she is surrounded by a group of* **Reporters**, *who shout questions at her.*

Reporter 1   Mrs. Graham, will you testify in there?

Reporter 2 Mrs. Graham, is it true that the *Post* considered not publishing the Papers?

Reporter 3 Mrs. Graham, are you prepared to go to jail to protect your principles?

Graham We're prepared to do what we can to get the presses rolling again. Please excuse us; we're running late.

Bradlee Okay, fellas, we'll have plenty to say after the hearing.

Sound of footsteps as they talk and press their way through the crowd.

Graham God, I was terrified. Why is it my knees turn to rubber every time I see a microphone or camera?

Bradlee Don't worry about it. Your reputation is secure

Graham In any case, I want you and Fritz to run interference with the press from now on. I'll stay in the background. Way back.

Courtroom doors open and close. Inside we hear the buzz of voices.

Clerk-Bailiff (*in the customary loud voice*) All rise. (*Everyone in the room stands up.*) The U.S. Court for the District of Columbia is now in session, the Honorable Martin Peel presiding.

Judge Peel *enters and, as he takes his seat, so does everyone else in the courtroom.*

Clerk-Bailiff Civil Action number 1235-71, United States of America versus the *Washington Post* Company, et al.

Judge Peel The court wishes at the beginning of these hearings to thank counsel for supplying several extremely helpful documents. These affidavits from *Washington Post* reporters and editors contend that government officials use the secrecy stamp for political purposes, and that secret documents are given to reporters by top officials on a regular basis. The government's affidavit identifies several documents that it says, if published, will injure the United States. That affidavit is stamped "Top Secret". It will be discussed, but only in a special *in camera* session that will be closed to the press and public. Mr. Kelly, are your clients present in the courtroom?

Kelly (*rising*) They are, Your Honor. Mrs. Katharine Graham, Publisher of the *Washington Post*. Mr. Benjamin Bradlee, Executive Editor of the *Post*. Mr. Frederick Beebe, Chairman of the *Washington Post* Company. And the Post's eminent Defense Department correspondent, George Wilson, who will be joining me at the counsel table.

Judge Peel Thank you, Mr. Kelly. Mr. Vanderhall, could you please introduce the gentlemen at your table.

Vanderhall Yes, Your Honor. The man sitting to my left is Robert Mardian, Assistant Attorney General for Internal Security.

Judge Peel All right. Now Mr. Vanderhall, as counsel for the government you have the burden of proof. Are you ready to present your case?

Vanderhall Yes, Your Honor . . .

*Before **Vanderhall** can complete his sentence, **Kelly** is on his feet.*

Kelly Your honor, I move that this case be dismissed. In its case against the *New York Times* last week, the government predicted grave danger to national security if another word of the Pentagon Papers got printed. Since then the *Post* has printed several more excerpts, and the Republic still stands.

There is some laughter in the courtroom.

Judge Peel (*gaveling for order*) Frankly, I don't see anything funny about the fact that the Republic still stands.

Kelly (*defensively*) Nor do I, Your Honor.

Judge Peel Mr. Kelly, I don't understand why a free and independent press can't, as a matter of simple patriotism, sit down with the Justice Department and screen the documents—not to censor them in any way, except from a limited security point of view. I wish you would explain that, because it is troubling me.

Kelly (*uncomfortable*) At first blush that might sound like the decent thing for us to do, Your Honor, but we can't go along with a prior restraint. My clients are convinced that it would be utterly inconsistent with the First Amendment.

Judge Peel Are you claiming an absolute privilege under the First Amendment? What about secret codes? What about troop movements?

Kelly Your Honor. I was referring to this case. I concede that in time of war, the government could stop a paper from publishing the departure date of a troop ship leaving New York harbor, if the story would inevitably lead to the destruction of the ship and crew.

Judge Peel Well, suppose in this hearing I find something that would lead to the death of a hundred young men whose only offense was that they were nineteen years old and had low draft numbers. What should I do?

Kelly We do not believe that Your Honor will find such a document.

Judge Peel Yes, but suppose I do. Would you say that the Constitution requires that I let it be published? That I let those men die? Is that what you would do?

Kelly No. I'm afraid that in that case, my concern for human life would overcome my somewhat more abstract devotion to the First Amendment. I would find it almost impossible to resist the inclination to prevent publication of the information.

Judge Peel In plain English, Mr. Kelly, I interpret that to mean you concede that there might indeed be instances where even free speech must be curbed to save lives. I'm denying your motion to dismiss. Mr. Vanderhall, you may proceed with your witness.

Vanderhall Yes, Your Honor. At this time we would like to to call to the stand Mr. Dennis Doolin.

Clerk-Bailiff Please raise your right hand. Do you swear or affirm to tell the truth, the whole truth, and nothing but the truth, so help you God?

Doolin I do.

Vanderhall Very well, Mr. Doolin. As Assistant Secretary of Defense for Security Affairs, did you have cause to examine the security classification of the Pentagon Papers study?

Doolin Yes, I did.

Vanderhall What was that cause?

Doolin Senator Fulbright, Chairman of the Senate Foreign Relations Committee, asked for a copy of the entire study. After reviewing the forty-seven volumes, we determined it was too sensitive to be transmitted outside the executive branch.

Vanderhall So sensitive that it must be declared off limits even to a distinguished U.S. Senator?

Doolin Yes.

Vanderhall What specifically was in those documents to lead you to that conclusion?

Doolin Well, candid messages between heads of state, eyes-only messages from ambassadors to the Secretary of State, and in some instances to the President. They dealt with operational plans. They dealt with troop movements. They revealed information about our codes, about our ability to break the codes of other countries.

Vanderhall Thank you. To your knowledge, what is the security classification of these materials at present?

Doolin Still top secret sensitive

Vanderhall No further questions.

Kelly Mr. Doolin, how many pages are there in the forty-seven volumes?

Doolin Approximately 7,000 pages.

Kelly Did you actually read each of those 7,000 pages?

Doolin No, I did not.

Kelly I thought you examined the entire study for sensitivity.

Doolin Not every page. We were looking at the totality of the study.

Kelly Isn't there considerable material in the study drawn from unclassified sources—newspaper clippings, for example?

Doolin Correct.

Kelly Why shouldn't the *Post* be free to publish the unclassified material in this study, the material that has already appeared in print.

Doolin　I suppose you could, but what would be the purpose? (*Turning to* **Judge Peel**.) Your Honor, they can find the unclassified material in any public library.

Kelly　Mr. Doolin, you mentioned earlier that the study contains operational plans. Do you recall that statement?

Doolin　Correct.

Kelly　And you said it concerns the movement of troops.

Doolin　Yes.

Kelly　Were any of these current operation plans?

Doolin　They were. They are.

Kelly　Are you stating that these papers contain information relating to current troop movements?

Doolin　I am.

Kelly　Could you be more specific?

Doolin　Certainly, but . . .

Vanderhall (*angrily interrupting*)　Objection, Your Honor, this is precisely the kind of material that Your Honor ruled should be dealt with in a closed session.

Judge Peel　Sustained.

Kelly　In that case, we have nothing further of the witness in the public session, Your Honor.

Vanderhall　We have nothing further.

Judge Peel　Very well. The court will at this time take a brief recess and exclude from further proceedings all persons except counsel, the defendants, the witness, and Mr. Wilson.

Clerk-Bailiff　All rise.

During recess, **Bradlee**, **Graham**, *and* **Beebe** *confer.*

Graham (*to* **Bradlee**)　Ben, why in the world did Kelly admit that the government should ever be allowed to stop us from publishing? Whose side is he on?

Bradlee　Damned if I know. I think he read the First Amendment for the first time coming down here on the Eastern shuttle.

Graham　Frankly, I'm getting worried. *The New York Times* is represented by a constitutional law professor from Yale, and we've got a guy who sounds like he specializes in parking violations. (*To* **Beebe**, *who has now joined them.*) What do you think, Fritz?

Beebe　They say he's their best litigator, but he doesn't seem to be winning Judge Peel's heart and mind.

Graham   He may be a perfectly nice man, but he doesn't seem to have a clue about how this town operates.

Bradlee   Or how newspapers function.

Wilson (*who has joined them*)   Hey, look. I worked with this guy all weekend. Don't count him out yet; he's no dope.

Graham   Maybe I'd better go into the hallway and buck him up a little.

She exits to hallway.

Graham (*to* **Kelly**)   Hi. I'm Kay Graham. We're terribly pleased that you came down here to handle this. Fritz says that you're the best litigator in the firm.

Kelly   Thank you, Mrs. Graham. That's very gracious.

Graham   Tell me, Brian, truthfully, how do you think it looks? I got very uneasy when we decided to retreat so quickly on the First Amendment. I agree, there are things the paper shouldn't publish, but don't you think the paper should make those decisions?

Kelly   Mrs. Graham, we're not going to win this on the First Amendment. We've got to strip away the veneer of secrecy—the idea that these are dangerous documents that belong in a spy novel. We've got to prove that those volumes just contain a lot of papers that happen to be stamped "top secret."

Graham   That would be a pretty narrow victory, wouldn't it?

Kelly   It's our best shot. As you said earlier, we want to get the presses rolling again. You heard the judge. An absolute First Amendment stance won't have a chance.

Graham   What about the testimony about current troop movements? They scored some points on that, don't you think?

Kelly   I've got to admit that was a surprise. But George and I have some surprises of our own. I hope to God it's enough to keep the *Post* publishing, and its editors out of jail.

Clerk-Bailiff   The court is now in session. Judge Martin Peel presiding.

Judge Peel   Bailiff, I want those doors closed and locked. (*Sound of doors being locked.*) Thank you. We just found a tape recorder that someone had concealed in here. I didn't know it until after it happened, or I would have had the people arrested and locked up. I gather they got away.

The court will now make the following order: No one attending this *in camera* hearing shall reveal anything divulged herein to anyone outside the hearing. All notes or other writings made by the defendants, or witnesses or counsel shall be surrendered at the close of the hearing. Now, Mr. Vanderhall, you may proceed with your case.

Vanderhall   Your Honor, at this time the government wishes to introduce in evidence the top secret affidavit by Dennis J. Doolin, who previously testified. I suggest that it be marked as United States Exhibit Number 2.

Judge Peel   It will be so identified.

Kelly   Your Honor, I would like to ask Mr. Doolin to resume the stand.

Judge Peel   You are still under the same oath, Mr. Doolin.

Doolin   Yes, sir.

Kelly   Mr. Doolin, the affidavit that you have presented to the court lists several parts of the Pentagon Papers study which you say would have dire consequences for our national safety if made public. The first item says that press leaks will endanger our peace negotiations with the North Vietnamese. You specifically refer to a peace overture by an Italian diplomat named LaPira. Do you regard the LaPira peace feeler as a "top secret" matter?

Doolin   I don't recall specifically, but I would say in my judgment, yes, it would still be secret, if not top secret.

Kelly   Still secret?

Doolin   Yes, it would compromise our intelligence operations.

Kelly   In what respect?

Doolin   We have used, and are using, third countries to convey messages to Hanoi and to receive messages from Hanoi. Those channels may well dry up if material keeps getting in the press.

Kelly   But Mr. Doolin, hasn't the story of the LaPira peace feeler already been well publicized?

Doolin   I don't know, sir.

Kelly   If that were the fact, would it change your opinion?

Doolin   I would still maintain that the principle of confidentiality is in jeopardy.

Kelly (*whispering to* **Wilson**)   Which book is that, George?

Wilson   It's the one by Kraslow and Lurie. (*Finding it.*) Here it is. And here's the Cooper book.

Kelly   Thanks. (*To* **Doolin**.) Mr. Doolin, have you ever seen a book called *The Secret Search for Peace in Vietnam*? It came out in 1969.

Doolin   I'm not familiar with it.

Kelly   You're not? Well, let me show it to you. (*Hands book to* **Doolin**.) Please take a look at pages 129 to 131. Those pages discuss, do they not, the background and substance of the LaPira peace feeler?

Doolin (*after reading for a moment*)   I am not quite clear from the book what the feeler was.

Kelly (*incredulous*)   You mention it in your affidavit. Don't you know what the LaPira peace feeler was?

Doolin   No, I don't.

Kelly   Well, how did you reach a judgment that this might endanger the United States, if you didn't know what the LaPira peace feeler was?

Doolin   Well, counsel, if you will read what I said in my affidavit, I wasn't addressing the contents of the peace feeler itself. My concern is with confidential diplomacy. The people who can help us most will not deal with us if these confidential discussions are going to appear in the papers. This is for real. For example, relations between the People's Republic of China and the United States are going to warm up. It didn't start with the ping-pong teams, and it isn't going to end there. But we are not going to make progress if diplomats from other countries lack confidence in our ability to keep a secret.

Kelly   Mr. Doolin, please answer my question. Would the LaPira overture—already public—create a danger if it showed up in the *Washington Post*?

Doolin   I stand by my original assessment.

Kelly   All right, let's turn to the next item. You identify a document that indicates that a Canadian diplomat was acting as an American agent. His name is J. Blair Seaborn. Do you contend that Mr. Seaborn's mission is still secret?

Doolin   To the best of my knowledge.

Kelly   Still secret. Are you aware of a book entitled *The Lost Crusade* by Chester Cooper?

Doolin   I've heard of it. I've never read it.

Kelly   When you prepared your affidavit, were you aware that this book describes Mr. Seaborn's mission?

Doolin   I answered that. I said I never read the book.

Kelly   You were not aware that on pages 325 to 327 this book tells how America "borrowed" a Canadian diplomat named Blair Seaborn to present its views to officials in Hanoi?

Doolin   No. I have not read the book.

Kelly   You're not aware that this book states that the Canadian Prime Minister approved of Mr. Seaborn's mission?

Doolin (*coldly*)   I told you, I haven't read the book.

Vanderhall (*trying to interrupt*)   Your Honor . . .

Kelly (*driving his point home*)   The truth is, is it not Mr. Doolin, that you could find this so-called "classified" material in any public library . . .

Vanderhall   (*persisting*)   Your Honor, he's badgering the witness.

Kelly   Not true. It's the facts that are badgering him.

Judge Peel   Mr. Kelly . . .

Kelly Excuse me, Your Honor. Now, Mr. Doolin, let me direct your attention to the next item. You say that disclosure of some of these documents will damage our efforts to release the prisoners of war . . .

Judge Peel May I interrupt?

Kelly Certainly.

Judge Peel I am more interested in another statement in your affidavit. You say that if these documents are published, prisoners of war are going to be killed in the prison camps.

Doolin I didn't say "killed," sir.

Judge Peel All right, I am looking at the text of your affidavit. You said that they will "die."

Doolin I said that they "*may* die."

Judge Peel In either event, are you saying that prisoners are likely to die if the *Post* publishes the fact that certain countries are helping us with our efforts to get the POWs released?

Doolin I said that they "may" die. I stand by that statement.

Judge Peel Will you explain it to me?

Doolin Some of these governments require guarantees of secrecy and confidentiality. If we can't guarantee that, then they won't help us. The more channels we lose, the longer those men will be kept in North Vietnam—and the more of them will die.

Kelly But Mr. Doolin, is it not a well-known fact that other governments have been attempting to serve as a channel of communications with Hanoi?

Doolin Some yes, some no.

Kelly How about the British?

Doolin On the prisoner issue? I don't believe so.

Kelly (*holding up the copy of* Life *magazine*) Are you aware of the description in Prime Minister Wilson's memoirs, published by *Life* Magazine?

Doolin No.

Judge Peel (*exasperated*) Gentlemen, this is simply becoming a policy discussion. Mr. Doolin, you say it would be better for the United States to conduct our affairs in private. That well may be. But counsel for the *Post* has books and articles that seem to show that all of the facts you are upset about are already public.

Doolin Your Honor, it is one thing for some of these contacts to be mentioned in a book. It is quite another matter to have the precise text of our cablegrams and memos printed in a newspaper. The impact on foreign governments is much greater.

Judge Peel   But what does that have to do with this proceeding? Your real problem seems to be that your own internal security controls aren't adequate.

Vanderhall (*jumping in*)   I submit, Your Honor, that the only mistake the government made was that we were betrayed by a person who had proper access.

Judge Peel   I don't know that. I don't know how the *Post* got these documents. I have affidavits from ten to fifteen *Washington Post* reporters who say that they constantly got top secret documents from government officials. When we met over the weekend, I directed the government to particularize the matters that were of greatest concern. Here we get to three or four of them, and up to now they all appear to be in the public domain. All right, you may proceed, Mr. Kelly.

Kelly   Mr. Doolin, the last item in your affidavit refers to a document about SEATO Operation Plan Number 5.

Judge Peel   Is that what you were talking about to when you said that these documents referred to troop movements?

Doolin   This particular one? I don't know whether this one does or not.

Judge Peel   Well, what were you referring to?

Doolin   To the buildup in Viet Nam . . .

Judge Peel (*showing some anger*)   Now wait a minute, that was years ago. Mr. Doolin, the clear impression you gave me this morning was that the disclosures involved *current* troop movements.

Doolin   I'm sorry. I didn't mean to give you that impression.

Judge Peel   You were talking about *past* troop movements?

Doolin   I was talking about past troop movements, about the strategy of the buildup and so forth.

Kelly   In any event, Mr. Doolin, you are stating now that the document does not contain any references to current troop movements.

Doolin   No. I'm sorry that I left that impression.

Kelly   Your Honor, I admire your patience, but how long must we go on with this charade? Each hour brings us closer to another day of suppressed publication, and the government has failed to come up with a scrap of evidence, a single document that even remotely endangers this nation's security.

Vanderhall (*jumping to his feet*)   Your Honor, we have just such a document but we have been reluctant up to now to bring it to the court's attention because of its extreme sensitivity. Therefore, I move that Your Honor examine the document in chambers, in the absence of any of the parties.

Judge Peel   The answer to that is a flat no. I've never excluded counsel for people who are being accused, and I'm not about to start now. It's foreign to my make-up. Mr. Mardian, you have something to say?

Mardian (*rising to address the court for the first time*)   Up to now, Your Honor, we have had our hands tied behind our back. We want to show you something, but we are most reluctant even to bring it into this courtroom. Nevertheless, we will agree to have counsel for the *Post* present, but all of the other representatives of the defendants must be excused from the room. This is an extraordinarily sensitive document.

Judge Peel (*to* **Kelly**)   Is that acceptable to the *Post*?

Beebe (*whispering*)   Just a moment, Brian.

Kelly   May we have a moment, Your Honor?

Judge Peel   Of course.

Kelly   Do you have a problem with that, Fritz?

Beebe (*slightly indignant*)   Hell, yes! What about George Wilson?

Kelly   But Wilson's not a lawyer.

Beebe   Look, they're about to bring in their ICBMs, and we can't afford to scuttle our fail-safe system. When they bring that new material, we'll need George's expertise more than ever.

Kelly   You're right. (*To the court.*) Your Honor, a more secure session is agreeable to us if Mr. Beebe is included as a lawyer, and if we can also have our national security advisor, Mr. Wilson, present to assist me.

Mardian   We insist that it be limited to the lawyers.

Judge Peel   No, I think the *Post*'s request is reasonable. I'm prepared to close the hearing further on that basis.

Mardian (*reluctantly*)   Very well, Your Honor.

Judge Peel   All right. We will clear the room. Thank you Mrs. Graham, Mr. Bradlee, Mr. Doolin, you will have to be excused. (*Sound of doors opening and closing.*) All right, Mr. Mardian, Mr. Vanderhall, you may proceed.

Vanderhall   The affidavit that we propose to introduce is from Vice-Admiral Noel Gayler, Director of the National Security Agency. It is in the safekeeping of his top aid, Lieutenant Darryl Cox.

Judge Peel   Lieutenant Cox, please come over to the witness stand. Do you swear or affirm that the testimony you are about to give is the truth, the whole truth, and nothing but the truth, so help you God?

Cox   I do.

Vanderhall   Would you please state your full name for the record.

Cox   Darryl William Cox.

Vanderhall   Where are you presently employed?

Cox   I am a Lieutenant in the Navy, attached to the National Security Agency as an aid to Vice-Admiral Noel Gayler.

Judge Peel   Could I ask—just what is the National Security Agency?

Cox   It is the government agency responsible for all cryptographic work.

Vanderhall   Simply put, you break and decipher codes, is that correct?

Cox   Among other things. Yes, sir.

Vanderhall   Do you have with you an affidavit from Vice Admiral Gayler?

Cox   I do.

Vanderhall   Could you please give it to Judge Peel.

Cox (*he stands up*)   Your Honor, my instructions are to give you the briefcase and these keys. The affidavit is in the briefcase.

Judge Peel   Why don't you proceed with your testimony while I open these locks?

Cox   The briefcase contains an affidavit from Admiral Gayler describing a specific document that we believe to be in the *Post*'s possession. The document is an August 1964 Defense Department cable that quotes from a radio intercept made by our agency during the Gulf of Tonkin crisis. If the text of the cable is published by the *Post*, the security of our code-breaking capability will be seriously threatened.

Judge Peel   Young man, there's a sealed envelope inside the briefcase. I take it that I am to open this as well.

Cox   Yes, sir.

The Court (*inside, there is a smaller envelope*)   And another one inside that?

Cox   Yes, sir, that one as well.

Judge Peel (*opening the second envelope*)   All right. Here it is. (*The document is a single page.* **Judge Peel** *reads it quickly.*) Give me a moment to read it.

Vanderhall   We request that this document be marked for identification as United States Exhibit Number 3.

Judge Peel   It will be so marked. (*He hands it to the* **Clerk**, *who marks it.*) Please give it to Mr. Kelly to read.

Kelly *reads it and hands it to* **Beebe**, *who then gives it to* **Wilson**.

Kelly (*to* **Judge Peel**)   Won't you please give us a moment to review it? Obviously we are seeing this for the first time.

Wilson *and* **Kelly** *walk over to the edge of the stage.*

Kelly   Jesus Christ, George. Those bastards never warned us about this one. This is it. This is a red-hot piece of intelligence. Peel isn't about to let the *Washington Post* tell the Viet Cong that we've broken their codes.

Wilson Can you stall for a little time? I could swear that I've read this somewhere before.

Kelly For Christ's sake, don't fake it, George.

Wilson I'm not. Just get me a few minutes so I can look this thing up.

Kelly (*to* **Wilson**) I'll try. (*To the* **Court**.) Your Honor, in all fairness, this is our first viewing of this document. A minimal recess is in order.

As **Kelly** *talks,* **Wilson** *is frantically rifling through papers and documents.*

Vanderhall What are you trying to do, Kelly, put Wilson up against the National Security Agency?

Judge Peel Mr. Kelly, wasn't it you who said just a moment ago that every minute is precious?

Kelly Indeed, but . . .

Judge Peel Well, you've got the document here, and you've got your own expert. Go ahead and question the witness. That seems the appropriate procedure.

Kelly Very well. Lieutenant Cox. This is a document from 1964. Is the code still in effect?

Cox To the best of my knowledge, yes sir.

Kelly Don't governments change their codes on a regular basis?

Vanderhall They certainly will if your stories are published.

Kelly So . . .

Wilson (*excitedly interrupting in a loud whisper*) Brian!

He shoves an open book at **Kelly**.

Kelly Your Honor, could you excuse us for a moment?

Wilson Here it is! I found it in the open literature.

Kelly (*quickly passing from incredulous, to stunned, to thrilled as he scans the page*) Incredible. (*Then, barely able to contain his excitement.*) Your Honor, this may be a sensitive document. Maybe it should even be a secret document. But it's not a secret, despite the Academy Award-winning performances we have witnessed here this afternoon. The government gave this precise document to the Senate in 1968. It was cleared by the Pentagon. Congress published it in a Hearing Report later that year. (*He hands the report up to* **Judge Peel**.) This is the Report of the Senate Foreign Relations Committee. I call your attention to page 34. This so-called "secret" document has been available to the public—and, need I add, to our enemies—for more than three years!

Judge Peel, *feeling somewhat used, reads the document hastily and hands it to the government's lawyers.*

Judge Peel   It sure looks the same to me. What do you have to say, Mr. Vanderhall?

Vanderhall and **Mardian** *are as surprised as* **Judge Peel** *and* **Kelly**. *They look at the document and caucus for a moment.*

Mardian   Your Honor, in light of the fact that this is new material, the government requests a short recess.

Judge Peel   I'm going to deny your request, Mr. Mardian. This was your document. This is your proceeding. You had the burden of proof. I will issue a formal written opinion, but gentlemen, I can tell you right now that I intend to deny the government's request for an injunction, and allow the *Post* to resume publication of these papers. This hearing is adjourned.

The courtroom decorum begins to disassemble.

Beebe (*rushing up to* **Wilson**)   Scoop Wilson! (*He shouts.*) Scoop Wilson saved the day.

Beebe *hugs* **Wilson** *and lifts him in the air. We hear the sounds of "Hip, hip hooray," the clicking of glasses and the buzz of Voices, making it clear that the scene is moving from the courtroom to a victory party for the* Post. *A few voices shout "Mrs. Graham" and "Speech! Speech!"*

Graham (*narrating*)   Late that evening, we had a victory party at the *Post* . . . (*To the men.*) Yesterday I saw a bumper sticker. It said: "Free the Pentagon Papers." Well, today we liberated them! I'm so damned proud of all of you. (*Applause.*)

Bradlee (*to* **Graham**)   Katharine, You've won your stripes on this one. To Katharine. (*Their glasses clink.*) You must be feeling very good.

Graham   I am. I feel as if I made a three-point landing on my first solo flight.

Bradlee   More than that. You showed world-class courage.

Graham   Careful, Ben. It only takes one sloppy sentiment to ruin a fellow's reputation. (*They laugh.*) You know, I have a feeling we haven't heard the last of this.

Bradlee   I think you're right. There's a movement in this administration to silence the press. They don't think we are the fourth estate. They think we're the fifth column. To them, we are all traitors.

In the background, we hear the Crowd calling for **Wilson** *to make a speech. "Scoop," "Scoop Wilson," "Speech."*

Wilson   I used to be a newspaperman myself. I've been a lawyer for the last few days. And one thing has become clear to me. It's easy for the *Washington Post* and the *New York Times* to take on the U.S. government. We had the resources. We could pay the lawyers. But we didn't wage this battle just for the giants of journalism. We waged it for the little guys, the poor guy out there covering some zoning committee, for some paper you never heard of. There're city councils all over the country that would love to have a precedent that would give them the power to cover something up, or freeze out the local reporter. It's hard for some little guy in a one-horse town to take on the city council. So, if for no other reason, we had to do it for him. You know, you can't really gain freedom, you only can lose it. And that's what this case was all about. You had to take them on at the top, and win. You had to win.

Wilson *finishes to a moment of silence, alone on the stage. Then* **Mrs. Graham** *walks over to him.*

Graham   Bravo, George. I wish I had said that.

Wilson   I wish you had, too. I was nervous as hell.

Graham   Well, it looks like the party's breaking up.

Wilson   Thank God. I haven't been home in three days. Now comes the really heavy lifting. I have to help my wife move into our new house.

Graham   Good night, George.

Wilson   Good night, Mrs. Graham.

Graham   Good night, gentleman . . . see you all bright and early.

Bradlee   Goodnight, Katharine. (**Beebe** *ad libs good night.*)

Everybody ad libs goodnights as most of the people at the party leave. Sounds of break-up of the party.

Bradlee   Looks like nobody's left but the three subversives: Bradlee, Bagdikian, and Beebe.

Beebe   Wilson made a hell of a speech.

Bradlee   Frankly, I didn't know he had it in him.

Bagdikian   I don't think Wilson knew it.

Beebe   Don't knock it. If George Wilson wants to play Jimmy Stewart, let him do it. I figure he saved this newspaper at least a hundred million bucks.

Bradlee   Still counting pennies, huh, Fritz? I bet you keep your money in a sock underneath your mattress.

Bagdikian   Wrong. I happen to know that Fritz Beebe has invested his money in the best growth stock he could find: *The New York Times*!

Beebe (*amid guffaws*)   You're both wrong. When you guys started this caper I put my money in an unnumbered bank account and prepared for a fast getaway.

Kelly *enters amid guffaws.*

Bradlee   Brian, I didn't know anybody else was still here. Come join us.

Kelly   Sorry, I just finished filing with the court. You're sure I'm not interrupting?

Beebe   Not at all. Have a drink.

Kelly's *presence changes the tone in the room.*

Kelly   Thanks. I could use one. I feel like I have just lost my virginity—and I don't know whether to celebrate or cry.

Bradlee   When in doubt, celebrate.

Kelly   No, I mean it. I learned a lot. I learned some things about government that shocked the shit out of me. I thought the government was concerned about national security. I still don't understand it. What were they afraid of? My kid's out there on the streets getting his head busted for exercising his constitutional right to protest, and it seems the servants of the people are mainly concerned about protecting the government's right to lie.

Bradlee   That's why God created the Pulitzer Prize.

Kelly   I keep thinking how lucky we were. What if there had been some real secrets somewhere in that mass of documents.

Bradlee   That wasn't luck. That was George Wilson.

Kelly   But what if that cable about the code hadn't been printed in the Senate record? You couldn't know that in advance. Or what if a batch of real secrets fell into the hands of some kid reporter at the *Village Voice*? We are fighting for a court decision that will apply to activist weeklies as well as professional dailies. What kind of precedent are we setting?

Bradlee   You *do* know we won this case! Because if this is how you celebrate a victory, then I'd hate what a defeat looks like.

Beebe   But Brian has a point, Ben. Remember JFK's speech to the newspaper publishers right after he took office. I was at that lunch. At the Waldorf Astoria. Kennedy charmingly asked us to avoid the unauthorized disclosure of national security information.

Bradlee   Come on, Fritz. You know that Jack called that one of his biggest mistakes.

Beebe   Of course he did. The press had such a crush on him that he never had to worry about what it would publish.

Bagdikian   Ben had a crush. The rest of us were just infatuated.

Beebe   Either way, everyone was smitten by the moonlight. Hell, Ben, the paper wouldn't even look into Jack's alleged peccadilloes. But God help nerds like Nixon.

Kelly   And God help the nation if the press doesn't consider some stories off base. This decision protects your right to publish. But what about your responsibility to keep some things secret? I admire your competitive spirit, Ben, and you proved that the *Post* has the guts to say "yes." But when your competitive juices flow will you have the guts to say "no"? At what point do we draw the line on stolen documents? Do we sanction stealing? How far will we go with anonymous sources? Do we ask? Do we want to know?

Bradlee   Of course we do. But right now I just want to know what you're having to drink.

Kelly Oh, hell, you're right, Ben, this is a victory party, not a wake. Tonight we speak of rights, not responsibility. Here's to the freedom to publish, long may it wave. Now how about some scotch?

Bradlee You're on. I'll open the good stuff.

Graham Although the *Post* won its case in District Court, the battle continued for another week. The Justice Department immediately filed an appeal, blocking publication of the Pentagon Papers while the case made its way to the United States Supreme Court. On June 30, 1971, in his last decision from the Supreme Court bench, Hugo Black wrote that the *Times* and *Post* "should be commended for serving the purpose that the Founding Fathers saw so clearly." In a landmark ruling, the Supreme Court allowed both newspapers to resume publication of the documents.

Years later, Erwin Griswold, who was Nixon's Solicitor General, described what he called "massive over-classification" by the government. Griswold said that the real concern of the classifiers is almost always to prevent government embarrassment, rather than to protect national security.

We also learned that almost all of the secrets identified by the government as most damaging had never been given to the *Times* or the *Post*. Despite his image as a wild-eyed zealot, Daniel Ellsberg had held back almost 3,000 pages that he deemed too sensitive to publish.

What we didn't yet know was that this series of events would help lead to the exposure of an even larger pattern of lying and deception by our government. The door was now open for the Watergate revelations by our great reporters Bob Woodward and Carl Bernstein. Revelations that ultimately would bring about the resignation of President Nixon.

And finally, we could not yet know that the publication of the Pentagon Papers—by creating a more informed public and a more skeptical press—would actually play an important role in bringing the divisive and painful war in Vietnam to an end.

End of play.

www.ingramcontent.com/pod-product-compliance
Lightning Source LLC
Chambersburg PA
CBHW072124290426
44111CB00012B/1770